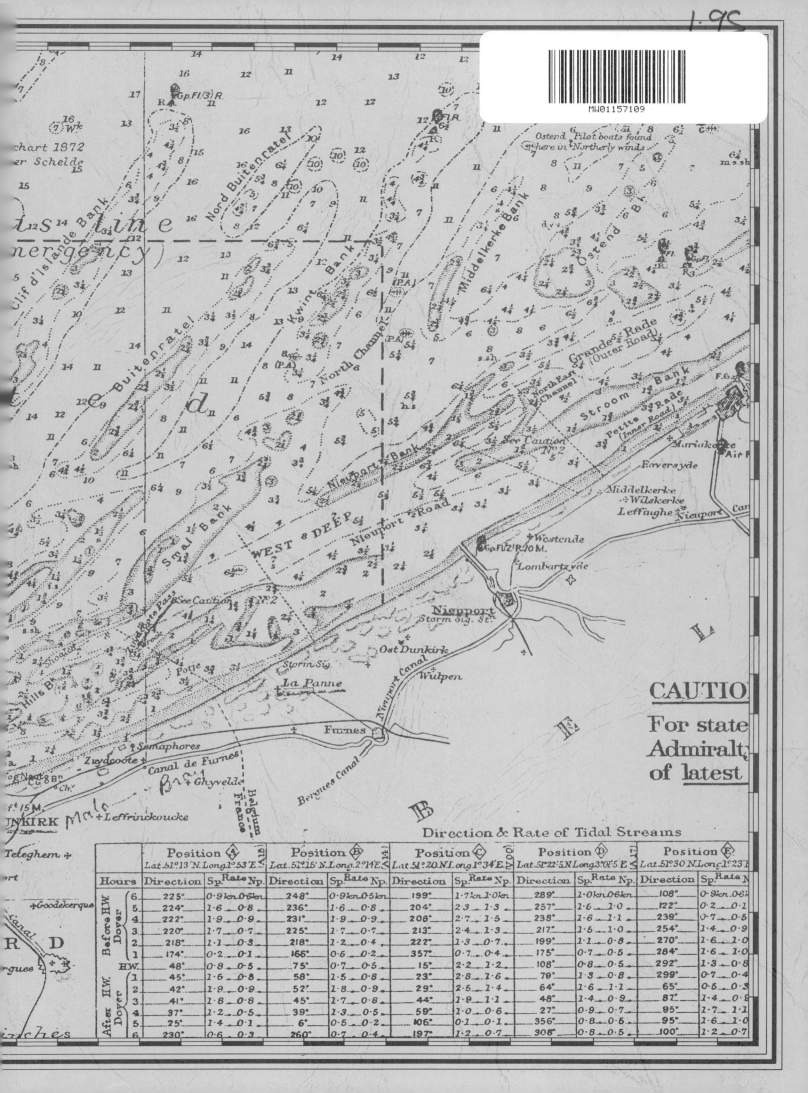

To Douglas with Best Wishes
Xmas 1997
From Judy & Gavin.

To Douglas with Best Wishes
Xmas 1997
From Judy & Gavin.

1940 1990

THE
LITTLE SHIPS
OF
DUNKIRK

COLLECTORS' BOOKS LIMITED

1940   1990

THE
LITTLE SHIPS
OF
DUNKIRK

Christian Brann

COLLECTORS' BOOKS LIMITED

First published in Great Britain, 1989
by Collectors' Books Limited, Bradley
Lodge, Kemble, Cirencester,
Gloucestershire GL7 6AD. Copyright
© Collectors' Books Limited, 1989

ISBN 0 946604 02 9

Printed in Great Britain by
HunterPrint Group plc

Colour Separations by Charles Elsbury
(Graphics) Ltd.

Designed by Brian Blake, Cirencester

Research by Mark Child

F O R E W O R D

For all who remember the dramatic evacuation of the British Army from Dunkirk in 1940, it was little short of a miracle, and the most moving, and unexpected, element of that whole astonishing event was the intervention of what have become known as the Little Ships of Dunkirk.

Cockle fishermen, lifeboatmen, yachtsmen and members of the Royal Navy put to sea in anything that would float and they braved the mines, the 'E-boats' and the Luftwaffe, to play their part in the rescue of 385,000 British and French troops in those fateful nine days in the summer of 1940. With outstanding courage and resourcefulness — and with Providence playing its part by providing unusually good weather and calm seas — they turned what might have been a major disaster into a remarkable success.

Thanks to the care of their present owners, 150 of these, now elderly and fragile, Little Ships survive to celebrate the 50th anniversary of those proud days. This book pays tribute to their service and it will be a lasting record of one of the most remarkable feats of seamanship in Britain's long maritime history.

1989

(Above) A view of Dunkirk from the
approaching ships

(below) Military situation around
Dunkirk on 28th May, 1940

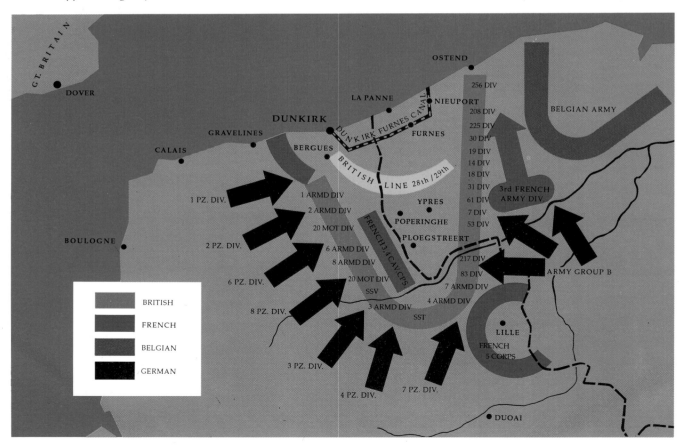

GT. BRITAIN

DOVER

OSTEND

256 DIV

LA PANNE   NIEUPORT

208 DIV   BELGIAN ARMY

DUNKIRK   225 DIV

GRAVELINES   FURNES   30 DIV

CALAIS   BERGUES   19 DIV

14 DIV

18 DIV

BRITISH LINE 28th/29th   31 DIV   3rd FRENCH
                                        ARMY DIV
1 PZ. DIV.   1 ARMD DIV   61 DIV

2 ARMD DIV   YPRES   7 DIV

20 MOT DIV   POPERINGHE   53 DIV

BOULOGNE   PLOEGSTREERT

2 PZ. DIV.   6 ARMD DIV

8 ARMD DIV   217 DIV

6 PZ. DIV.   20 MOT DIV   83 DIV   ARMY GROUP B

SSV   7 ARMD DIV

3 ARMD DIV   4 ARMD DIV

8 PZ. DIV.   SST

LILLE

FRENCH
5 CORPS

3 PZ. DIV.

4 PZ. DIV.   7 PZ. DIV.

DUOAI

BRITISH

FRENCH

BELGIAN

GERMAN

DUNKIRK FURNES CANAL

FRENCH 3,4 CAV CPS

6

INTRODUCTION

A memorable page of world history was written in those nine days between 26th May and 5th June 1940 when the quiet Flanders port of Dunkirk lent its name to a legend which will rank in fame with Agincourt and Waterloo. Some of the great names of World War II had received their baptism of fire: Major-General Erwin Rommel in command of the 7th Panzer Division and Major-General Bernard Montgomery of the British 3rd Division were little known then, but would rise to fame when they crossed swords again in the North African desert. Winston Churchill had just moved from the Admiralty to Downing Street to take his nation's helm and in his words, the Battle of France was over and the Battle of Britain was about to begin.

"The Battle of France is over and the Battle of Britain is about to begin"

Many good books have been written about the Generals long dead, the battles they fought, the things they did and might have done and about the warships of the French and British Navies - destroyers, mine sweepers and auxiliary ships - which braved the German dive bombers to evacuate French and British troops from the harbour of Dunkirk until the port was blocked with their sunken wrecks.

This book is about the Little Ships of Dunkirk, a strange, unlikely collection of heroic small craft, not built for war, which came from the rivers and coastal waters of England: the Thames, the Medway, the Solent and some who first crossed the sea to England as refugees: 49 sturdy *schuyts* from the Netherlands. There were river launches, old sailing and rowing lifeboats, yachts, pleasure steamers, fishing boats, working sailing barges; fire boats without as much as a compass, many of which had not been

to sea before. Some were formally chartered in the name of King George VI, some were commandeered without notice and given a hand written slip for a receipt by the naval crews who took them to their assembly point at Ramsgate under orders from Admiral Ramsay, who masterminded 'Operation Dynamo' from his command post deep in the white cliffs by Dover Castle. Tugs accompanied some of them across the channel like mother ducks but many made three or more journeys on their own amid dive bombing and strafing by the Luftwaffe. Unlit and unable to comprehend, or respond to naval signals when challenged in the night, they risked being sunk by their own side. They were desperately needed to negotiate the shallow waters off La Panne on the French-Belgian border, where no deep draught ships could approach and pluck the exhausted waiting troops from the beaches of Dunkirk, where they were tending their wounded and vainly trying to shelter from air attack among the dunes.

Of the seven hundred brave little craft almost a hundred perished but 385,000 troops, more than 100,000 of them French, were ferried to the waiting ships or taken direct to England to fight again another day. Ships can live longer than men and some two hundred of these veterans have survived their wartime owners and most of the soldiers they saved.

Some have been lovingly restored in keeping with their great past; some,

Within days of coming to power, Churchill was faced with the crisis of Dunkirk

Vice Admiral Ramsay was responsible for "Operation Dynamo"

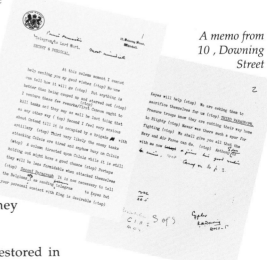

A memo from 10, Downing Street

INTRODUCTION

Cdr. Charles Lamb,DSO,DSC, RN first Hon. Admiral of the ADLS

Raymond Baxter, co-founder and first Commodore - later Hon. Admiral

like forgotten war veterans with no further practical function, have been left to decay and many have simply disappeared. This book depicts and tells the story of those we found.

In 1964, Raymond Baxter, the well known writer and broadcaster, who is the owner of Dunkirk Little Ship *Surrey,* now called *L'Orage* , was flying with his family to France. As they approached the coast near the Franco-Belgian border East of Dunkirk he pointed out to his son Graham who was with him that they were above La Panne, - the beaches of Dunkirk. They then realised that the next year it would be 25 years since the evacuation of the British Expeditionary Force by the Little Ships through the dangerous shallow waters just below them.

It was his son's idea that they should try to organize a commemorative return to Dunkirk by a small fleet of surviving veterans to mark this anniversary. Raymond Baxter wrote a letter to the Editor of The Sunday Times in the hope that this would attract replies from the current owners of any Little Ships that were still afloat. No less than 43 owners came forward

and took part in the 1965 Return to Dunkirk.

John Knight, Hon. Archivist of the ADLS

Early in 1967, Commander Charles Lamb DSO DSC RN, himself a veteran Fleet Air Arm pilot and the owner of *Lady Frances* and John Knight, then owner of *Elizabeth Green* and later of *Fedalma II* joined with Raymond Baxter in forming the Association of Dunkirk Little Ships. Charles Lamb became the first Commodore, later Hon. Admiral, and Raymond Baxter subsequently succeeded him to both flags. John Knight took on the onerous task of Hon. Archivist. He has compiled a card file of 700 Little Ships which took part in the operation and it is thought that between 400 and 500 may still be in existence - some as far away as Canada, Israel and Turkey.

More than 120 of these Little Ships are members of the Association and meet regularly. The British Admiralty has

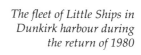

The fleet of Little Ships in Dunkirk harbour during the return of 1980

granted them the right, traditionally reserved for Admirals of the Royal Navy, to fly the Cross of St. George: a plain red cross on a white field, on the jackstaff (at the bow end of their ships) on special occasions or when cruising together in company, and the town of Dunkirk added its crest to the cross of St. George which forms the Association's house flag flown by members from the starboard yard-arm. Wherever a member ship is seen, this proud emblem is now recognised.

What of the future? Each year the number of survivors diminishes and at the time of the 50th anniversary of Dunkirk, more than a hundred of them made strenuous efforts to join another ceremonial return. The Royal Navy promised an escort and the town of Dunkirk a festive welcome. But many of the Little Ships will never be fit to go to sea again. Some of the owners are too old or can't afford to make them seaworthy. Some would gladly *donate* their ships to anyone willing to restore them as a continuing memorial to part of Britain's maritime history.

This book is dedicated to the Little Ships of Dunkirk and their Association in the hope that some will survive to celebrate their hundredth anniversary in A.D. 2040.

No single individual can take credit for the contents of this book because so many have generously contributed all the records and pictures they had. In many cases the identity of photographers was not recorded. Tribute must here be paid to members of the Association of Dunkirk Little Ships and especially their Hon. Archivist, John Knight, without whose contributions and painstaking work this book could not have been compiled.

Bob Tough, whose father played such an important part in assembling more

A leaflet dropped on French and British troops by the Luftwaffe as the Panzers closed in on the BEF at Dunkirk.

than 100 Little Ships for Operation Dynamo on the Upper Thames, entrusted us with his precious charts and many pictures to reproduce. Beken of Cowes gave us access to his priceless collection of photographs from before the war and took new ones specially for this book. Finally, Mark Child was responsible for the painstaking research which has made this book as complete as possible.

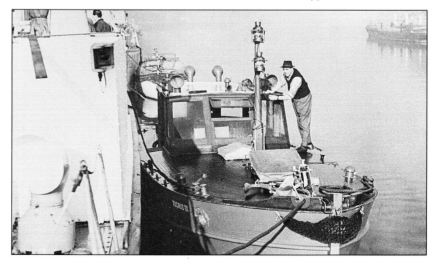

Douglas Tough , who assembled the flotilla of Little Ships on the Upper Thames in 1940.

Angele Aline

Angele Aline is a Dunkirk Little Ship with a remarkable, romantic history. She is a 'Dundee' - a French corruption of 'Dandy' - the name given by British East coast fishermen in the 1860s to an elegant new type of ketch later adopted by the Fécamp yard where Angele Aline was built. Jules Talleux and his two partners ordered her as a sturdy sailing trawler to go as far as Newfoundland and Iceland for cod, and to follow the shoals of herring off the Scottish coast in summer to Normandy in winter. The barrels in which the catch was salted down in her spacious hold did double duty as floats for the trawl.

She was named *Jean* when she was launched on 3rd November, 1921. Sixty-five feet long, with a 17ft beam and 8ft 6in draught, she is carvel built of 1 3/4 in. oak planks on oak frames and with 3in. teak decks. Her handsome rounded counter stern and beautiful, yet rugged lines can be appreciated in Leonce Bennay's model. It was he who built her nearly 70 years ago and his detailed hand-written notes survive to this day. When she first went fishing from the port of Gravelines, just West of Dunkirk, she had no engine, but was towed out to sea where she would hoist her brown gaff mainsail, mizzen, gallant topsail and two foresails on her way to the distant fishing grounds.

Later she was fitted with a succession of powerful diesels which enabled her to fish under power, and her sails were used less often. She belonged to various members of the Talleux family and was then sold to a Gerard Schollaert of Nieuport, who named

Leonce Bennay's original notes for the construction of Angele Aline in 1921.

her *Angele Aline* - the Christian names of his twin daughters. He had her until 1948 and so was her owner at the time of Dunkirk. During the night of 28th May 1940, when she was sailing from St. Valéry en Caux, where she had

A 1:15 model of Angele Aline made by her builder in his later years, showing her characteristic round stern.

gone for a new propeller, she was commandeered by the French navy to assist in the evacuation. She must have embarked her passengers in the port of Dunkirk, because her deep draught would not have allowed her to come close to the beaches. There is no record of the number of trips she made - presumably ferrying troops from the harbour to the warships anchored in deep water off the coast.

Her next record tells that she was sunk by British aircraft while fishing off St. Vaast-la-Hougue in 1941. Permission was given by the Germans to refloat her on 17th April and they used her to blockade Nieuport harbour entrance in 1943. Later she was allowed to continue fishing, sometimes carrying German guards to prevent her being used by the Resistance. One of her guards once caused her to be stuck high and dry on top of some submerged piles in Nieuport harbour, when the tide went out, by dictating which course she should take. There she remained until the incoming tide refloated her. No damage was done, except to her guard's pride. Meanwhile someone ashore risked his life taking a photo of the shaming event.

After the war *Angele Aline* continued as a fishing boat under several owners, until she was sold in 1963 to a Dutch couple, Binne and Dagmar Groenier. They fell in love with her, and not only restored her to her former beauty as a splendid gaff ketch, but converted her into their floating home. They lived and brought up their children in *Angele Aline* over the next 20 years, often sailing her along the coast and across the channel until one day the children demanded to "live in a proper house ashore, like other children."

The Groeniers sold *Angele Aline* to Gareth Wright, an Englishman who brought her to London and St Katherine's Dock. It was then that her latest owner saw her, and it was again

love at first sight. He took some pictures and then returned home to his wife to say: "I've found my dream boat". But it was three years before he could buy her. Meanwhile she sailed thousands of miles, taking part in some of the Tall Ships Races, including

Sailing off Bodrum, on the South-West coast of Turkey

By contrast, here she is, still as a fishing boat , in Northern France soon after the war.

Angele Aline

NAME:	Angele Aline
TYPE:	Gaff Ketch
LENGTH:	56 ft + 18 ft bowsprit
BEAM:	17 ft
DISPLACEMENT:	29.17 tons
DRAFT:	8.5 ft
ENGINE:	Perkins 6350 Diesel
HULL CONSTR. :	Carvel, oak-on-oak
BUILT BY:	L.Bennay,Fécamp
DATE BUILT:	3rd November, 1921

a modern fibreglass boat, and will surely be there when the time comes to celebrate the 100th anniversary of her service at Dunkirk.

Her restoration and conversion were tastefully done in traditional style and materials and she is meticulously maintained by George and Meriel Thurstan.

two crossings of the Atlantic. In December 1984 George and Meriel Thurstan realised their dream and spent the next eighteen months on a major programme of restoration before leaving England in their new home during May 1987 to start a voyage around the world. In 1989 they had got as far as Turkey, where they now charter the boat out of the lovely ancient port of Bodrum.

Angele Aline is one of the fortunate Little Ships. To begin with she was built to last. Her oak planks and frames still bear the marks of her trawling hawsers; honourable scars which witness her early years as a working boat earning her living in all weathers way out in the Atlantic. But inside she has all the comforts of a home and she is pampered with constant caring, coats of varnish and new paint. Her sails, though in traditional brown are now made of long-lasting Duradon but her blocks and bowsprit are in traditional gleaming wood. Her baggywrinkles protect her mainsail from chafe and contribute to the lovely look of an old timer. Though 70 years old, she is more fit to cruise the oceans than many

Her rugged construction and the fine craftsmanship, with the best traditional materials employed in her extensive refit, make Angele Aline a joy to look at and a pleasure to sail in.

Angele Aline looks quite at home among the local wooden boats where she now takes holiday makers to explore the sunbaked coast of Turkey. But George Thurstan is already beginning to dream of their next adventure. What a joy to see an old timer so well taken care of in her later years, after such a distinguished history!

Naiad Errant

The formal charter agreement for the use of the motor yacht Naiad Errant by the Royal Navy during World War II.

Pleasure cruiser ready for war

Built in June 1939, the last Summer before the war, at William Osborne's yard in Littlehampton for Wimbledon solicitor Ralph Nightingale, *Naiad Errant* was a new prototype of the then popular Swallow Senior class of pleasure cruisers. She had twin Morris petrol engines capable of 9 knots and cost her owner just over a thousand pounds - a substantial price in those days. He had little chance to enjoy his lovely new boat. War broke out just three months later. He was away from home on a visit to Bath in May 1940 when the Navy came to Horace Clark's yard in Sunbury-on-Thames, where she was lying, and requisitioned her. It was not until a year later that the formal agreement for the ship's charter was signed "between Major Nightingale and His Majesty the King".

NAME:	Naiad Errant
TYPE:	Motor Yacht
LENGTH:	32 ft
BEAM:	8 ft 3 ins
DISPLACEMENT:	8 tons
DRAFT:	3 ft
ENGINES:	2 x Perkins 4107 Diesel
HULL CONSTR.:	Carvel wood
BUILT BY:	Osborne, L'hampton
YEAR BUILT:	1938/39

Members of the Sunbury Fire Brigade took her down to Ramsgate where she was handed over to Able-Seaman Samuel Palmer who commanded her with great distinction during her remarkable exploits at Dunkirk for which he was awarded the Navy's Distinguished Service Medal. He was

*Back in civilian dress,
soon after the war*

one of the few Naval personnel manning the Little Ships whose identity and stories are precisely recorded. John Masefield the Poet Laureate who was also a war historian mentions it in his book: *The 9 Days' Wonder* about Operation Dynamo. He corresponded with Palmer, for whom he had a great admiration and invited him to tea.

A.-B. Palmer set out on 31st May with his Naval crew, in company with the motor launch *Westerly* and a small fleet of similar boats to cross the Channel that night. During the 20-mile crossing there was an aerial battle overhead in which a German plane was shot down. The pilot fell into the sea, but by the time *Naiad Errant* reached him it was too late to be of any help.

A few moments later he saw the *Foudroyant*, a French Destroyer, on its way to Dunkirk at 25 knots, sink in a matter of minutes when she received a direct hit from a German bomb. Palmer and the *Naiad Errant* picked up 20 French sailors -the only survivors- and transferred them to the next

French vessel they encountered before they continued towards Dunkirk. There they found a larger ship anchored some way off and swarms of soldiers waiting on the beach. Three of their little convoy of eight boats had arrived and the first had already loaded up and was soon on her way back to England. The second had gone aground on the sand. *Naiad Errant* made a number of trips, ferrying soldiers from the beach to the warship and then tried to tow the other boat off the sands, but had the tow rope round her propeller and went aground herself. Palmer and his crew jumped into the water and helped to carry wounded soldiers off the beach to the large ship's skiff. The Luftwaffe was dive-bombing and then machine-gunning the troops on the beach and their flotilla of rescuers who were waiting for the

Her call-up orders in 1939

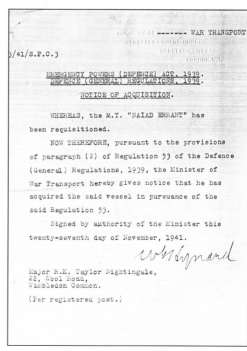

incoming tide to refloat their stranded craft.

While Sam Palmer was in the water and later on the larger ship, some Tommies from the beach had boarded the stranded *Naiad Errant* and after clearing the tow rope from her propellers, got her engines going. The fast rising tide (it was between seven and eight o'clock in the evening by then) refloated the ship so she could start with her full load towards England. They paused on the way, to scrounge some more fuel from a boat full of petrol cans, moored in the fairway, but as they continued their journey, the engines died. There were bombs and shells all around them and they were in danger of drifting onto Dunkirk pier or of being run down by other craft.

While the more mechanically-minded among the soldiers on board got to work on the engines, the weak and exhausted A.-B. Palmer ordered the cabin doors to be broken up and used as paddles. A flask of rum put fresh life and warmth into them. At ten o'clock the starboard engine came to life. Still without the port engine they headed home, avoiding the main shipping lane, for fear of being run down by the host of traffic in the night.

While Sam was having a brief rest, the soldier at the wheel misread the primitive compass and started to steer due East. But A.-B. Palmer soon got on course again. He knew the coast well, passed Dover, and by 11.00 a.m. next morning put his troops ashore at Ramsgate. He refuelled, got his engines seen to, had a bath and some food and then returned twice more to Dunkirk.

At the end of one of these trips there was a lady dispensing sandwiches, cigarettes and hot cups of sweet tea to the tired, cold and starving troops as they landed. One of them, overcome with joy and gratitude, removed the ship's bell and gave it to her as a memento. Thirty eight years later she found it, advertised it in Lloyd's Register and restored it to the present owner.

Naiad went through several hands after decommissioning in 1946. Sandy Evans was looking for a Dunkirk Little Ship and first saw her lying on the river Hamble but lost her to a boat yard where she was stripped and sold un-named. He spent seven more years looking for her, acquiring along the way her mast, ship's papers, her bell and her navigation lights used on patrol after Dunkirk. Then by chance one day he saw another Dunkirk Little Ship, coming through Boulter's Lock. On board was the Association's Secretary who had just located *Naiad,* for sale at Southampton. Three days later - 3rd September 1981 - she was Sandy's. He has restored her, cherished her and taken her to every Little Ships' rally and Return to Dunkirk ever since. He keeps her on the Thames at the bottom of the garden of his waterside home in Bray.

A letter about Naiad Errant from John Masefield, poet and war historian.

Telephone:
Clifton Hampden 77 BURCOTE BROOK ABINGDON

25 April.

Dear Sir,

I thank you for your letter of the 23rd, and for so kindly sending me the photographs of your Motor Yacht, the NAIAD ERRANT.
I return these, thinking that you may prefer to write to the applicant direct. He is
S. Palmer, A.B. D.S.M. No 1, Mess, H.M.S. JACKAL c/o G.P.O. LONDON.
May I hope that if this famous little ship pass my door when Peace returns, her owner will tie up and come in for a cup of tea?
This lies about half way, between Dorchester and the Barley Mow.

With my thanks,
Yours sincerely, *John Masefield.*

Naiad Errant's bell, given to a tea lady after Dunkirk and restored to the ship 38 years later.

On the Thames, in 1989

Trawler (Scottish Yawl) **W i l l d o r a**

When they were built in Scotland, soon after the turn of the Century, the *Willdora* and her sister ships, the *Willmarie* and the *Willanne*, were named after their owner's wife and his two daughters.

These Scottish yawls were fitted out as fishing trawlers, 55ft long, with a 16ft 6in beam and a displacement of over 70 tons. They were sturdy ships, fit to go out on their dangerous work in all weathers, yet their modest 5ft draught enabled them to come quite close inshore.

At the time of Dunkirk they were working on the south coast of England when the call came for all three of them to cross to Dunkirk and help in the evacuation. They were among the first to arrive and the *Willdora*, who was badly damaged by shellfire, was credited with saving 200 troops. Here, off the beach of La Panne, she was spotted, packed with troops by a soldier who, years later, identified her rotting hulk in a northern English dock and triggered the effort to save her.

After the war she went back to fishing, was later sold as a pleasure craft and eventually ended up in Sunderland, on the east coast of England, where she was intended as a training vessel for the district's schoolchildren. But the local council ran out of funds and before they could fully rebuild her, the hulk became prey to vandals and she ultimately sank at her moorings.

For three years she lay in Sunderland's south dock at a steep angle: her bow on the rocks, her stern embedded in the mud beneath 30ft of water at high tide. The local authority offered her free to anyone willing to raise her and several attempts failed. Then, one day, George Fraser, a local garage owner, met the soldier who first saw *Willdora* at Dunkirk - a local man, who had followed the boat's sad decline over the years. Inspired by his story, George dreamed of fitting out *Willdora* as a pleasure cruiser. He persuaded Gordon James and Joe Williams of the Hartlepool Diving Club, with the aid of a crane and ten helpers, to undertake the dangerous task of raising her from the muddy bottom and they succeeded in bringing her to the surface. But the cost of restoration once more proved too much and she has now been given to the Ousebourne Water Association whose members intend to adapt the ship for use by handicapped children.

So there are still enthusiasts left who want the war veteran once more to have a useful life.

NAME:	Willdora
TYPE:	Trawler (Scot. Yawl)
LENGTH:	55 ft
BEAM:	16 ft 6 in
DISPLACEMENT:	70 tons
DRAFT:	5 ft
ENGINES:	80 h.p. Kelvin
HULL CONSTR.:	Carvel built in wood
BUILT BY:	Unknown
YEAR BUILT:	1901

Willdora raised from Sunderland docks

Alusia at anchor on the south coast of England, enjoying her peace-time role as a comfortable family cruising yacht .

The nineteen thirties were a time when the well-to-do English middle classes developed elegant leisure pursuits. Mrs Louisa Alexander had a most comfortable 45-foot motor yacht built and named after her by Rampart Boat Builders, in Southampton in 1938.

Alusia was not only considered luxurious, but extremely innovative. Instead of having access amidships, from the narrow side deck, she was designed to be boarded aft, through the cockpit. From there one conveniently enters the saloon, the tiled galley and heads.

The raised wheelhouse provides excellent visibility all round and separates the public and entertaining areas of the yacht from the magnificent forward stateroom.

This was beautifully fitted out in varnished mahogany, with deep-sprung mattresses on two comfortable berths, a large wardrobe and even a full-length mirror.The stateroom has its own separate heads and washbasin. Oak floors were laid throughout the ship to give her not only durability, but an air of elegance to match any country house.

Forward of the stateroom is the foc'sle with a further guest - or crew berth and a large locker.

Alusia was strongly built in wood on oak frames and powered by twin Morris Commodore petrol engines which gave her an easy cruising speed of 9 knots. One engine was fitted with a powerful pump, which could serve as a most efficient bilge pump or as a salt water power wash for the decks. The engine was well insulated to make the ship glide through the water with hardly a murmur. There was even room between the engines for a mechanic's workbench.

Alusia's strong davits were fitted to support her exceptionally fast 12ft 6in dinghy, which had an Elto outboard, capable of propelling it at a reputed 27 knots - suitable for water skiing.

Mrs Louisa Alexander pronounced herself well pleased with the performance of her boat on its south coast trials in the year before war broke out. Her sleek lines gave the impression of length, and her owners had in mind to slip through France to the Mediterranean. Yet the Alexander family were to have but a few months use of her in the next nine years.

NAME:	A l u s i a
TYPE:	Motor Yacht
LENGTH:	45ft
BEAM:	10ft 6ins
DISPLACEMENT:	19.9 tons
DRAFT:	3ft 7ins
ENGINES:	80 hp. Kelvin
HULL CONSTR.:	Carvel, timber on oak
BUILT BY:	Rampart, S'hampton
YEAR BUILT:	1938

Alusia only enjoyed a single season fulfilling the role for which she was built: cruising in French waters as an ideal pleasure boat. Soon after the outbreak of war she was called up for more serious duties, first as a patrol boat (some members of the Royal Navy must have blessed the day!) and then, at the end of May 1940, under the command of Gunner A J Northcott RN, with a civilian crew, she assisted in the evacuation of Dunkirk.

After the war she was bought back from the Admiralty by her original owners, the Alexander family.

Since then, the *Alusia* has changed hands five times. Her original petrol engines were replaced with twin BMC diesels in 1958 and she now belongs to Mr. M.R.Woods, a member of the Association of Dunkirk Little Ships.

An old black-and-white-picture of Alusia with a former owner, which shows her elegant lines and her dinghy on her davits

The cockle fishermen of Leigh-on-Sea on the shallow northern, Essex shore of the Thames estuary were used to handling their cockle *Bawley* sailing ships in all weathers and in tricky, shallow waters. For a little extra income - and excitement - they used to crew in the famous J-Class yachts of the gentry during the nineteen-twenties. It was after four of these racing yachts that the *Resolute* and her sister ships, the *Reliance, Defender* and *Endeavour* were named.

The *Bawleys* were broad-beamed, flat-bottomed gaffsail cutters, typically of some 36ft length, designed to be beached at high tide on the sandbanks, while the fishermen got out to gather cockles and shrimps for the London market. They were therefore ideal for the shallow waters off Dunkirk. At sea they could drop their lifting centreboards for better sailing and their powerful Kelvin petrol/paraffin engines made them less dependent on sail when it suited them. The *Resolute* was built for Cecil Osborne by Heyward's at Southend in 1927 for £375. She was gaff-rigged, with a main, jib and foresail and had a

Resolute as a solid cruising boat in the nineteen eighties

16ft bowsprit. Her gaff was held to the mast by large wooden hoops and her sails were made of the traditional red cotton. She would go cockling from Easter to October and shrimping in the winter.

During the war she went fishing all the year round. At that time there was an honorary 'Commodore' appointed at Leigh, who determined where they could fish on a particular day. Forty-nine years later, the 68-year-old Eric Osborne recalled how he came into harbour on the last day of May 1940 to be told that the Navy at Southend, just down river, wanted their boats with volunteer crews to go to Dunkirk. They were to be at the pierhead, ready for sea, by eight o'clock on Friday morning. Once there, Naval ratings provided drums of fuel, rations and an extra deckhand: Vincent Joscelyne, to join Eric and his cousin Horace Osborne. As the Navy stored *Renown*, alongside *Resolute*, one of them turned her hatch cover upside-down: a bad omen among Thames bargemen. Cousin Luke, who sailed on the *Renown* had already signed a form number 13 the night before and wasn't pleased. *Renown* never came back from

Dunkirk. The six boats sailed line-ahead for Dunkirk, which they easily recognised in a mass of flames and covered under a pall of smoke from the burning oil storage tanks. They were told to go to the beach, but the tide was ebbing fast and the fishermen were too canny to get grounded with a full load of troops, a sitting target for the German bombers. So they went to the outside of the Mole of Dunkirk harbour instead. Although the sea was calm, there was a 4ft swell and they had no ladders.

There was no option but to go inside. They embarked a full load of soldiers whch they ferried to a trawler anchored some way off. Then a second load to a coaster and then a third.

By then it was dark and they went inside once more. A destroyer lay sunk across the entrance; oil barrels and debris floated on the oily water. On one side of the harbour one of the *Eagle* steamers lay sinking after a bomb scored a direct hit down her funnel. The debris of vehicles showed here and there above the water. Marked by their phosphorescent wake and after picking their way through this mess, they drew alongside the pier. There seemed to be less men waiting and they were getting choosey: ".. not going back on that bloody thing" they shouted. Eric quite understood: "when you're not a cockle fisherman and consider the idea of a 36ft. boat, seen from 36ft. above, it doesn't inspire a lot of confidence!"

The fishermen decided to go ashore, partly so that they could say they had been on French soil and partly to persuade the reluctant soldiers to come aboard since, they maintained, their ship was equal to any weather. "At that moment", Eric recalls, "we had our narrowest escape: Jerry found his range, - sparks and shrapnel were

NAME:	R e s o l u t e
TYPE:	Gaff Cutter (Bawley)
LENGTH:	36ft
BEAM:	11ft
DISPLACEMENT:	5.88 tons
DRAFT:	2ft
ENGINES:	Kelvin J3
HULL CONSTR.:	Carvel,pitch pine on oak
BUILT BY:	Haywards, Southend
YEAR BUILT:	1927

Cecil Osborne who built Resolute in 1927 and whose son Horace commanded her at Dunkirk, together with 1989 owner "Dusty"Miller

Resolute

Resolute as she was, a traditional Leigh Cockle Bawley boat

flying all over the place and we came down that ladder faster than we ever went up; it only lasted three or four minutes. We had our full load and motored outside the harbour. It was 5 or 5.30 and *Defender* was close by us. We couldn't find a large passenger ship or coaster and the Sub-Lieut. on *Defender* told us to head for Ramsgate."

Admiral Ramsey, who as Vice-Admiral Dover, was in command of 'Operation Dynamo' had high praise for the Leigh Cockle *Bawley* boats:

"The conduct of the crews of these cockle boats was exemplary. They were all volunteers who were rushed over to Dunkirk in one day. Probably none of them had been under gunfire before and certainly none of them under Naval discipline. These were Thames estuary fishing boats which never left the estuary and only one of their crews had been further afield than Ramsgate. Yet they maintained perfect formation throughout the day and night and all orders were obeyed with great diligence even under shellfire and aircraft attack."Now *Resolute* lives in happy retirement, well cared-for since

1969 by "Dusty" Miller, who has fitted her out for comfortable cruising under sail out of Rye Harbour, on the South coast of England. He has made numerous voyages along the Dutch, Belgian and French coasts and belongs to the Association of Dunkirk Little Ships.

The memorial at St. Clements', Leigh to the fishermen who died in the Renown.

*L*etitia's rudder was damaged while she was close inshore at Dunkirk and she took a tow from the drifter *Ben and Lucy*. The *Renown's* engine had also broken down and she made fast to *Letitia's* tow. Half-an-hour later she struck a mine and a shower of splintered wood came down on *Letitia's* deck. The *Renown* was lost with skipper Noakes and her crew: Frank and Leslie Osborne and Harry Noakes - all cousins - and Harold Porter, a naval rating from Birmingham. A.J. Dench, the *Letitia's* skipper said: "In the pitch dark we could see nothing and could do nothing - except pull in the tow rope, which was just as we had passed it to

Renown three quarters of an hour before." Today Leigh has its own memorial to those brave men.

The *Resolute* and *Letitia* made it back to Ramsgate, as did the *Defender*. There they were told by the Navy that they now wanted only ships that could do 10 knots or more, so they returned to Leigh. "On the lighter side," Eric recalls, " we went to Naval Headquarters to collect our pay - I think mine was just under £4 and the deckhands' just over £3 each. Waiting for the train at Southend Central Harold King, the Deckhand on *Reliance* suggested a game of cards. Ten minutes later, on arrival at Leigh, he had one shilling left. As Eric put it with his characteristic humour: ". . . . easy come, easy go, they say! "

Letitia is once again engaged in fishing on the Essex coast. Not for her the comfortable retirement of a pleasure boat. But she looks well cared for and with plenty of life left in her.

NAME:	Letitia
TYPE:	Aux. motor sailer
LENGTH:	30 ft
BEAM:	10ft 6in
DISPLACEMENT:	7.09 tons
DRAFT:	5 ft
ENGINES:	Petter PJ 4M
HULL CONSTR.:	Carvel,pitch pine on oak
BUILT BY:	Johnson & Johnson
YEAR BUILT:	1938

Endeavour

*E*ndeavour, with skipper F. Hall, was one of the little fleet of Leigh Cockle *Bawley* boats that set out in convoy at half past midnight on 31st May 1940 for Dunkirk. They went under power of their engines that night in order to keep in convoy under command of their Naval Lieutenant. They were soon attacked from the air, but the Royal Air Force provided cover for them.

The *Endeavour* played her full part - first in embarking soldiers from the beach and then, as the tide went out and threatened to strand them, from the Mole and finally from the inner harbour of Dunkirk.

Her rudder was smashed during the rescue operations and, together with *Letitia* and *Renown*, she was towed back by the coaster *Ben & Lucy.* which had been ferrying troops from the beaches all the previous day before working almost exclusively with the cockle boats.

Unlike the ill fated *Renown*, the *Endeavour* got back to Ramsgate safely with her load of soldiers, to be congratulated for her valiant efforts.
After the war *Endeavour* went fishing

NAME:	Endeavour
TYPE:	Cockle Bawley
LENGTH:	34ft
BEAM:	12ft
DISPLACEMENT:	11.78 tons
DRAFT:	3 ft 6in
ENGINES:	Ford 80
HULL CONSTR.:	Carvel, pitch pine on oak
BUILT BY:	Cole & Wiggens
YEAR BUILT:	1926

on the south coast of England and changed owners several times. She is still a licenced fishing boat and Spike Thorrington now also uses her for tourist trips. In 1986 she won two prizes in a trawler race, with a fancy dress competition for her crew.

A year later she sank in the great storms of 1987, when tied up at Thunderbolt pier off Chatham Historic Dockyard. The Nautilus Diving Club, with Thames side sub-aqua divers and some huge inflatable bags, raised her in a two day exercise which began at midnight. It was all done free and for the love of a great old boat.

Cockle Bawley Defender

Defender was built in 1920 by Haywood of Leigh-on-Sea, gaff cutter-rigged, with a short mast, bowsprit, three foresails and a powerful diesel engine. Traditionally, the Leigh cockle boats were only 36 feet long and not only had a shallow draft, but were also light, so that they could be beached as the tide went out, allowing their crews to collect the cockles before the tide came in to refloat their craft.

Defender was the first of a new design, which was heavier, so that she could carry a crew of up to ten. This was to enable her to be more productive. But they soon discovered that her greater weight meant that she had to be beached further out, with a longer walk for her crew and a shorter time before the tide refloated her. Only two of the new design were ever built.

NAME:	Defender
TYPE:	Cockle Bawley
LENGTH:	42ft
BEAM:	12ft
DISPLACEMENT:	16 tons
DRAFT:	2ft 6ins
ENGINES:	Ford 80 diesel
HULL CONSTR.:	Carvel, pitch pine on oak
BUILT BY:	Haywood, Leigh-on-Sea
YEAR BUILT:	1920

On 31st May 1940, she and her sister ships left for Dunkirk. *Defender* carried one RNVR officer, Sub Lieut. Soloman - later to receive the Navy's Distinguished Service Cross for valour. - in charge of the Leigh cockle boats *Letitia, Renown, Endeavour, Reliance* and *Resolute.* Between 18.20 and 18.40 the flotilla had scattered during an enemy air attack. By 18.50 RAF Spitfires had driven off the attackers and 5 Dorniers had crashed into the sea. At 19.15 the flotilla, now reunited, reached Dunkirk Roads but found it

Defender converted to a cruising yacht

impracticable to work off the beach. At 21.30 they therefore started embarking troops from outside the jetty and transferring them to the schuyt *Tilly* and other ships. By 22.40 the strong swell made work from the outside of the mole difficult, so they entered the harbour in formation and loaded troops to be transferred to other ships, including the *Sarah Hyde* and the *Ben & Lucy.*

At 03.00 it was time to return to Ramsgate where *Defender* arrived in company with *Resolute* landing her load of soldiers, including the Colonel commanding the Royal Worcestershire Regiment, several officers of the Cameron Highlanders and 60 men. In all, the Leigh Cockle ships had rescued about 1,000 soldiers.

After the war the *Defender* was converted into a comfortable sea going cruising boat with a 50ft mast and a Bermudan rig. Under her shallow draft hull she has a drop keel and she was much loved by her owners, which included Cmdr. P.F. Clayton RN, his wife and six children.

Defender, in need of someone to restore her.

On 22nd January 1965 they received a letter from the Sunday Times

explaining that, to mark the 25th Anniversary of Dunkirk, a return by the Little Ships was planned in May. This was the first they knew that *Defender* had taken part in the Evacuation. It took them three weeks and thirty-one telephone calls to confirm the fact and to get in touch with one of her Dunkirk crew members.

Defender returned to Dunkirk in 1965, this time with Ted "Edge" Harvey and George "Pie" Osborne on board. The latter had lost his brother, Leslie and cousin Frank Osborne when the *Renown* was sunk on the way home from Dunkirk, in 1940 so it was fitting that he was asked to lay the wreath from *Defender* in memory of all those killed at sea.

Richard Dimbleby was the commentator for the live television coverage of the return on 6th June 1965, and *Defender* became a film star. The final shot showed a flag-bedecked *Defender* slipping out of the Bassin de Commerce with the message: "au revoir" spelled out in signal flags at her mast head.

Her flirtation with the film world nearly proved fatal for the illustrious Little Ship. She was chosen again as an extra by Television and a clever young film director had the bright idea to burn her as a climax for an episode of a soap opera, but she escaped on that occasion.

But the future of *Defender* does not look bright. She has fallen on hard times and can be seen rotting and rusting on her moorings in St. Aubin Harbour in the Channel Islands. No-one, it seems, can afford to restore her to seaworthiness. Old wooden boats cost a lot to maintain.

*R*ania was built by Rampart Boat Building Works in Southampton who, during the years before the war, acquired an enviable reputation for well built traditional gentlemen's motor yachts, scores of which are still sound fifty years later. These boats were primarily intended for Channel crossings and cruising the extensive European inland waterways. Constructed in pitch pine over oak frames, the interior and wheelhouse of *Rania* are finished in finest mahogany.

She was built in 1938 for a Mr McLoughlin who named her *Zelia*. With her length of 43ft. and a 10ft. 6 in. beam, she is a comfortable boat. She has a raked transom and a semi-clipper stern and is now powered by two diesel engines. Originally, she had two 6 cylinder Morris petrol engines which gave her a speed of 9.5 knots.

In 1939 *Zelia* was collected from Rampart Boat Building Works not by her intended owner, but by the Royal Navy who had need of her on H.M. service and re-named her *Rania*.

She became part of the Royal Navy's motley collection of hastily acquired civilian ships. They served as the 'mosquito navy' which performed a great variety of tasks, as patrol boats, communications vessels and transport for naval personnel who needed to move around on the rivers and estuaries of southern England.

Under naval command, *Rania* took part in the Evacuation of Dunkirk, but no details are recorded. After the war *Rania* had four civilian owners in forty years. The 1989 owner, Ian Davidson, spent two years restoring the boat, re-named her *Arkian* (Ian's ark) and uses her as a demonstration vessel for communications equipment. Today, *Arkian* has an idyllic home alongside the Double Locks Hotel halfway up the Exeter Canal. Her owner is determined to find the means to maintain her in perfect order by using her for commercial purposes, he has even thought of forming a charitable trust. Although the Association of Dunkirk Little Ships is reluctant to become involved with commercialisation and sponsorship, there does seem to be a case for using all modern means to defray the considerable cost of maintaining these historic craft. *Arkian* is a member of the Association of Dunkirk Little Ships and is being prepared to join the return to Dunkirk in 1990.

NAME:	Rania
TYPE:	Motor Yacht
LENGTH:	45ft
BEAM:	10ft 3in
DISPLACEMENT:	13 tons
DRAFT:	3ft 9in
ENGINES:	Twin Morris Petrol
HULL CONSTR.:	Pitch pine on oak
BUILT BY:	Rampart, S'hampton
YEAR BUILT:	1937

A year after Queen Victoria died in 1902 the bearded, pleasure loving Prince Edward, Prince of Wales was crowned King Edward VII. As one of the many ways of celebrating this, the end of the Victorian Age, Harry Tagg of East Molesey on the river Thames, built an 81ft Hurlingham-style passenger steam-boat, not in iron and steel, but in teak. She was christened *The King* and became sister ship to *The Windsor*, owned by Thames Launches Ltd, of Eel Pie Island, Twickenham.

Year after year, *The King* would take up to 200 passengers at a time to and from Hampton Court, Richmond and Kew. Powered by a single steam engine and immediately recognisable by her bowsprit, clipper stem and classic lines, she was a charabanc afloat at a time when most motor cruising was confined to the wealthy.

On 28th May 1940, *The King* was one of the 540 privately-owned vessels commandeered for the evacuation of the British Expeditionary Force from the beaches of Dunkirk. Her elegant shape and low freeboard were ill-suited to the open sea and even the wash from a destroyer would have swamped her, especially when she was fully laden with troops. But it was one of the miracles of Dunkirk that the sea was calm and she returned without mishap.

When the war was over, she was returned to Twickenham to continue her peacetime activities. Her steam engine was replaced by a 75hp 6 cylinder Thornycroft internal combustion unit of 1947 vintage.

Moored on the Thames by Westminster Bridge is Fuel Barge *Freddy* and it was in 1985 that her owner, Gary Beckwith,

The King on the Thames in Westminster where she still works in 1989

purchased *The King* from Thames waterman C.H. Wyatt, with the intention of returning her once more to the former splendour of Edwardian days.

When the 1986 season was over, *The King* was taken to Len Bowman's Eel Pie Island Boatyard and dry-docked. Here, during the winter months, Gary Beckwith's marine engineer/shipwright, Ron Oemering, carried out her face-lift.

Externally two of her teak planks were replaced, her 3ft bronze propeller was sent away to Streamline Props of Hampshire for reconditioning, whilst new bearings were found for her shaft. Her oak decking was replanked where necessary, then recaulked and re-tingled and Len Bowman's Eel Pie Island team gave her a new coat of gloss blue and white. Perhaps more elegant was the transformation of *The*

Period scene of an English crowd enjoying a bank holiday on the river - ca. 1938

and one covered, together with her magnificently carved dining saloon seating thirty-two guests, *The King* is an ideal ship for wedding receptions and private parties. Guests can board her at any of the Thames piers between Putney and Greenwich and there will be few places for a party that can boast such facilities for guests!

NAME:	The King
TYPE:	Thames Pass. Launch
LENGTH:	81ft
BEAM:	14ft 6in
DISPLACEMENT:	40.80 tons
DRAFT:	5ft 5in
ENGINES:	Thornycroft 75
HULL CONSTR.:	Teak on oak
BUILT BY:	H. Tagg, East Molesey
YEAR BUILT:	1902

King's interior. The ceiling was rebuilt using 22 panels covered in washable suede-style material. When 80 years of variegated paintwork was stripped from the rafters, they were found to be solid mahogany. *The King,* the oldest timber-hulled passenger ship working the tidal Thames can, in 1989, still be privately chartered for special occasions, or boarded by fare paying customers at Westminster Pier on her daily excursions to Kew and back.
With two spacious decks, one open

Those who crossed the channel in *The King* in 1940 would smile to see her now and surely their spirits must still hover around her ornate and durable timbers.

Passenger Motor Launch Tigris I

Harry Hastings, born 1908, Freeman of the City of London and the Company of Watermen & Lightermen was thirty-two years old when, on Tuesday 28th May 1940, he was asked by the Admiralty to take a ship down river to Southend for an undisclosed purpose. Harry was then a lighterman, working for Clemence Nolan. His father, elderly publican of The Gloucester Arms at Kingston, owned *Tigris I* as well as a number of pleasure steamers and motor boats for public hire. These had already been checked out, categorised and numbered by the Admiralty; earmarked as either hospital ships or fire floats should the need arise.

Tigris I, a former first World War submarine-chaser, had been converted by Tough Brothers at Teddington to a passenger boat, and worked as a summer pleasure cruiser carrying tourists - up to 350 at a time - between Richmond and Hampton Court. She had just been fitted with a new engine which had not even been properly run in. Harry's father asked his son if he, together with fellow-lighterman Bill Clark, then thirty-three and Harry's brother Warren Hastings, who was three years younger, would be prepared to take *Tigris I* to wherever the Admiralty had in mind. Despite great secrecy over the ultimate destination, they speculated that she was needed to take people - perhaps children - out of London.

Bill Clark later recalled being offered "a day's work and the fare back home" to join Harry and Warren on the trip. Since work was short at Nolans, Bill and Harry were given the week off, and at 7 o'clock on Monday morning *Tigris I* set off for Gravesend in company with a Billingsgate fish market boat which had also been appropriated. Passing the Royal Albert Docks, they noticed a lock full of ships' lifeboats; the first indication that "something big was on".

Ordered alongside at Westminster Pier which was packed with officers and naval ratings, the crew of *Tigris I* were despatched to the ship's chandlers and other local shops to exchange chits for sufficient provisions for four days. They bought tea, bread, eggs, bacon, sugar, meat, candles, cigarettes ... and filled a trolley which was then trundled back to the boat. With provisions stowed, they were sent first to Southend pier where there were no free berths to be had and *Tigris I* was moored to another boat. Still believing they could be home by nightfall, the crew prepared to leave the boat, packed with provisions, and return by train. The order to proceed to Sheerness put paid to that.

They lay outside Sheerness harbour until nightfall. Once inside, the crew was ordered ashore by naval ratings with fixed bayonets, who marched them into the office where they were asked to volunteer for Dunkirk. After a 'phone call to the Admiralty and another to alert relatives, they all signed on in the Royal Navy at around £20 pay for a month. Ever afterwards Harry was to say: "We joined up for a month, but one bloody day was enough!" He also tells the story of a man who was not prepared to sign. He went back to the Barley Arms at Twickenham where a woman overheard him explaining that the boats were going to France. She called the police who arrested him, and in a closed court, because the matter was top secret, he was sent to prison for three months..

At Sheerness, the Navy installed their own personnel both in command and as extra crew, then brought on more provisions and two ladders which would be needed across the Channel.

Then the convoy went to Ramsgate, moored overnight, and next morning sailed to Dover. They were led by a fish-cutter with two machine guns and a triangle of three red lights on the mast. At Dover, Harry recalls, a voice over the tannoy shouted: "Does anyone want to turn back? Those who want to go on, follow the light on the top of my mast." Forty-five boats set off on convoy, knowing that if they lost the light they could be on their own in a sea of mines. Part-way across the same voice shouted: "I'm turning back now. Where you see the smoke coming up, that's Dunkirk. Make for it." *Tigris I* followed behind *Princess Freda* - another peace-time passenger boat - and Mears' *Margherita*. The latter never made the journey. In Harry's words: "A destroyer ran by and put out a huge wave. *Margherita* went under and didn't come up again, but the two ratings on board surfaced through a hole in the aft end and were picked up".

Bill Clark recalled his first impression of Dunkirk: "Destroyers were coming towards us loaded with troops, some of whom were fully dressed, some half dressed. Away to starboard on the beach some hundreds - no thousands of men. Some lined up in companies, columns and groups, down to the water's edge. Others in the background, lying on the sand, some sheltering in the sand dunes. Ahead of us there was a lot of noise. The Germans were above us, dropping bombs from the air."

When the bombs were not falling, the sea was calm. There was no wind and the sky was blue. One and a half miles off shore the big destroyers were waiting, unable to sail closer to land. About 250 yards out to sea *Tigris I* touched the sand and lowered her ladders. But being of wood, these floated on the water making it hard for

NAME:	Tigris I
TYPE:	Pass. Motor Launch
LENGTH:	Approx. 80ft
BEAM:	15ft
DISPLACEMENT:	50 tons
DRAFT:	5ft
ENGINES:	Thornycroft
HULL CONSTR.:	Pitch Pine on oak
BUILT BY:	Unknown
YEAR BUILT:	1914

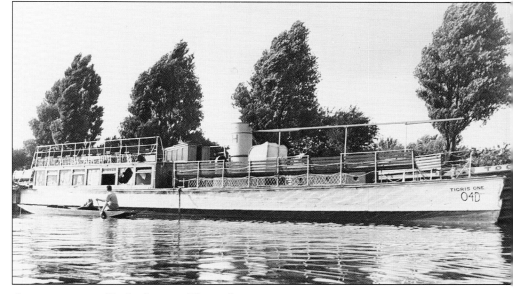

the troops to climb them. Then the first man, the head of a column, climbed aboard after 72 hours waiting on the sands. Others used the rubbing strakes on the outside of the hull to climb up. But they were two feet apart and hardly wide enough to get a toehold so that they could heave themselves aboard with their packs and rifles. The first run rescued over 400 men; altogether *Tigris I* is credited with saving 900 lives from the beaches of Dunkirk.

They soon found that they could not get close enough to be of any help on the beaches, so they went into Dunkirk harbour under very dangerous conditions, ferrying troops to the bigger ships outside. Bill Clark again: "On the way out to our destroyer we had to dodge lots of little boats, all loaded and ferrying troops or else empty and on their way to the beaches." On the fourth run a bomb fell close to *Tigris I* and Harry Hastings was blown out of the wheelhouse by the blast of a bomb, while machine guns strafed the boat. When Harry was hauled out of the foul-smelling and oily sea, from among floating corpses, *Tigris I* had bullet holes in the deck and funnel and shrapnel had torn into her hull. He was badly shaken, but they went into Dunkirk again.

"Some of those men", Harry says, "had been on the beaches for days; they were in a terrible state, hadn't washed or shaved and stank something awful." *Tigris I* suffered further damage later that day in collision with a Thames barge.

The breakwater, which had been used for embarkation had suffered a direct hit and lorries had immediately been driven into the water on top of each other to form a makeshift jetty. *Tigris I* used this to pick up French troops and the last load was delivered to one of Nolan's Tilbury mud-hoppers. With *Tigris I* badly hit, it was felt that she could not make it home. The naval command ordered her engine to be broken up and the ship to be beached and abandoned. Holed by enemy action, opened up at the seams by the collision and with her pumps unable to cope, she was left amid the debris and carnage of Dunkirk.

Harry Hastings and his crew were taken back to Ramsgate. Not surprising, they slept most of the way home. "We felt like death" was Bill Clark's description "I don't know when we last had a wash. No shave since the Saturday. My face was beginning to itch; my feet were swollen and my body sore all over. We were all the same".

At Ramsgate the quay was lined with stalls of tea, coffee, sandwiches, chocolate and tobacco. At the end was a barrier, manned by naval ratings. Harry recalls being marched round to the *Merry England* for a wash and brush up.

They feared that they might be sent back to Sheerness or, if they left for home, that they would be arrested by the Navy for desertion. Nevertheless they made for Ramsgate station with only six shillings between them. They took a train to Rochester where they borrowed thirty shillings from Warren's mother in law (out of her rent money under the mantle-piece clock) That got them back to Kingston where they were toasted as heroes in their local pub.

But this was not the end of the *Tigris I*. Found and refloated by a group of desperate French sailors who plugged up her holes, she was towed across the channel into Ramsgate harbour by a naval tug who had found her crippled off the Goodwins. Taken to Sheerness and then to Teddington where she was repaired, *Tigris I* was put back into civilian use after the war as a houseboat. She was finally broken up in 1985.

Motor Yacht **B o u n t y**

Bounty was an ideal ship for the Navy to take over. She was constructed by Camper & Nicholson at Gosport in 1936 as a substantial 78ft motor yacht of 67 tons with two Gardner engines. Fast and powerful, she carried a dinghy and a 14ft motor launch.

At Dunkirk her owner, Lieut. C A Lundy RNVR, was in command of his ship throughout the operation and he kept a detailed log. At one time she was used as Flagship by Commodore Stevenson and Lord Gort, the C.-in-C. of the BEF, was taken in the *Bounty* from the minesweeper *Hebe* to the destroyer *HMS Keith*. Between 2100 hours and 2400 hours on May 31st the *Bounty* took troops from the beaches out to the destroyers. During one of these runs, while carrying 150 troops, the *Bounty* fouled her propeller and *HMS Seriola* towed her back to Ramsgate. After the war a succession of owners cruised in her, but latterly her condition declined. Although she

NAME:	B o u n t y
TYPE:	Motor Yacht
LENGTH:	78ft
BEAM:	15ft
DISPLACEMENT:	67 tons
DRAFT:	5ft 6ins
ENGINES:	Twin 4 L 3 Gardners
HULL CONSTR.:	Teak
BUILT BY:	Camper & Nicholson
YEAR BUILT:	1936

returned to Dunkirk for the 1985 reunion, the captain feared for her safety and would not go above 5 knots. She lay unused for two years, partly vandalised and was discovered on a slipway at Torpoint, Plymouth, by Dr N E Harvey. Now she has had a complete re-fit with new masts, hydraulic steering, air conditioning and electronic equipment. Her engines have been re-built, her frames and floors renewed and she has been re-wired throughout. So *Bounty* is once more set for cruising in home waters.

In the 1920s and '30s when boats and often motor car bodies were hand-built, private yacht designs were often based on ships' tenders and life-boats. The *Gay Venture*, a 45ft Watercraft cruiser was built for ex Brook-lands racing driver, Douglas Briault. He took up the more leis-urely sport of yachting and wanted a boat that he could use as a floating home. *Gay Venture's* design was based on the hull of a naval pinnace. She was rigged as a ketch, but her two short masts only carried 267 square feet of sail. Despite her 2-ton iron keel, she had a mere 4ft draft which would not have given her much of a perfor-mance to windward.

Gay Venture's machinery below decks was more impressive. Her two 58 h.p. 6-cylinder Gray engines with reduction gears gave a cruising speed of $9^1/_2$ knots at only three quarters of her available power. Her well-insulated engine room, beneath the bridge deck lined with asbestos and perforated zinc, was built for almost silent running.

Gay Venture was the largest boat ever built by Watercraft at Molesey, and her 12ft beam (wide for those days) provided space for a comfortable in-terior. Forward of the bridge one stepped down into the state room which led into a comfortable bathroom. Be-hind the wheelhouse was a large saloon with access to the spacious galley. The ship was built for two; any professional crew would have to sleep on the settee in the wheelhouse.

The Briaults planned her as a floating home, first to be moored at Bosham and then to cruise the French canals from Brittany and the Garonne down to the Mediterranean Riviera. Against the British climate, she had a coal-fired stove and central heating system. This could have been the cause of a serious fire which troops returning from Dunkirk were thought to have started by accident. However, her solidly built hull, with $1^1/_2$ inch pitch pine planks on oak and decks of teak with grooved pine survived. The low, well pro-portioned wheelhouse was made of mahogany and teak. The panelling

NAME:	Gay Venture
TYPE:	Auxiliary ketch
LENGTH:	45ft
BEAM:	12ft
DISPLACEMENT:	23 tons
DRAFT:	4ft
ENGINES:	Twin BMC diesel
HULL CONSTR.:	Pitch pine on oak
BUILT BY:	Watercraft of Molesey
YEAR BUILT:	1938

and the floors of the saloon and state room were of American oak. She cost her first owner £2,100 in August 1938.

The Briaults had every reason to be proud of *Gay Venture* and sold their home to pay for her. But just a year after they launched her on the Thames, war broke out. She was requisitioned to become His Majesty's Yacht *Gay Venture* - a Royal Navy Patrol Ship in the Thames Estuary, flying the White Ensign. Her owner joined the Royal Navy and three years later took part in the raid on St Nazaire as skipper of a Naval mine-laying craft.

For the last 25 years Gay Venture has been owned by Don Waddleton and his wife Joan. He gives full credit to his wife for "many years of agonising work on the boat". For fifteen years they lived on board and cruised extensively.

In 1985 Lesley Jurd bought a share in *Gay Venture* whose strong construction combined with the loving care of her owners should ensure her survival for many years to come.

Barge **Tollesbury**

NAME:	Tollesbury
TYPE:	Barge
LENGTH:	84ft
BEAM:	20ft
DISPLACEMENT:	Approx. 57 tons
DRAFT:	6ft
ENGINES:	80 h.p. Rus. Hornsby
HULL CONSTR.:	Pitch pine on oak
BUILT BY:	H Felton, Sandwich
YEAR BUILT:	1901

Around 1850 the age of stage coaches was at an end and transport by rail had only just begun. At that time, there was a thriving trade between the East Coast of England and the Pool of London below London Bridge. At first, grain was shipped from the farms of East Anglia to the Metropolis and a variety of merchandise from coal to manufactured goods was loaded for the return journey. The breweries of London had an insatiable need for malt and there was a good market in straw and oats.

Later, when cheaper wheat in greater loads was imported into London Docks from Canada, the Continent, the Mediterranean and Black Sea ports, it had to be trans-shipped into 100-ton loads for the millers on the rivers Stour and Orwell. For this a very special kind of craft was required, which could come alongside cargo ships and liners in the Pool of London, negotiate the shallow waters of East Anglia and handle small cargoes economically. The age of the spritsail barges created a whole new industry, a special kind of ship and a tough new breed of sailors. The sailing barges were adaptable, fast, economical vessels typically manned by only three men: a skipper, a mate and a boy, with small wages and their keep while sailing and extra pay for loading and unloading their ships. Often, the three of them manhandled 200-tons unloading and loading their barges in a single day. It was dusty and back-breaking labour dealing with coal, grain, straw and manure alike. They would take on any load to avoid returning under ballast to keep their ships stable in heavy weather .

Their large hatches gave easy access for lightering and quick turnrounds. The spritsail barge was fast even in light airs and the bargemen sharpened their skills by racing their boats. They were in great demand as crews in the age of the J-class yachts. The flat-bottomed barges had leeboards which enabled them to sail close to the wind and close to the shore in shallow waters. Although they were mainly coasters, they were quite able to cross the Channel when required and it is easy to see why they were pressed into service for the evacuation of Dunkirk.

Tollesbury is a fishing village in Essex, on a tributary of the river Blackwater, which was a loading port for the stack barges. They could lie alongside for horse drawn waggons to unload them. It was after this village that the barge Tollesbury was named by Mr Fisher, her owner in 1901. She was built at Feltham's Yard at Sandwich on the Kentish Stour. It was this as much as her squat profile that earned her the name *Sandwich Box*. In 1912 she joined the fleet of R & W Paul Ltd, the most famous wharfingers in East Anglia, who traded in grain, malt and animal feeds and, to perfect their fleet, became barge builders themselves. The skipper of the Tollesbury was Lemon Webb who earned his keep - and the Tollesbury's - by carrying stone from the West Country, as well as coal, coke and pitch from both sides of the Channel during the First World War.

Once, in 1932, Paul's contacted Webb at Colchester and ordered him to pick up 130 tons of Canadian feed oats at Antwerp. His crew had just left the

barge, but he was told to find another crew and get under way. In due course Lemon arrived back at Ipswich and reported the completion of his job. When asked whether he found a crew alright, he explained laconically that he had not found anyone worth having and so he sailed by himself - some measure of his skill as a sailor in a ship without an engine and of his craft's ideal design for sailing short-handed.

At the end of May 1940, Lemon was sailing his ship up the Thames near Erith when a naval launch came alongside and instructed him to proceed to Cory's jetty for orders. There, Lem and his young lad of nineteen, were given a choice to leave the ship or to volunteer to help evacuate the BEF from Dunkirk. Neither of them hesitated and by two o'clock in the afternoon, the Tollesbury, with the larger *Ethel Everard* of London, towed by the tug *Sun XI* took their place in a motley armada of pleasure boats, fireboats, tugs and barges. It was planned to sacrifice the barges by beaching them to be used as embarkation platforms for the troops waiting patiently ashore. From there they could be transferred to small boats and launches and eventually to larger transports lying in deep water.

The wooden hulls of the barges made them relatively safe from magnetic mines. Their flat bottoms would enable them to come in closer to the beaches than other craft.

At midnight they arrived and were abandoned by their tug. Their orders were to beach their craft. There was little wind and they used their 'sweeps' (24ft long oars) to close the shore. As they approached, they heard the shouts of soldiers warning them of the shallows. So they let go their anchor and tried to provide access for the troops with their wooden ladder, but the surge soon broke it. They then provided a makeshift gangway by lowering their tender. Then 273 wet, sunburnt and exhausted soldiers came aboard desperate for food and water. Lem Webb had sufficient water and a supply of biscuits together with a few loaves of bread which he gave them gladly.

They tried to re-launch the barge but it had grounded on the falling tide. Two hours later, the tide re-floated them and they pushed off into deep water setting their sails, but in the light winds they made little headway. So they dropped anchor again and the mate, who had seen naval service in the First World War, signalled a Destroyer to ask for their troops to be transferred. Another air raid delayed the operation, but the bombs and shrapnel from anti-aircraft shells again left the Tollesbury unscathed. Later, a barge tried to tow them off too quickly and the towline snapped. Finally, they got under way and set sail for Ramsgate.

Again, an air raid seemed to be directed specifically at them with dive-bombers dropping their lethal loads within feet of the barge. However, she was spared and a Destroyer together with an MTB drove off the attackers. They saw two Destroyers sink during their voyage. Near the North Goodwins a mine exploded in their way, but without sinking them.

At Ramsgate Roads they transferred their passengers to motorboats to be taken ashore and one soldier looked at them in wonder saying, "she is a lucky ship, skipper!" She certainly turned out to be so and she is still afloat today, being used as a houseboat by her present owner, Dave Paling at Pin Mill.

Sailing Barge Ethel Maud

Built by Howard's at Maldon in Essex in 1889, the *Ethel Maud* is a well preserved centenarian. Originally she worked for Parkers and then for Green Brothers, the millers in Maldon, until they sold out in 1964. Her type were known as stack barges or 'stackies'. These were loaded with hay and straw from the farms of Essex, Kent and Suffolk, to feed and bed the working horses on the streets of east London. Their appearance when loaded also earned them the name of 'haystack barges' and they frequently returned with cargoes of 'scrapings' - horse manure swept from the streets of the City and put to good use by the farmers of East Anglia. They carried a variety of cargoes which were quicker and cheaper to transport by barge than by horse-drawn wagon or even by the early railways.

When Tilbury docks opened in 1958, the old traffic to the docks of London diminished and the working boats gradually lost their importance. Despite her age, the *Ethel Maud* was a fast sailer whose moveable bowsprit could carry two staysails, a jib and a foresail. She had a mainsail, topsail and mizzen and could, on occasion, add two more foresails used like spinnakers. She sailed competitively in barge races until 1970. Yet her rigging allowed for her spars to be lowered easily to pass under bridges and despite her three-foot draft, her lee boards gave her a good performance to windward.

Ethel Maud was finally sold into retirement in 1963. Her present owners, David and Jean Maude, (no connection with her original name) converted her into a houseboat in the Kentish seaside town of Sheerness and she is now at Rochester. At Dunkirk she was loaded with stores for the BEF, but her precise role has not been recorded.

NAME:	Ethel Maud
TYPE:	Sailing Barge
LENGTH:	80ft 2ins
BEAM:	19ft 2ins
DISPLACEMENT:	57 tons
DRAFT:	3ft
ENGINES:	BMC diesel 56 h.p.
HULL CONSTR.:	Pitch pine on oak
BUILT BY:	Howard, Maldon
YEAR BUILT:	1889

Ethel Maud on a run in 1936

Cabby is believed to be the last of the full-size wooden sailing barges to be built. The Gill brothers who had constructed many of her type, were left with one on their hands when a client went bankrupt. They began to trade with her and soon discovered that this was a more profitable occupation than boat building. They formed the Rochester Barge Company, using the profits to buy land and to plant fruit. By 1924 they had all their interests in the London and Rochester Trading Company. The building of Cabby was begun in 1925, but due to a slump in the trade, was not completed for another three years. For more than a decade she carried grain, animal feeds, timber and other bulk cargoes between

London docks, Colchester, Whitstable, and various ports on the south and east coast. She was at Ipswich in 1940 when ordered to London and loaded with drums of fresh water for the troops at Dunkirk. Instead, she was sent to the Downs to await further instructions which, coming after several days, ordered her to Brest. She was well on passage when fresh

NAME:	Cabby
TYPE:	Thames Sailing Barge
LENGTH:	92ft
BEAM:	21ft 6ins
DISPLACEMENT:	96.8 tons
DRAFT:	3ft 9ins
ENGINES:	88 h.p. Kelvin diesel
HULL CONSTR.:	Pitch pine on oak
BUILT BY:	Lon. & Roch. Tradg. Co.
YEAR BUILT:	1928

instructions returned her to Plymouth. From there, under war service, she went to Ireland, to the Clyde, and then the Hebrides where she was given a new wheelhouse. Finally *Cabby* spent the rest of the war years at Greenock.

Many of the requisitioned sailing barges came back from the war in a poor state, too old to go back into trade, and were sold for as little as £500 each to be converted into houseboats. *Cabby*, however, went back to work until trade in the London docks declined. Alec Rands, who took her over from his father and first master Harry Walter, recalls loads of "just about anything" - cement, asbestos tiles, china clay, portland stone - and trips as far away as Antwerp. She carried her last load in the late 1960's and was converted to passenger use, spending the winters laid up at Snape Maltings and the spring/autumn season earning her keep out of Rochester. With the exception of the engine and the conversion below into comfortable

conference accommodation, *Cabby* has been restored to her original appearance. She is very much a commercial venture for Crescent Shipping Limited, direct descendants of the original builders. Sailing on the Medway, her sails advertising products above, whilst businessmen are in conference or at lunch below, she reckons - given favourable weather - to reach Sheerness and the Thames Estuary in a couple of hours.

*Captain John Fairbrother
at the wheel on Cabby*

Thames Spritsail Barge **Ena**

NAME:	Ena
TYPE:	Thames Spritsail Barge
LENGTH:	88ft 2ins
BEAM:	20ft 6ins
DISPLACEMENT:	90.48 tons
DRAFT:	4ft
ENGINES:	80 h.p. 6 cyl. diesel
HULL CONSTR.:	Pitch pine on oak
BUILT BY:	McLearon, Navy Yard
YEAR BUILT:	Harwich, 1906

Robert Paul started as a wharfinger in Ipswich during the eighteen forties. When he died in 1864 at the age of fifty eight his sons, Robert aged nineteen and William aged fifteen, proved to be true Victorian entrepreneurs. During the next fifty years they expanded their trade in grain, malt, coal, manufactured goods and animal feed, between East Anglia and the Pool of London and built a fleet of coasting barges and tugs, lighters and steam-ships - many at their Dock End yard in Ipswich.

But the *Ena* was built by W McLearon at the Navy Yard slip at Harwich in 1906 and Paul's bought her for £875 and then spent another £232 fitting her out. She was rigged as a 'mulie' - a compromise between a more substantial ketch and a spritsail barge. She was given a tall mizzen mast, with a large gaff sail, well forward of the wheel and a smaller spritsail.

In World War I the fleet of R & W Paul carried a whole range of supplies for our armies on the continent of Europe. Often there were 100 barges loading and unloading in Boulogne and Dieppe. Their small draft gave them access to shallow waters, they were less likely to be sunk by mines and German U-boats were often reluctant to disclose their presence, or even to waste a precious torpedo, attacking a mere sailing barge. Between the wars barges, like the *Ena*, largely escaped the ravages of the depression because Paul's own shipyard kept them in immaculate order, they had the company's own cargoes to carry and each skipper cherished his craft and spent much of his own time keeping hull, spars and canvas painstakingly maintained.

Twenty years later, the fleet of R & W Paul's barges was still intact, lightering on the river Orwell and trading with London docks. They avoided carrying brick rubble from London bombsites, for the building of East Anglian airfields, which destroyed the wooden linings of other barges. Sugar beet and maize were more popular cargoes.

No less than six of the sixteen barges which sailed to Dunkirk were owned by R & W Paul. The *Ena* survived the one hundred mile outward journey across the English Channel which was strewn with mines. During their crossing they endured constant air attacks. Finally, Alfred Page, her skipper was ordered to beach her close to the smaller sand barge *H.A.C.* As the Germans closed in, the crews of both barges were ordered to abandon their ships and escape on a mine sweeper to England.

There are two eye-witness accounts of what happened next. Alex Smith recalls how he, with 30 men of the Duke of Wellington's Regiment commanded by Captain David Strangeways their Adjutant, arrived on La Panne beach. They could not believe their luck when they saw two barges in seaworthy condition anchored and almost afloat. They took possession of the barge *H.A.C.* while Colonel McKay with his men of the 19th Field Regiment, Royal Artillery boarded the *Ena* which was beached not far away. Captain Atley of the East Yorks Regiment, also remembers the

event. He was at the mole at Dunkirk and together with one of his men, made a raft. Using shovels, they rowed out to the *Ena*. They helped 36 other men on board including three wounded and by 0800 hours they were under sail.

Then, according to Alex Smith, the two ships got involved in one of the most remarkable barge races of all time. Under constant enemy bombardment and machine-gun fire, they crossed the Channel. Captain Atley recalls that by midnight they took a back-bearing on Dunkirk and found they had gone too far south west. His only sailing experience had been on the Broads and he had forgotten to put the leeboards down. So they altered course to north-north-west and finally sighted the North Goodwin buoy. They then had to tack again towards the South Goodwin lightship. Eventually, the *Ena* was picked up by a tug or fleet auxiliary and taken into Margate. Since the harbour was full, the empty barge was then towed out and left anchored off Deal.

The shipping manager of R & W Paul, who had presumed the *Ena* lost on the beaches of Dunkirk, was amazed when he was told and asked what he proposed to do about it. Alfred Page, her skipper, by then back in Ipswich, was sent to recover her. He found the *Ena* seaworthy but stripped of all her gear. "They had taken the sweeps, mooring lines, fenders and even my false teeth which I had left behind in a glass of water by my bunk!" he said "you can't trust these men of Kent!" So he sailed her back to Ipswich. In 1974 the *Ena* was transferred to the Social and Sports Club of Paul's and she still competes in sailing barge races on the Thames, the Medway, Blackwater and Orwell keeping the great tradition of the spritsail barges alive.

The race is on! Ena making good time to the delight of all on board

Brightlingsea, on the river Colne in Essex, is another boatbuilding town famous for its barges. *Greta* was built there in 1891, at Stone's yard, for a barge sailmaker called Hibbs. John Leather in his book "Barges" (Adlard Coles, 1984) records how Hibbs perfected the process which gave a fifteen-year life to the sails of the working boats. Apparently he devised a dressing including horse fat which gave them their shine, resistance to hard wear and traditional colour. Later, oil and red ochre were also used.

Hibbs sold the *Greta* to Owen Parry, a barge owner with a fine fleet of working boats which had a high reputation for their smart turnout and racing success. After a hundred years it is their quality as fine sailing boats that has kept the barges alive and still highly prized today.

Felix Mallett was the first skipper of *Greta* appointed by Owen Parry to sail under his yellow and black house flag. She carried the usual cargoes of grain, malt and building products and some unusual ones like the spars for the German Kaiser's racing schooner, destined for Kiel. The *Greta* was sold to the Rochester Barge Company in 1918 but Mallet remained as her skipper until 1926 when he returned to Owen Parry.

NAME:	Greta
TYPE:	Thames Sailing Barge
LENGTH:	80ft
BEAM:	20ft
DISPLACEMENT:	49 tons
DRAFT:	3ft
ENGINES:	Perkins 6354
HULL CONSTR.:	Oak on oak
BUILT BY:	Stones, Brightlingsea
YEAR BUILT:	1892

Greta

Early in World War II *Greta* was chartered by the Ministry of Supply to carry ammunition from the army depot at Upnor near Rochester in Kent to naval vessels anchored in the Thames estuary. At that time seagoing ships picked up all other loads at London docks but the danger of a large explosion, especially in an air raid, made it far safer to trans-ship dangerous cargo outside the dock area, further down the river. *Greta* would come alongside ships where they lay at anchor allowing them to transfer her explosives down river.

She certainly took part in the evacuation of Dunkirk and then continued her work as a lighter. The Admiralty discharged her from war service in 1946. After a thorough overhaul and refit she returned to normal trading; carrying grain, timber, animal feed and miscellaneous cargo and taking cargo from ships in the port of London for distribution to smaller ports. *Greta* mostly served the Medway wharves, but also sailed as far as Colchester in Essex.

John Tooke of Crescent Shipping Limited, recalls a particular cargo for which she was favoured. Towards the end of 1947 she started carrying beer from Chatham to Nine Elms, Battersea in London. This developed into a continuous trade for a very special reason. Both her master and his mate were teetotalers and the brewery requested that *Greta* be kept permanently on this run. The goods were shipped under bond, there was never any pilfering or "accidental breakage" and H.M. Customs could always be sure that the exact number of bottles and kegs loaded at Chatham were discharged at Nine Elms. Following the decline in work at the London docks throughout the early 1960's, *Greta* was sold off and laid up at Whitewall Creek pending restoration.

Despite extensive alterations when she was turned into a houseboat (in 1989 she was being reframed and reskinned inside and out on the star-board side) *Greta* still manages to take part in the half-dozen or so east coast barge matches each year, and in 1987 was the outright champion barge at Southend. According to Robert Deards, her skipper in these events, old Felix Mallett always said that if Greta had only been given an extra couple of feet more run fore and aft she would have been a real racer. For a very old lady, she's still pretty fast!

In 1979 *Greta* was bought by Tony Ryan who lived aboard at Allington Lock, Kent. She is now at Hoo, Rochester where Steve Norris who has a half-share in *Greta* uses her as his home.

Thames Sailing Barge Beatrice Maud

Built in 1910 by Whites at Sittingbourne in Kent nothing is known about *Beatrice Maud* before the war - who owned her and who sailed in her.

Her involvement in Dunkirk is well recorded. She crossed the channel on 31st May and like many other barges, was left stranded on the beach. Perhaps her skipper relied on her shallow draft to enable her to re-float on the incoming tide. Or her crew may have been ordered to beach her to enable slightly larger vessels to use her as a boarding platform.

In the event it proved providential. Some two hundred and sixty soldiers, reported to be French, led by a Lieut. Heron, a yachtsman, boarded her on 4th June and she was found drifting in the channel on 5th June and towed to Dover by a British destroyer.

She must have ended her war service then because she was seen carrying rectangular bales of compacted straw from Colchester and Hythe to London, and seems to have been one of the earlier victims of the decline in trade with the old London Docks. Old barge masters were retiring with few apprentices to take their place. Craftsmen who could work oak, pine, brass and wrought iron were in short supply and the work was expensive. The old wooden barges simply couldn't economically go to Antwerp, Rotterdam, Hamburg and the French ports where the ocean-going transporter vessels preferred to dock and discharge their cargoes. So the wooden barges were sold off by their owners.

In the words of one barge fleet owner: "No-one back in the '60's was as conservation-minded as we are nowadays, nor were we ourselves particularly interested in the old barges. It seems we were only too glad to get rid of them and didn't bother to retain any documentary record". *Beatrice Maud* became a houseboat, but her present where-abouts are not known.

NAME:	Beatrice Maud
TYPE:	Thames Sailing Barge
LENGTH:	88ft
BEAM:	21ft 5ins
DISPLACEMENT:	Approximately 65 tons
DRAFT:	4ft 5ins
ENGINES:	None
HULL CONSTR.:	Pitch pine on oak
BUILT BY:	A White, Sittingbourne
YEAR BUILT:	1910

Nowadays few sailing boats - leave alone commercial vessels with cargoes of 150 tons or more - would be considered safe without a powerful engine. At the time of Dunkirk all but a few of the barges that went over managed quite well on sails alone. *Pudge* was an exception and her auxiliary engine, rarely used, saved her life as well as that of her crew and the soldiers on board.

War records show that *Pudge* was requisitioned on 29th May 1940 while she was in Tilbury docks waiting to load for Ipswich under command of Bill Watson, one of the senior captains of the London and Rochester Trading Company who was an old-time sailor and wore gold earrings.

When they got to Dover the naval officer in command asked for eight or ten volunteers from among the skippers and their mates but so many of them were ready to go that it was necessary to draw lots.

Three of the barges - *Thyra, Lady Roseberry* and *Pudge* were taken in tow by the steel-hulled tug *St Fagan*. To

keep them together, save fuel and increase speed, they were towed across to Dunkirk and they reached the beaches under cover of darkness. There the three barges were cast off from the tug. The *Lady Roseberry* was ordered to proceed in-shore to pick up troops. She had navigated ahead of the *St Fagan*, just astern of the tug, when there was a tremendous explosion as the *St Fagan* struck a mine. *Pudge* was lifted bodily out of the water, but in the words of her skipper, "she came down the right way up". When the smoke and dust had settled, the *St Fagan*, *Lady Roseberry*

tow to the great relief and loud cheers of those on board. Three hours later they arrived safely in Ramsgate. *Pudge* spent the rest of her war service on the Clyde in Scotland, together with other barges from the London and Rochester Trading Company: *Cabby*, *Mary May*, *Alderman* and *Knowles*. There they acted as lighters and transports for military stores and as mail boats to the Cunarders *Queen Mary* and *Queen Elizabeth* which were working as transatlantic troop ships.

After the war *Pudge* returned to her work with the London and Rochester

Beached and abandoned. Barbara Jean, stranded amidst Bren gun carriers; a fate which Pudge escaped

NAME:	Pudge
TYPE:	Thames Sailing Barge
LENGTH:	92ft 6ins
BEAM:	22ft 6ins
DISPLACEMENT:	Approximately 97 tons
DRAFT:	3ft 6ins
ENGINES:	Kelvin 66 h.p. diesel
HULL CONSTR.:	Pitch pine on oak
BUILT BY:	London Rochester Co.
YEAR BUILT:	1922

and *Doris* were no more. *St Fagan* had a crew of twenty five and only six survived the explosion. *Pudge* immediately launched her tender and picked up a large number of survivors, both from the tug and from other barges. In all she is thought to have taken on about three hundred men before the skipper and mate decided it was time to head back to Dover.

E G Fryer, a fifteen year old boy/cook serving on the tug *Tanga* recalls how they made three journeys across the channel during those fateful days and retrieved 1,300 troops from Dunkirk. On the second occasion of returning to England they encountered the sailing barge *Pudge* and at first thought her deserted. When they went in closer to investigate, they found that she had 300 troops in the hold and took her in

Trading Company (now called Crescent Shipping) and in 1968 when she was finally retired and sold to the Thames Barge Sailing Club, they re-rigged her faithfully in accordance with her original design, with advice from professional barge skippers. Now *Pudge* can be chartered by members for holidays out of Maldon in Essex and she cruises around the Thames and Medway and up the East coast of England.

Sailing Barge Glenway

Old barges have a habit of surviving through all kinds of calamities. The *Glenway* has lived through more than most. She was built in 1913 by James Little at Rochester in Kent. Her owners are recorded as Mr Hammond, and later a Mr Wilks. In 1933 she was bought by West's at Gravesend who in 1934 fitted a diesel engine.

During the evacuation of Dunkirk, she was towed across the channel by the tug *Crested Cock* with a consignment of bread, munitions and medical supplies for our troops. Sub-Lieut. Bruno de Hamel, on patrol off the beaches of Dunkirk in his anti-submarine vessel spotted her there on the beach with 190 battle-weary troops on board, unable to refloat and with her engine out of commission. He first armed her to resist enemy air attacks and then, being an experienced yachtsman, decided that she could be sailed home. He got her away laden with soldiers of the 27th Field Regiment, Royal Artillery, but during the sixteen-hour crossing twenty of them died of their wounds. When the *Glenway* reached Dover, she was picked up by a passing tug and towed into port.

After the war she went back to work for West's of Gravesend, but in 1951 had a bad accident in the Thames Estuary, went ashore and lost her load. She was then laid up for a long period and never worked again. Later she became a house-boat at Otterham Quay where she sank and was re-floated. New owners then took her to Strood.

She was fully restored at Ipswich and even regained her original rigging when she was caught at the top of the tide on the jetty . This caused her to fall off, badly damaging both herself and the *Hydrogen* which was caught underneath her. Again, it was planned to restore her for conversion into a restaurant but when this did not materialise she was given to the Maldon sea scouts. One day, full of water, she sank at her moorings. She changed ownership once more, had an engine installed and was moved to the Dolphin Barge Museum at Sittingbourne in Kent getting caught in a force nine gale on the way. Her present owner, Hugh Pore, is planning to rebuild her. There is life in her stout oak timbers yet and old barges simply refuse to die.

NAME:	Glenway
TYPE:	Sailing Barge
LENGTH:	86ft
BEAM:	22ft 6ins
DISPLACEMENT:	82 tons
DRAFT:	7ft 6ins
ENGINES:	Twin petrol/paraffin
HULL CONSTR.:	Pitch pine on oak
BUILT BY:	James Little, Rochester
YEAR BUILT:	1913

Another Dunkirk survivor at The Dolphin Barge Museum, Sittingbourne, Kent, is the old sailing barge *Viking*, once a well-known trader around the Medway and the east coast. Her origins are obscure. She was built in 1895 at Rochester's Co-operative Barge Yard, and her first master was William Jarrett of Upnor. By 1934 *Viking* had been converted into a yacht barge, and soon afterwards passed into the ownership of the Whiting family - well known Medway barge owners whose fleet numbered half a dozen vessels in the 1940s. After Dunkirk she continued her war service as a balloon barge, from which anti-aircraft barrage balloons were flown.

After the war she was re-rigged at Whitstable for cargo carrying as a coastal barge. At the end of that decade, Whitings were taken over by the London and Rochester Trading Company and throughout the '50s *Viking* worked for them.

She sailed around the east and south east coast ports: Norwich, Great Yarmouth, Ramsgate and Felixstowe, and twice crossed to Calais. With the London and Rochester she had Yarmouth - Dover limits, but a considerable diversity of cargo. This

NAME:	Viking
TYPE:	Sailing Barge
LENGTH:	87ft
BEAM:	17ft 4ins
DISPLACEMENT:	63 tons
DRAFT:	3ft 6ins
ENGINES:	None
HULL CONSTR.:	Pitch pine on oak
BUILT BY:	Co-operative Barge Yard
YEAR BUILT:	Rochester, 1895

included imported grain and animal feedstuffs from London's Victoria and Milwall docks consigned to the merchants of Ipswich; Canadian and American wood pulp for the big paper mills, and sawn timber from Scandinavia and Canada for the traders at Maldon, Essex. On her return journeys she often carried bags of cement, destined for the emerging third world countries, for industrial buildings and new airports.

In the late 1960s, *Viking* was beached in the Medway where she is still just afloat along with hopes - even now- that Les George, her owner and an enthusiast, will succeed in putting her together again.

Barge Yacht Nancibelle

Nancibelle's name appears in several official records of the Little Ships which helped in the evacuation of Dunkirk and is credited with bringing back ninety seven troops in a single voyage. But no further details are known.

After the heyday of the successful and romantic spritsail working barges in the nineteenth century, around 1890 the new concept of half-sized "barge yachts" was developed. Compared with the 80ft-90ft length and 22ft beam of the working boats, these "barge yachts" were 40ft in length, 11ft wide and had only a 2ft draft. In place of the cargo hold they had comfortable and roomy cabins which made them ideal to adapt as house boats and they were provided with a ketch rig and the traditional lee boards.

Unusually, the Nancibelle was spritsail rigged and her main mast was stepped above the coach roof. She was built by the Sittingbourne Ship Building Company in 1930 but her first recorded owner lived in Colchester. She changed hands three times before the war. After she came back from Dunkirk she had one more owner in the south of England and then moved up to Yorkshire - presumably through

NAME:	Nancibelle
TYPE:	Barge Yacht
LENGTH:	40ft
BEAM:	11ft 4ins
DISPLACEMENT:	22 tons
DRAFT:	2ft
ENGINES:	None
HULL CONSTR.:	Oak Carvel
BUILT BY:	Sittingbourne Ship Co.
YEAR BUILT:	1930

the canals, for which she would have been well suited with her narrow beam and especially modest draft.

In the mid 1970s she became a houseboat and a home for a number of families in succession. At that time she had her mast and rigging removed and when she had been taken on to the river Penryn, in the Fal estuary in Cornwall, she finally also lost her twin screw Thornycroft engine.

Denise Pipkin, who originally bought Nancibelle as a mobile home, has had a struggle to maintain her and is now looking for someone who might once more restore the veteran to her original condition.

There is rarely a good commercial reason for keeping a ship alive for more than fifty or maybe a hundred years. Water, especially saltwater, is the enemy of timber and steel and a boat needs to be cherished, out of proportion to its usefulness, to survive. Owners of Dunkirk Little Ships, many from outside the traditional boating fraternity, are motivated to do it by affection and respect for their heritage.

Ona II was built in 1931 by Staniland and Company at Thorne in Yorkshire, near the river Ouse, which flows down to the Humber, as a typical motor yacht of 36ft, designed for the enjoyment of English rivers. In 1940 she belonged to a Mr H Payne but we could not discover how she came to be in Southern England at that time. The official records show that she certainly crossed to Dunkirk and saved twenty soldiers.

Then the trail goes cold until 1984, when heating engineer Dennis Haresign found *Ona II* on the Thames at Oxford, vandalised, partly submerged and blocking the local boatyard's slipway. Her owner lived abroad and was eager to dispose of her for £500. *Ona II* was taken through the country lanes of rural Wiltshire, chocked up in a picturesque cottage garden near Swindon and tackled by a team of eight enthusiasts. They replanked the hull, stripped and repainted every inch of her woodwork, added mast and sails, re-wired and re-furbished the interior, renewing all her fittings. With financial help from the Swindon branch of the Dunkirk Veterans Association, *Ona II* was made seaworthy in time to sail to Dunkirk for the forty-fifth anniversary in 1985.

Now she is a handsome family cruising boat, for use on the Thames and in coastal waters. After some

NAME:	Ona II
TYPE:	Motor Launch
LENGTH:	36ft
BEAM:	9ft 6ins
DISPLACEMENT:	8 tons
DRAFT:	2ft 6ins
ENGINES:	2 x 30 h.p. Perkins M30
HULL CONSTR.:	Pitch pine on oak
BUILT BY:	Staniland & Co., Thorne
YEAR BUILT:	1931

years of alternating between Wiltshire and Portsmouth, *Ona II* has been acquired by Keith Carter - a man used to sailing boats in the Lake District of England - and his wife Anne. They wanted a motor yacht "of a certain age" and have been replacing her fittings with authentic examples from the '30s. *Ona II* is one of the fortunate ones and there is no reason why she should not remain one of the fleet of Dunkirk veterans for another fifty years.

According to owner Frank Hutchinson, *Monarch* was "little more than an open rowing boat" when she was towed from the Thames estuary to Dunkirk in 1940. He tells people, "she's fifty percent a Dunkirk boat; the bottom half went to the evacuation, the top half's mine!" In fact, *Monarch* was built by Heywoods at Southend as an open gaff-rigged day-sailer with a large centreboard. She had two petrol/paraffin engines at the time. These were exchanged for diesels with the profits from "white weeding" in 1958.

This is a trade in a particular type of seaweed which occurs randomly throughout the world, and is prized, particularly in Japan, for its decorative value. It was discovered in the Thames Estuary during the mid-1950s when *Monarch* spent her summer season at Westcliffe, Southend-on-Sea as a passenger vessel and her winters

NAME:	Monarch
TYPE:	Passenger Launch
LENGTH:	40ft
BEAM:	13ft 6ins
DISPLACEMENT:	13 tons
DRAFT:	3ft
ENGINES:	standard diesel x 2
HULL CONSTR.:	Pitch pine on oak
BUILT BY:	Haywoods, Southend
YEAR BUILT:	Not known

shrimping or fishing wherever the opportunity occurred.

She remained a passenger launch licenced to carry up to 73 at a time, until she was converted in 1972 to take out sea angling parties during the next five years. Frank, who owns a small marina, wanted somewhere to live when he sold his house to finance his business. *Monarch* has since been his home, his pride and his joy.

Passenger Launch New Windsor Castle

All those of us who love the river Thames retain romantic images of hazy meadows, willow trees, cows grazing beside the river, of rowing eights, punts and skulls, of men in boaters and girls in pretty summer dresses enjoying strawberries and cream in marquees at Henley regatta.

We think of the Thames as a narrow stream at Lechlade, of the Isis and Cherwell meandering through Oxford, the widening river at Wallingford and Shillingford Bridge. All along we see a variety of craft taking happy summer parties down to Windsor Castle, Hampton Court, past Westminster and under Tower Bridge to Greenwich. An unforgettable part of this picture are the elegant river steamers, brightly painted and some with gleaming, varnished hulls, full of happy people, bands and bars, the epitome of an English summer. What a contrast it must have been when war broke out to disrupt the carefree, leisurely world of the 1920s and '30s. Suddenly we demanded undreamed-of sacrifices from a pleasure-loving generation.

NAME:	New Windsor Castle
TYPE:	Passenger Launch
LENGTH:	105ft
BEAM:	15ft 6ins
DISPLACEMENT:	Not known
DRAFT:	3ft 9ins
ENGINES:	Ford 6 cylinder diesel
HULL CONSTR.:	Carvel
BUILT BY:	Arthur Jacobs, Windsor
YEAR BUILT:	1923

The *New Windsor Castle* was built in 1923 by Arthur Jacobs at Windsor as a sister ship to the *Grand Duchess*, to join *Windsor Belle* and *Empress of India* in the Jacobs fleet. They were all then driven by steam. The *New Windsor Castle* had a varnished hull and inverted compound engines by E Hayes & Sons. She did not have the lovely clipper bow which added so greatly to the elegant appearance of her sister ships, but she is to this day a beautiful river boat, an ideal vessel to carry her passengers in holiday mood through her beautiful environment.

When war began, the Ministry of Transport first called her up as part of the Emergency River Transport Service at the time of heavy air raids in the capital. This scheme was designed to relieve the congestion suffered by

commuters through the shattered streets of London. Then she was one of twenty similar Thames passenger boats to go to Dunkirk.

Her low freeboard could only have survived the crossings in a flat, calm sea and this of course was one of the miracles of Dunkirk. One dreads to think what would have happened if the English Channel had adopted its more common angry mood. The *New Windsor Castle* is now owned by M J Turk, by Appointment Waterman to Her Majesty the Queen. Turk Launches still maintain their service on the Thames and are available for charter and for summer parties on this loveliest of all rivers. The *New Windsor Castle* is the oldest, largest wooden pleasure boat of its kind on the river.

Motor Yacht Hilfranor

Hilfranor was built at Walton-on-Thames and was one of the Little Ships collected from the Upper Thames by Douglas Tough, who assembled such a great part of the Dunkirk flotilla in May 1940. She is said to have been named after the original owner's three daughters: Hilda, Francis and Nora. Soon after, she was extended by 6ft, given a pretty canoe stern, a steel keel and two bilge keels to make her into a seagoing vessel. Her deck was made of great slabs of mahogany.

At Dunkirk she was crewed by Jock Christie, W Hills and V Hissons and when she was attacked by German dive bombers, two near misses cracked her ribs down both sides and she was abandoned. But a group of soldiers, desperate to get home, re-floated her and bailing furiously all the way, got her as far as the Goodwin Sands, off the English coast. There she was stranded until a naval minesweeper, commanded by a young lieutenant, towed her into Ramsgate. Despite her damage she was repaired, her ribs were doubled up and she remained in naval service for the rest of the war.

When peace came, her petrol engines were replaced by two diesel tractor engines and her new owner, an ex-naval officer, kept her in Ramsgate for another thirty-seven years.

In 1984 Fred Miskimmin found her, with grass growing on her deck, and gave her a new lease of life. Now she belongs to the British computer firm ROCC Computers Limited, who have restored her and take the same pride in her as they do in their products, as something uniquely British.

NAME:	Hilfranor
TYPE:	Motor Yacht
LENGTH:	41ft
BEAM:	9ft
DISPLACEMENT:	6.56 tons
DRAFT:	3ft
ENGINES:	Twin Perkins
HULL CONSTR.:	Carvel
BUILT BY:	Walton Yacht & Launch
YEAR BUILT:	1936

The plaque presented by the people of Dunkirk to participate in the 25th anniversary return

Auxiliary Ketch Cygnet

Cygnet was another example of the great variety of Little Ships that made up the flotilla which crossed the channel, answering the call for help in those last days of May 1940. She was then owned by AA Rowse of Oxford. The wind and weather were kind to her when her Royal Navy crew made the crossing and on that occasion she returned safely.

With her 6ft draft she was hardly ideal for the task. A 42ft Hillyard ketch with a canoe stern, white hull and mahogany superstructure, she was a handsome looking yacht with 6ft 6in headroom and 6 berths but Major M P Morris, who owned her from 1960 to 1974, was well aware of her limitations. She leaked by the keel bolts. Water, once it got aboard, could run the full length of the yacht and her bilge pump was inadequate, working through a weird arrangement of lead pipes. She did not handle well in a strong breeze and was reluctant to go about in certain conditions. Her ballast was provided by 30lb chunks, kept loose in the bilges.

NAME:	Cygnet
TYPE:	Auxiliary Ketch
LENGTH:	45ft
BEAM:	9ft 10ins
DISPLACEMENT:	19 tons
DRAFT:	5ft
ENGINES:	Morris. Comm. 40 h.p.
HULL CONSTR.:	Mahogany
BUILT BY:	Hillyard,Littlehampton
YEAR BUILT:	1930

wedding. Many people, including Dennis Fairfield, the Swansea coastguard, tried to dissuade him.

Crossing the Bay of Biscay in autumn can be a severe test for a well-found yacht and an experienced crew. The *Cygnet* was never seen or heard from again. Having survived her brave war-time exploit, she succumbed to the merciless sea.

For 14 years she was moored at the Bight, near Starcross in Devon and she wintered at Odhams Wharf on the river Clyst at Topsham where Chris Rowe at one time took 8ft off the top of both her masts in an attempt to make her handle better. Then she was sold to John Hurrell, a design draughtsman who kept her in South Wales. From there he set out in October 1984 with a crew of three, with poor equipment and very limited experience, to sail to South Africa to attend his daughter's

Motor Yacht **Llanthony**

Rear-Admiral Robert W Timbrell of the Royal Canadian Navy (Retired) was a newly-fledged Sub-Lieutenant stationed at Whale Island, Portsmouth, in May 1940 when he was summoned by an old naval captain sitting at his desk with a pile of paper in front of him. Twenty young officers had been told to report rather hastily after getting their gas masks, toothbrushes and shaving kit and they wondered what it was all about. Robert Timbrell knew better than to

ask an irritable old captain for details when he brusquely told him "to join the *Llanthony*". He had no idea what kind of ship this was and was amazed when he had been chosen to command her. He was even more astonished to find that she was a gentlemans' yacht built for Lord Astor of Hever Castle and ill-equipped for naval duty. Her compass had not been swung and the only armament was the 1914 Colt 45 on Timbrell's leather belt.

With his crew of two civilian diesel engineers from London Transport and six sailors from Newfoundland (they were actually lumberjacks), he was ordered to proceed to Ramsgate where the yacht was fuelled and provided with charts. They were then told to set course for Dunkirk. There they were to anchor off the beach and embark as many troops as they could using the two tenders swung from their davits.

On the way, they encountered a strange variety of craft: sailing yachts, mud hoppers and Thames pleasure steamers. One of these they found broken down half way across. This boat was loaded with troops and so

Sub-Lieut. Robert Timbrell in 1940

they towed her all the way back to Ramsgate.

Forty years later, Admiral Timbrell told his story to Cameron Graham of the Canadian Broadcasting Service:

"It was a very shallow beach and at low tide, the water went out a long way. We were being shelled by the Germans, the town was in flames and after we had anchored, I sent the Petty Officer in with the boats; I stayed with the yacht. We could take about 120 on each trip and our instructions were to return as soon as we were loaded. We did that for a couple of trips. Then, on the third or fourth trip, we got bombed. Although the RAF were doing a marvellous job, the odd German got through. We were hit on the fo'cs'le. I lost about five of the crew and both my anchors snapped. The fuel tanks were forward of the engine room and the fuel pipes were severed so that both engines died. We drifted up on the beach. It all happened so quickly - one minute we were there and the next we were damaged, drifting and running aground.

It was a sunny afternoon and there were shells falling all the way down the beach with thousands of soldiers asking to be taken back to England. It was day four of the evacuation and a stream of ships were going in and out. We drove some trucks into the water to form a small jetty. Then, at high tide, we could go alongside the trucks and men could walk on top of them and jump aboard.

While I was high and dry, I heard the English voice of a sergeant marching some troops down, calling out the order to halt. He was tired and his uniform was not parade ground standard, but he was still smart. He turned out to be from a Guards regiment. He asked if he could help and I told him to get a Bren-gun carrier and drive it out as far as he could in the water until the engine stopped so that I could use it to anchor by. That is what he did and my two civilian diesel engineers repaired the fuel pipe, got the capstan going and winched us off. They put a plate over my bombed fo'cs'le and we sailed back to England.

By then I was an old hand, in the eyes of the authorities, so I was given four trawlers to add to my fleet. They had come down from Scotland and their old skippers had twenty years' experience - more sea time than I will ever get in my life. I told them the form: 'We'll sail from Ramsgate. You stay close to me and we will go straight into Dunkirk, anchor, load and come back.' As simple as that . We sailed by night and loaded by day because at night the German E-boats were coming down the coast. My Guards sergeant had got me some Bren-guns and anti-tank weapons so now the *Llanthony* was armed with

NAME:	Llanthony
TYPE:	Motor Yacht
LENGTH:	77ft 5ins
BEAM:	14ft 6ins
DISPLACEMENT:	61 tons
DRAFT:	5ft 5ins
ENGINES:	Daimler Benz x 2
HULL CONSTR.:	Steel
BUILT BY:	Camper & Nicholson
YEAR BUILT:	1934

something more than my Colt 45. The trawlers stayed close to me - almost too close - and the port one went over a mine. She disappeared in a flash and we were not able to pick up survivors. The rest of us did two or three more trips. On one of them we had a fight with an E-boat. Thanks to my sergeant and his troops we were able to hold it off and they were surprised at our volume of fire. The Guards sergeant stayed with me for the whole time. While we were on the beach, one of the soldiers came towards us on a zig zag

course which miraculously avoided all the German shells. This was not good fieldwork, but due to a whole day spent in a French pub! He was drunker than anyone I have ever seen and he told us not to go back to England without him. He said he would come back with his ticket. He staggered back to his pub and returned with a case of brandy. 'Here's my ticket, sir, to get back to England. Don't leave me behind'. With this, he shoved his case of brandy aboard and fell asleep in the wheelhouse.

Our last trip was the tightest. The Germans had started to enter the town and to close the ring around Dunkirk. There was no way we could return any more. Back at Portsmouth I had a job to find anyone who would take over *Llanthony* from me. She was beaten up with bullet holes in her funnels and her boats were smashed. We took off the Bren-guns and anti-tank weapons as well as our case of brandy and tried to get back to Whale Island, three and a half miles away. I stopped a bus and asked the conductor the best way to

get back to our ship. The conductor said, 'Have you just come back from Dunkirk?' and when I told him we had, he walked around to the front of the bus and told the driver to take us there - with apologies for the detour to the civilian passengers. We got back to Whale Island complete with the brandy despite some protests concerning our army crew from the duty officer."

The *Llanthony* rescued 280 troops from Dunkirk and Lieut. Timbrell was awarded the Navy's Distinguished Service Cross. The Guards sergeant got the DSM - a rare naval award for a soldier.

Now called the *Golden Era, Llanthony* was bought by her present owner in 1985 in Cyprus and has been lovingly restored to her former glory. She is now an elegant charter yacht operating among the Greek and Turkish coasts and islands.

Cabin Cruiser Jockette II

Judge Adam Partington had *Jockette II* built as a sturdy but modestly-sized Thames cruiser by Watercraft of East Molesey in 1938 and took a keen personal interest in her construction. He only had two summers to enjoy her, before the war, and took her down river to Leigh-on-Sea, by the Medway, in Essex.

There she received her call to Dunkirk. Judge Partington, a generous man, took good care to stock her with beer and provisions for her naval crew. "Ricky" Latham, a young midshipman in the Royal Navy was put in charge. He was given a young 6ft 2in seaman called Bruce as his crew and a Petty Officer engineer called Jimmy - who knew all about "deep sea steam" but little about small cruisers with petrol engines. However, he proved a good cook and was much appreciated for that. Ricky Latham remembers *Jockette II* fondly: "A good little boat, strong - take you anywhere - rolls a bit in a rough sea, but will always get you home." Well, at the time of Dunkirk the sea was kind to them and *Jockette II* survived. At that time a gun was mounted on her wheel-house roof and she was painted in battleship grey. Since 1964 she has belonged to the Gingell family who keep her at Ripley in Surrey, on the river Wey. Long after they bought her, they were astonished to learn of her distinguished history and since Mr Gingell died, his widow Joan and her sons have worked hard to maintain their historic Little Ship, which they hope to pass on to her grandchildren.

NAME:	Jockette II
TYPE:	Cabin Cruiser
LENGTH:	30ft 3ins
BEAM:	9ft
DISPLACEMENT:	Approximately 9 tons
DRAFT:	3ft 3ins
ENGINES:	BMC Diesel x 2
HULL CONSTR.:	Mahogany
BUILT BY:	Watercraft
YEAR BUILT:	1938

Jockette II's wartime crew come off patrol

Motor Yacht **Lijns**

L*ijns* is a substantial steel-hulled motor yacht built and well fitted out by Devries Lensch in Holland just before World War II.

Although the records show that she took part in the evacuation of Dunkirk, nothing is known about her precise history at that time - or indeed before the war.

Being substantially built, she has survived many years of neglect since the war and a number of owners have tried to restore her. For some time she lay under tarpaulins at Beacon Boat Yard at Borstal on the river Medway and Stephen Peel, who owned her then, fitted two reconditioned BMC Commodore diesels as well as new hydraulic steering gear.

Now she has been bought by Morris Tolhurst who is finally determined to make her seaworthy and fit to take part in the 1990 reunion when he plans to sail her to Dunkirk with the fleet.

NAME:	Lijns
TYPE:	Motor Yacht
LENGTH:	42ft
BEAM:	10ft
DISPLACEMENT:	18 tons
DRAFT:	4ft 2ins
ENGINES:	BMC 3.8 L x 2
HULL CONSTR.:	Steel
BUILT BY:	Devries Lensch,
YEAR BUILT:	Holland, 1939

The eastern bulge of England, from the Thames estuary to the Wash, contains a much loved holiday area. Along the coast there are shallow sandy beaches where seals and rare species of migrant birds can still be seen and inland are the Norfolk Broads, whose largely unspoilt waters with their reed covered banks offer a protected refuge to a great variety of vegetation and wildfowl. This is an idyllic cruising area for holiday sailing and motor yachts.

Along this coast are the important commercial and fishing ports of Lowestoft and Great Yarmouth, used by freight and passenger ships and ferries shuttling between Suffolk and the continent of Europe. The weather on the east coast is unpredictable and seagoing passenger ships must be

NAME:	Oulton Belle
TYPE:	Motor Vessel
LENGTH:	84ft
BEAM:	16ft 6ins
DISPLACEMENT:	75.20 tons
DRAFT:	6ft 6ins
ENGINES:	Gleniffer 8 cylinder
HULL CONSTR.:	Steel
BUILT BY:	Fellows & Co.,
YEAR BUILT:	Gt.Yarmouth, 1930

designed to withstand easterly gales and rough seas at times. The *Oulton Belle* was built for these conditions at the Fellows shipyard in Great Yarmouth in 1930 with an Elliott and Garood steam engine, high freeboard and strong bulkheads down below. She was built to a proven design, that of the old river steamers *Yarmouth* and

The Oulton Belle dressed overall on the Norfolk Broads

Oulton Belle

Gorleston, both built in 1895. She is a 'double-ender', with a canoe stern and the ability to go into a berth forward and emerge backwards with equal ease and she was greatly respected as a fast ship, commanded by her skipper, George Cates, who later became a river Yare pilot. The *Oulton Belle* had the edge on all the other riverboats, including her sister ship the *Norwich Belle*, in the friendly races that were often arranged between them. She could "roar into Lowestoft, unload and

A pre-war picture of the Oulton Belle in holiday mood

load up again and as she did not have to turn around was able to get back to sea first." The war ended the trips to Lowestoft, and they were never to start again for *Oulton Belle*.

Despite their size and obvious ability to accommodate large quantities of troops, not all the passenger cruisers called up actually went to Dunkirk. Some were placed on the reserve list, and whether or not they actually went across remains a mystery. This might have been so in the case of *Oulton Belle*, but for an 'unofficial' source: the

handwritten notes made at the time by Commander V.A.L. Bradyll-Johnson. He was in charge of the eastern arm at Dover breakwater throughout the operation, and kept his notes and messages relating to the preparation, manning, despatch and reception on return from Dunkirk of the Little Ships placed at his disposal by the Navy. Decades later they were to re-appear proving the active involvement of *Oulton Belle* amongst many others. Both she and *Norwich Belle* were requisitioned soon after war began. After Dunkirk the latter went back to Lowestoft. (She was last heard of owned by a London-based Japanese company and is still thought to be afloat.)

Oulton Belle became a fleet tender in the Gaerloch, on the river Clyde in Scotland. Just two months after war ended in 1945, *Oulton Belle* was back in Great Yarmouth; but great changes were in the offing for the Company's fleet. Their Broads steamers and harbour service vessels were taken over by Pleasure Steamers Limited, leaving the two larger vessels to ply alone.

Originally her top deck was open, offering little protection for her passengers, who sat on deck in cane chairs in all weathers, but in 1950, after the war, she returned to her peace-time role as a pleasure steamer. At that time the main deck was enclosed and a smaller upper deck added. This gave her passengers a better view above the overgrown banks on river cruises. In fact the first post-war alterations made to both *Oulton Belle* and her sister ship were intended to make both vessels resemble *Brit II* which had been built at Great Yarmouth in 1935 for E.W. & S.H.D. Longfield, a competitor in the tourist trade. *Brit II* had also gone to Dunkirk as *HMS Watchful*.

Then, in 1970 *Regal Lady* was bought by Blakes who still specialise in holidays on the Norfolk Broads. She was then one of the largest passenger ships operating in that area with soft seats and carpets, music, dancing, bars and a variety of good food available on board. From her top deck she provided lovely views over the Yare Valley, up-river from Great Yarmouth. But the passenger trade in this area declined and she was finally laid up until 1984.

Then *Regal Lady* was given another fresh lease of life by Tom Machin who took her back to Scarborough, completely modernised her with a new wheelhouse and new decks and she now operates pleasure trips out of Scarborough every year from April to October. She is much changed in

appearance since she was *Oulton Belle,* but she is still a handsome old lady who will not only be remembered by those thousands who have enjoyed their holidays on board but will be remembered all her life for her gallant service when she went to the rescue of the British Expeditionary Force from Dunkirk in 1940.

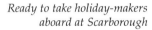

Ready to take holiday-makers aboard at Scarborough

Motor Vessel Southern Queen

Seaside towns just like the ships and those who earn their living in them, have two different faces. From June to September (or October in a good year) they have their summer face, seen by holiday makers, and much dependant on the English weather. They wear a bustling, festive air and when the sun shines, there is a good living to be earned from introducing their world to townspeople and trippers who would not relish the sea when winter seas and storms lash our coasts. During that time of year, the seaside is wilder and lonelier. The seamen return to their more traditional, less lucrative tasks of fishing and ocean transport. To earn their keep the year round, the ships have to be adaptable to both their roles and when the need arose for them to go to Dunkirk, their tougher, more rugged character came into its own.

The *Southern Queen* is a robust open boat, 51ft long, with a 12ft beam and a displacement of 20 tons. Although she might roll a little with her 3ft 6in draught, her oak construction and copper fastenings make her sound and strong. Before the war, she worked out of Folkestone and at Dunkirk she was commanded by Sub-Lieut. B.G.P de

NAME:	Southern Queen
TYPE:	Motor Vessel
LENGTH:	51ft
BEAM:	12ft
DISPLACEMENT:	20 tons
DRAFT:	3ft 6ins
ENGINES:	Barracuda Mk.II Ford
HULL CONSTR.:	Oak
BUILT BY:	Short Bros., Leics.
YEAR BUILT:	1926

Mattos. She would have been towed across by one of the tugs and must have been invaluable getting troops off the beach and taking them to the destroyers anchored off. After Dunkirk, she remained in naval service throughout the war. Once hostilities were over, she returned to carrying trippers out of Folkestone and gave a great deal of pleasure to holiday-makers at the seaside.

Later, she was taken out to the beautiful Isles of Scilly, 30 miles west of Land's End, with their rugged scenery and balmy climate warmed by the Gulf Stream. There, since 1957 and with a crew of two, she has been taking up to 81 passengers on sightseeing trips to see the seals, the puffins and the spectacular scenery of the islands. Often she copes with up to 300 visitors a day. In winter, she becomes a fishing boat again and she is one of a 10-strong voluntary Association of St Mary's Passenger Craft.

When she first went to the Scilly Isles, her owner equipped her with a large gramophone, loudspeakers and a good supply of popular recordings. At that time she still had an iron roof held up by a massive stanchion, which had been constructed to accommodate a gun for her defence during her service on war time patrol.

When Frank Pender bought the *Southern Queen* in 1967, he took all this away, renovated the entire ship and rearranged the accommodation to make room for more passengers. She was later sold to Alec Hicks who owns her at this time and the manner in which she is now maintained augurs well for her future.

Southern Queen with her skipper
at St. Mary's, Isles of Scilly

Pinnace **Dorian**

When she was originally built in 1918, *Dorian* was a pinnace - a 41 foot harbour launch with a Gardner or Kelvin petrol engine. A Mr Findlay bought her in 1937 from the Admiralty. He lengthened and converted her to a cruising yacht for charter but when the war started she was commandeered once more by the Admiralty for the duration. The navy took her to Dunkirk and she then spent the rest of the war at anchor in Chichester harbour.

After the war, she had a single Scripps V8 petrol engine fitted (a conversion of the Ford V8 engine), the type used for landing craft. The Findlays felt safer with a second engine and both were converted to run on paraffin. Despite her two masts, the *Dorian* was never much of a sailing boat, but she was a handsome cruiser and towed a 9ft mahogany tender which could also be hoisted on to the stern cabin. Her old brass binnacle and oil navigation lamps still exist, although her compass had a massive 14-degree deviation and was therefore replaced after the war

NAME:	Dorian
TYPE:	Pinnace
LENGTH:	41ft
BEAM:	21ft 1in
DISPLACEMENT:	16.61 tons
DRAFT:	5ft
ENGINES:	None
HULL CONSTR.:	Teak on oak
BUILT BY:	Portsmouth Yard
YEAR BUILT:	1918

with a 30-shilling government surplus one. For many years the *Dorian* cruised extensively from the Thames as far east as Great Yarmouth in Norfolk and south through the Solent to Yarmouth on the Isle of Wight. She frequently crossed to France and spent holidays on the French canals. The Findlays then had her on the Thames and lived on *Dorian* at Benson in Oxfordshire. They visited Oxford with their infant son lashed into his playpen on deck.

In the 1960s she was sold to Ted Cattle, an electrical contractor who re-organised her electrical system, re-covered her decks and continued her modernisation. When he died, *Dorian* was next seen at Ash Island on the Thames. Lord Soper, the Methodist minister and President of the Methodist Conference, once used her for a religious revival campaign based on the 'Dunkirk Spirit' which was reported in the Sunday Times. She carried a large banner lashed to her guardrails saying 'Jesus Saves'. Now

Dorian's cruising days are over. Her engines, which seized up many years ago, have been removed and she has been retired to become a houseboat, still with a brave face and a fresh coat of paint, but no longer likely to go to sea and leave a bright foaming wake crossing the channel.

From time to time the sons of previous owners see her lying on the Thames and are inspired to consider the idea of restoring her to her former state. Then the cost causes them to think again. But those who love boats are seldom motivated by mathematics; it is an affair of the heart which sometimes makes us do foolish things.

Motor Yacht Lamouette

Like so many old tars, most Dunkirk Little Ships have changed their occupations several times in their lives, as need and opportunities dictated. When *Lamouette* was launched in Portsmouth in 1937, as a naval pinnace built after the design of a Norwegian whaler, she served, rather grandly, as an Admiral's barge. So, at the time of Dunkirk, she was still in her prime. She was one of the little fleet assembled on the Thames by Douglas Tough at Teddington. From his hand-written records of the time, Bob Tough his son, could see that *Lamouette* came back without her dinghy, which was replaced at a cost of £8.10s.

When her pre-war owners did not reclaim her after 1946, she was bought for £201 by Marshall Hayes, an engineer, who used her as a home for his wife Grace and their daughter when his work caused him to move to the south of England. They lived on board while they overhauled her and on their journey south, experienced some engine trouble while in Norfolk. They so loved the area that they spent their subsequent winters there. In summer they cruised the south coast,

NAME:	Lamouette
TYPE:	Motor Yacht
LENGTH:	45ft
BEAM:	13ft
DISPLACEMENT:	19.68 tons
DRAFT:	4ft 6ins
ENGINES:	BMC Commodore
HULL CONSTR.:	Teak on teak
BUILT BY:	The Admiralty
YEAR BUILT:	1937

with excursions across the channel to Calais. She was a comfortable home with calor gas lighting and an anthracite stove for the winter.

Ian Rennie, a builder, has owned her since 1964. He was demolishing some houses in Plaistow, in the 1970s, when he discovered that one of them had belonged to the man who sailed *Lamouette* across to Dunkirk in 1940. The records showed that her crew at Dunkirk included Hugh Knowles of Great Bookham, G.H. Minton of Twickenham and L. Gates. Now Ian Rennie has taken *Lamouette* to the Costa Brava in Spain where he hopes to enjoy her in his retirement.

Motor Vessel Silver Queen

Silver Queen, now re-named *Fermain V* was built by Horn Brothers in Southampton in 1926 as a harbour launch. With a 2ft draught she was certainly never designed to cross the channel.

At the time of Dunkirk, she was towed across, because she was ideal for ferrying soldiers from La Panne beach to the larger destroyers and transports which brought them back to England. Boats of her kind were considered expendable once their task had been fulfilled and no-one would have expected her to come back unscathed. In fact, she was reported to have sunk, but was later re-floated.

She then found her way via Sheerness, where she was briefly owned by a Commander Carter, to Guernsey in the Channel Islands. This may have been when she was re-equipped with a Ford 6-cylinder diesel. At the time of Dunkirk she almost certainly had a petrol engine. Her next owner was C.B. Ferguson and when he died, he left her to his son Percy, who operates her on a daily run carrying 65 passengers on a ferry service (started in 1928) between St Peter Port and

NAME:	Silver Queen
TYPE:	Motor Vessel
LENGTH:	40ft 6ins
BEAM:	12ft 6ins
DISPLACEMENT:	Not known
DRAFT:	2ft
ENGINES:	Ford 6 cylinder diesel
HULL CONSTR.:	Carvel
BUILT BY:	Horn Bros. S'hampton
YEAR BUILT:	1926

Fermain Bay. This is a favourite holiday beach, difficult to get at by any other means. Her 2ft draught, which was so beneficial at Dunkirk, still makes her ideal for her present ferry work.

Because she has to pass her annual Department of Trade survey, she has to be well maintained and is likely to continue earning her keep for many years to come.

Silver Queen now re-named Fermain V working as a ferry out of St. Peter Port

Motor Yacht Chico

Sir Malcolm Campbell, the holder, between 1924 and 1948, of several of the world's land and water speed records, owned three fine yachts in succession and named each of them in turn *Bluebird* after his famous record-breaking car.

One of his yachts was later re-named *Chico*. She was a Watson design, built in Scotland in 1932 of pitch pine on oak, with a copper-sheathed bottom and she had luxurious accommodation for ten guests and two crew. Later, for a time, she was owned by the Countess of Onslow. On 28th December 1939 she was requisitioned from her for service with the Rear-Admiral, Minelaying Squadron. She was fitted out with echo sounding gear at Camper and Nicholson, Gosport and in January 1940 was then re-named *Chico*. Her career in the navy was a

particularly illustrious one and well recorded in her log, preserved from those days:

On leaving the fitting out yard she worked up as necessary at Brightlingsea before proceeding to her base in Dover. Here, as the *Chico*, she was commissioned on 6th March 1940. In May 1940 it became obvious that the British Expeditionary Force would have to be evacuated from France. At 2130 on 25th May a force of seven trawlers, three yachts (the *Grey Mist*, *Conidaw* and *Chico*), and two drifters sailed for Calais Road ready to evacuate troops from Calais the moment an order to do so was received. Five of the trawlers towed motor boats. Commander W.V.H. Harris, R.N. (Commander, M.S. Dover), in the *Grey Mist*, was in command and the destroyers *H.M.S.*

Windsor and *H.M.S. Verity* left Dover at 2300 to cover the withdrawal of this force. On arrival off Calais, two of the motor boats were ordered into Calais harbour. At about 0300 on the 26th, a signal was received that Calais was to be held at all costs; furthermore, it was ordered that this signal was to be sent by hand to the Brigadier commanding our forces on shore. *The Conidaw* went in to deliver the signal. All ships were then ordered back to the Downs.

On 30th May the *Chico* (under Sub-Lieut. J. Mason, R.N.V.R.) left Dover for Dunkirk where she embarked 217 troops and returned to Dover. On the 31st she ferried nearly 1,000 troops from the Dunkirk shore to ships, disembarking a further estimated 100 troops herself on her return to Dover. On 2nd June, she was transferred to life-saving duties on Route X - a new

NAME:	Chico
TYPE:	Motor Yacht
LENGTH:	73ft
BEAM:	16ft
DISPLACEMENT:	Not known
DRAFT:	8ft
ENGINES:	Gleniffers Twin Screw
HULL CONSTR.:	Carvel
BUILT BY:	J.N. Miller & Son Ltd.
YEAR BUILT:	Fife, 1932

middle route prepared between Dover and Dunkirk, from the North Goodwin to the Ruytingen Pass and thence into Dunkirk Road. On 20th March 1941 the small ships of the Dover Command assisted in the destruction by the minesweeping force off Dungeness of an enemy bomber, almost certainly a Junkers 88. At about 1400 hours the minesweeping trawler *Fyldea*, the senior ship, reported an attack by enemy aircraft. The machine dived to attack and was greeted with machine-gun fire from the drifters *Young Mon*,

and *Forecast* and from the *Chico*, all serving with the mine sweepers. Possibly the most credit was due to the *Young Mon*, whose gunlayer, with a single Lewis gun, coolly withheld his fire, but once he started continued until the plane coming up from astern was within fifty feet. The *Chico*, two or three hundred yards astern of the *Young Mon*, and also the *Forecast* on the beam joined in. The *Chico* claimed to have shot the tail off when the aircraft was between her and the *Young Mon*, while the latter put a pan straight into the nose. Whoever was responsible, the *Young Mon* had her masts carried away and received large pieces of aeroplane on her after deck, the fuselage having, fortunately, dis-integrated just before reaching the ship, leaving one engine to fall into the water on each side, with nothing very solid ending up on board. There were no casualties in any of H.M. Ships but none of the crew of the aircraft survived.

On 4th April, while engaged on survey work in the Downs, the *Chico* again received a little attention from an enemy aircraft. The latter was being hunted by British fighters and let go some bombs which fell not far from the yacht but without causing any damage. Although not seen to crash, the enemy was considered by the fighters to be a 'probable'.

The *Chico* was compulsorily acquired by the navy on 7th May 1941. On 15th May aircraft again figured in her life. She had left Dover at about 0800 hours to work at C 2 Buoy, servicing it and fitting a rescue ladder. At about 1510 , in the vicinity of C I Buoy during her return passage, she was close to MTB 50, who was on the opposite course, on passage from Dover to Portsmouth, when each was attacked by a separate aircraft. Two Dorniers appeared out of the cloud and carried out shallow dive attacks. Each aircraft opened fire with machine guns and cannon and dropped five bombs. Several near misses were observed. The MTB in particular had narrow escapes from two bombs within a few feet of her. Though her hull apparently suffered no damage, the MTB was badly shaken up. In the engine room, all her cast-iron engine bearers were badly fractured and all engines were damaged internally. Because of the engine room damage, the power-operated machine gun turret ceased to function and her armament could no longer be used. The *Chico* suffered no damage, only the disappointment of having the best of her many guns, a 20-mm cannon, jammed as a result of excessive zeal in over-charging the magazines.

Fortunately there were no casualties in either boat, but it was a pity that neither was able to take advantage of an easy target, although the *Chico* claimed some hits with tracer from the more ordinary part of her armament. Both aircraft made off, apparently undamaged. MTB 50 was taken in tow by the *Chico* and brought safely back to Dover, which was reached at about 2030 without further incident, thanks no doubt to a close escort provided by three fighters.

The *Chico* continued her activities without incident, but on 4th June 1942 she sustained minor damage when she collided with some MTB pens, breaking her sternpost and her covering board and all her planks from the deck to one foot above the water line. On 29th July, with a demolition cutter, she commenced work on the wreck of the trawler *Tranquil* which had sunk as a result of a collision in the Downs and was a hazard to navigation. On 5th January 1943 the *Chico* paid off and de-stored for an engine overhaul and was taken in

hand at the London Graving Dock, Poplar. In February she was re-allocated for service with the Royal Naval College, Greenwich, but in April 1943 she transferred to the Medway Mine Watching Patrol based at Chatham. There she remained until 16th February 1945 when she was laid up at Mears yard, Twickenham under the Director of Sea Transport's care and maintenance arrangements. She was disposed of in August 1946.

After the war she had a number of civilian owners, some of whom used her as a charter yacht and she now belongs to Carol and Phillip Goddard who live in Southampton.

Motor Yacht **Anne**

When she was built in 1925 by Frank Curtis in Cornwall, the *Anne* was sloop-rigged, of carvel construction, planked in pine on oak. She still has her two Ailsa Craig petrol/TVO engines driving her two propellers. Her draught is only 3ft 3ins so she could not have done very well under sail unless she had some sort of centreboard.

At the time of Dunkirk, the *Anne* belonged to Mr P.J. Darby and before the war end belonged to a Dr McCracken. As in so many cases of Dunkirk Little Ships, her precise war-time service has not been recorded, but her name appears in all the official records.

In January 1970 when she was lifted out of Bristol Docks by her present owner, Mr H.W. Bambridge of Winterbourne near Bristol, a mishap with a crane dropped her into the water, but the damage was restricted to sea water getting in her wiring and engines. Since then, Mr Bambridge has had the *Anne* in his garden and has

NAME:	Anne
TYPE:	Motor Yacht
LENGTH:	30ft
BEAM:	8ft 11ins
DISPLACEMENT:	Not known
DRAFT:	3ft 3ins
ENGINES:	Ailsa Craig petrol/TVO
HULL CONSTR.:	Pine on oak, carvel
BUILT BY:	Frank Curtis, Cornwall
YEAR BUILT:	1925

spent an almost unbelievable amount of time, money and effort in restoring her. When he stripped off the deck, he found 75% of the old ribs and some of the exterior planking were rotten and had to be replaced. She is a fortunate ship in having found a latter-day owner with such enthusiasm and skill.

The engines have been overhauled, the ballast keel shot-blasted and a new wheelhouse fitted. Now, after 20 years, she should be fit to go to sea again for the 50th anniversary return to Dunkirk.

Anne in Mr Bambridge's garden at Winterbourne near Bristol where she is being restored in March 1989

Thames Ferry Southend Britannia

When she was first built by Thornycrofts, the *Southend Britannia* operated a ferry service across the widest part of the Thames estuary from Southend to Sheerness. She was designed to carry 250 passengers on two decks and was virtually flat-bottomed, with a 3ft draft and only 2ft freeboard.

It is not hard to imagine Lieut. G.L. Norton, in command of the twin-funnelled ferry, packed solid with troops, returning from Dunkirk, low in the water, praying for the fair weather and smooth seas to hold out. Without this act of grace she would have sunk.

Like a much married old lady with an action-packed history, she has had many names - which speak for themselves: *Brightlingsea Belle*, when she worked on the Colne in Essex, then *Western Lady,* offering cruises and a ferry service for five years out of Brixham in Devon.

Once the scheduled cruises and ferry runs there had finished for the day, *Western Lady V* would have all her seating stripped out and stacked between her funnels, a band would arrive and her decks became a dance floor for the enjoyment of the locals and visitors alike, once a week. Normally, she would remain moored alongside for this entertainment but, if weather permitted, a trip around the bay was thrown in, or parties of teenagers - jiving to live music - were taken on evening cruises up the River Thames.

In 1960 Howard Thomas, the managing Director of ABC - now Thames Television - was looking for a suitable vessel to moor near the studios at Teddington Lock for use as a hospitality ship and floating restaurant by the company's clients and VIPs. The Western Lady *Fairmile* craft were

considered, but rejected. Then *Western Lady V* was inspected and finally chosen. The ferry company were persuaded to sell her. She was taken from Brixham to the River Thames by a crew of four plus two executives from Thames Television who were tempted by the thought of a 'nice little trip'. They lived to regret it! On their voyage around the coast strong winds forced her to seek shelter first at Weymouth, then at Newhaven and finally to drop anchor in Cowes Roads near Portsmouth. Her scant freeboard made her a dangerous craft for a journey up the English Channel. In all, it took over a week to complete the 'nice little trip' and her two joyriders became firm landlubbers in the process!

Once in the Thames, her funnels and her wheelhouse were removed to clear the bridges of the Thames on her journey up to Teddington Lock. When she arrived there, her engines and other surplus machinery were

NAME: Southend Britannia	
TYPE:	Thames Ferry
LENGTH:	107ft
BEAM:	27ft
DISPLACEMENT:	Not known
DRAFT:	3ft
ENGINES:	2 x 90 h.p. diesel
HULL CONSTR.:	Oak
BUILT BY:	Thornycroft
YEAR BUILT:	1924

removed to provide more room for her as a floating restaurant and she was re-named *Iris* after the wife of one of the directors.

She proved to be as popular in her new role as she had been as a ferry and she did a good job for Thames Television. But eventually, in 1987, at the grand old age of 63 and much to the regret of her owners, twenty years of static mooring in the strong tidal flow below Teddington Weir, took their toll. Thames fought long and hard to save her, even contemplating the idea of having her bedded in concrete or placed in a dry dock. But *Iris* was condemned as no longer viable and it was decided to scrap her. A sad loss indeed, but now another ship has taken her place. Newer and fully engined, this vessel can take her guests up and down the river whilst they dine, just as once *Western Lady V's* guests used to dance the night away in Torbay.

They thought that she had gone for scrap, but then she was seen again, re-named *Beverley*, at one time moored in the Docklands and later at Cadogan Pier in Chelsea. When we heard of this, we tried to find her, but to no avail. Perhaps it was her ghost? Dunkirk ships seem to have as many lives as the proverbial cat.

There is a postscript to the story of *Southend Britannia*. Her lifeboat, 14ft long with a 5ft beam and $2^1/_2$ ft draft, was used to carry troops from the beaches of Dunkirk to the ferry in deeper water. After the war, the lifeboat, re-named *Landscaper,* was sold separately. Lieut. Cmdr. John Sharman-Courtney (also a one-time owner of Dunkirk Little Ship *Thame II*) owned her for a while and then gave her to a London youth club which planned to restore her. There our trail went cold. The area is now built up and *Landscaper* has disappeared. Perhaps this book will come into the hands of those who know the whereabouts of *Southend Britannia* (*Beverley* ?) and *Landscaper,* so that both may qualify again to join the fleet of Dunkirk Little Ships and fly the cross of St. George on their jackstaff.

Motor Vessel Nayland

Commander J. Glendinning RNR, in his report dated 5th June 1940 to the Naval Officer in charge, Ramsgate, told tersely how he took command of the tug *Java* on 28th May at 1430 and proceeded to Dunkirk with four drifters and five motor launches including the *Nayland*. They arrived off Bray Dunes on 29th May at 1100 and he anchored in three fathoms of water sending the motor launches to the beach in search of troops which "seemed to be hiding in the sands". All the vessels under his command proceeded to transfer soldiers from the beaches to the bigger ships offshore. At 1000 hours he ordered the motor launches to transfer their troops to *HMS Calcutta*. By 1900 there were no more large ships and the small boats returned directly to Ramsgate with their loads. They arrived there at 0930 on 30th May and Commander Glendinning reports that all their men were in good heart "despite having had no meal from the afternoon of 28th until 1100 on 30th May."

Records show that the *Nayland* disembarked 28 troops at Ramsgate at dawn on 2nd June and more at 0740 and 1120, so she must have been ferrying these from off-lying ships to Ramsgate harbour. The following morning, she disembarked a further 55 troops directly from Dunkirk at Ramsgate and her total score for the duration of Operation Dynamo was 83.

NAME:	Nayland
TYPE:	Motor Vessel
LENGTH:	37ft
BEAM:	10ft 8ins
DISPLACEMENT:	16 tons
DRAFT:	4ft
ENGINES:	Perkins
HULL CONSTR.:	Clinker built
BUILT BY:	R J Perkins & Sons
YEAR BUILT:	Whitstable, 1937

In July 1940 the *Nayland* was transferred to auxiliary patrol duties at Ramsgate; later she became a despatch boat at Sheerness and she continued to serve the Navy until 17th July 1945.

After the war, her name was changed to *Peggotty* and Isabel Robinson, who runs a secretarial bureau in Eastbourne, describes how she found her advertised in *Dalton's Weekly* and bought her for £3,000. Little did she know that this was a Dunkirk Little Ship. When she first saw her in the pouring rain and full of water in March 1977, she nevertheless got a warm feeling about the boat and believed the yard manager who told her that she was basically sound, despite her sad condition.

Isabel Robinson was three days old when the *Nayland* went to Dunkirk, but the ship was originally built by Perkins in Whitstable in 1937 as a pilot boat. Before Isabel found her, she had been raised three times from the mud at Richmond-on-Thames where she had sunk, full of rain water, while she served as a floating home for a group of hippies. Now *Peggotty* lies at Swan Island Harbour, Twickenham and serves as a houseboat for Joe Eves, her present owner.

The *Warrior* was built in 1912 as a naval pinnace and she is a handsome roomy vessel - a real ship in miniature, so unlike a modern pleasure yacht. Her hull is constructed durably in double-diagonal teak on oak. Her own early records, including her Dunkirk log, were destroyed when an incendiary bomb struck her while she lay, still under naval command, at Greenwich, after Dunkirk.

At that time *Warrior* served as a coastal defence vessel and was used by Commander C.A. Lund to instruct naval officers in navigation and seamanship at H.M.S King Alfred in 1942.

After the war, *Warrior* had five owners. Stanley Crabtree had her entirely refitted at Dickie's Yard, Bangor in the late 1960s. In earlier days she had a fine figurehead of an Indian warrior which was maintained faithfully in its original colours even when *Warrior* was painted in battleship grey. Sadly she lost this figurehead during her restoration.

Later she was taken through the French canals to cruise in the Mediterranean and back. John and Mary Hornshaw lived aboard *Warrior* in Torquay during the 1980s. Now

NAME:	Warrior
TYPE:	Motor Yacht
LENGTH:	64ft 8ins
BEAM:	14ft 10ins
DISPLACEMENT:	40.39 tons
DRAFT:	5ft 10ins
ENGINES:	Russ. Newbery 40 h.p.
HULL CONSTR.:	Teak on oak
BUILT BY:	Camper & Nicholson
YEAR BUILT:	1912

Warrior belongs to Dennis Wells who is also the owner of the Dunkirk Ship *Inspiration II.*

This early photograph of Warrior was found in the Beken of Cowes collection and was taken in the 1930s

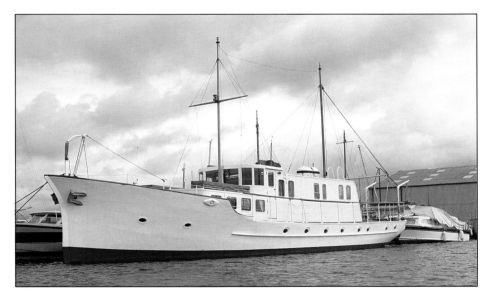

Motor Yacht **Moiena**

Moiena is the only Dunkirk Little Ship known to have a criminal record! In five trips between Turkey and Belgium during the 1970s, she carried a total of 10,000 kilograms of hashish before the authorities swooped in 1976 and confiscated both the boat and its illegal cargo.

But let us go back to her beginnings. Designed by John Baines and built at Rosneath, Scotland by James A. Silver in 1934, *Moiena* was commissioned by J.B.P. Weir of Hampstead who wanted her as a comfortable Thames cruiser and enjoyed her there for five years. She was then acquired by Mr Trower of Guildford less than a month before war broke out, but he had little chance to sail in *Moiena*. Within a few months she was at Dunkirk, credited with lifting 1,500 troops from the beaches and coming back loaded with men. She returned from Dunkirk with *H.M.S Wakeful* and *H.M.S. Grafton*, neither of whom survived the heavy enemy bombardment.

She was immediately put on auxiliary patrol at Brightlingsea, Essex and very soon afterwards sent to Lowestoft, Suffolk, for hydrophone training. The luckless Mr Trower then lost his ship, by compulsory purchase, to the Admiralty in 1941. When *Moiena* finished her distinguished war service she was owned for five years by Mrs Caroline Sears, in Northampton and then by a distinguished wartime RAF pilot, Wing-Commander Alex Ingle DFC, AFC who moved to Holland in the 1950s and used *Moiena* to explore the North Sea and the Baltic.

She changed hands twice more and then, in 1957, was acquired by John Stuart Marriner who registered her in Jersey and changed her name to *September Tide.* He was a travel writer who cruised as far as Scandinavia, the Baltic, Poland and France. Then he took *September Tide* to the Mediterranean, Spain, Italy, Malta, Yugoslavia, Greece, Cyprus, Lebanon, Syria and Turkey collecting material for his books. In 1966 she went along the Bulgarian and Rumanian coasts and up the river Danube to Vienna. These were the golden years of the ship's life. John Marriner sold *September Tide* in 1967 and it was in 1970 that the much-travelled ship got into bad company.

Her drug-running trips nearly ended her life. When the customs authorities caught up with her, her owners went

NAME:	Moiena
TYPE:	Motor Yacht
LENGTH:	55ft
BEAM:	12ft 4ins
DISPLACEMENT:	30 tons
DRAFT:	5ft 3ins
ENGINES:	2 x DAF diesel 6 cyl.
HULL CONSTR.:	Pitch pine on oak
BUILT BY:	James Silver Ltd
YEAR BUILT:	Scotland, 1934

to jail and she became the property of the customs who let her fall into neglect, so that she almost sank several times.

Her present owner, Eric Zandwijk bought her at a customs auction in September 1984. On board he found documents, correspondence and books which enabled him to trace her fascinating history. To his delight he learned that she was one of the heroes of Dunkirk and he set to work restoring her. She now lies at Ibiza in Spain where her owner has a restaurant. His great ambition is to sail her proudly - her criminal interlude forgotten - to the 50th anniversary celebrations at Dunkirk. We must remember it is not the ships but their owners who sometimes go astray.

Motor Yacht Marsayru

Although every one of the Little Ships of Dunkirk has a story, not all these are preserved in written records. The skippers and crews were too busy to keep a log and not all of them survived. The simple story of the *Marsayru* appears in Battle Summary 41 compiled by the historical section of the Admiralty and she is also mentioned in Walter Lord's book: *The Miracle of Dunkirk* and in A.D. Devine's book: *Dunkirk*

The *Marsayru* went over to Dunkirk on 31st May commanded by her civilian skipper, G.D. Olivier, who received a DSM and her engineer C. Loggins who was mentioned in despatches. They sailed in company with three lighters: *X217*, *X213* and *X149*, arriving off Malo beach at about 1600. During an air attack *X213* and *X419* were sunk. The *X217* was beached and with the help of a cutter towed by *Marsayru*, embarked about 200 British and French troops, some in the yacht *Llanthony* and some in the *Marsayru* which was then towed towards England. Shortly after sailing, the *Marsayru* broke adrift and in the darkness could not be found. Her skipper had been taken home aboard the towing vessel. Next day, Sub-Lieut. T.E. Godman RNVR, in

a naval steam pinnace off La Panne, sighted the *Marsayru* drifting with the tide and unoccupied but in working order. He left a petty officer in charge of the pinnace and, with the dinghy in tow, took the yacht to the western end of the beach where he anchored. The dinghy ferried 19 troops to her and at 2330 he made fast to a conical flashing buoy and waited for daylight. At 0430 on 2nd June a trawler took the *Marsayru* in tow to Ramsgate where, at 0800, she disembarked her 19 troops. Later, on 2nd June, the original crew took charge of the *Marsayru* and A.D. Devine reports that she was again working the beaches on that day. At one time, the nearest ship being about

NAME:	Marsayru
TYPE:	Motor Yacht
LENGTH:	40ft
BEAM:	10ft
DISPLACEMENT:	Not known
DRAFT:	3ft
ENGINES:	BMC Commodores x 2
HULL CONSTR.:	Steel
BUILT BY:	Timmer & Zoon
YEAR BUILT:	Holland, 1937

2¹/₂ miles away, she was attacked by four Messerschmitts who ineffectually machine-gunned her for half an hour from a height of more than 2,000 feet until three Hurricanes saw them off. *Marsayru* was credited in her various crossings with saving some 400 French soldiers. Built far more strongly than her size demands, the *Marsayru* was constructed of Swedish steel on steel frames by Timmer & Zoon in Holland.

Gareth Roe, her present owner, cruises in her from his home in Ramsgate, near the scene of her wartime service. Since the war, *Marsayru* has had a number of owners who have sailed in her for 3,000 miles or more through the canals of France to the Mediterranean.

The *Motor Boat* issue of 23rd October 1925 carried a two-page article about the conversion of the *Vere*, a naval pinnace built in 1905, into a handsome cabin cruiser. The strong seaworthy hull (with $3^1/_2$in. x 5in. solid oak frames planked in double diagonal teak) of the pinnace was retained and a teak and mahogany super-structure added for cruising comfort. Steel-covered rubbing bands were added to save her from damage when passing through locks. Inside, the 3 cabins were lined with tapestries. There were comfortable sleeping, cooking and washing facilities for six people. On the after deck there was room to lounge in deck chairs when the weather was kind and to launch the mahogany dinghy from its davits.

She had two engines of unequal power: a 25/30 h.p. Sterling and a 10/12 h.p. Universal as well as a 2 h.p. generator. For added safety she had a foresail, a gaff-rigged main and a small mizzen - a total sail area of 195 sq. ft. But Capt. B.G. Fray, the owner who had her converted, added a 98 sq. ft. square sail for running before the wind. She was indeed, as the 1925 magazine article claimed, "fitted out regardless of expense."

Despite her many means of propulsion the *Vere* broke down twice on her first crossing to Dunkirk. There is a simple explanation for these breakdowns - of the *Vere* and many other ships. They simply weren't prepared for the sudden call into service. There was a war on and their owners, in many cases, had no chance to use their pleasure boats or to get them ready for the 1940 summer season. Rear-Admiral Taylor and his staff of the Small Vessels Pool at Sheerness had little time, staff and spares to repair and equip the hundreds of different ships that were wished on them. Consequently some craft did not even make it all the way down the river. Neverthesless, the *Vere* is credited with saving a total of 346 men and survived to spend most of her post-war years as a floating home for three different families.

One of her owners, N. Perfect, a schoolmaster, who inherited the *Vere* from his father, recalls his surprise when he carried out restoration work to her timbers and came across 2 German machine-gun bullets imbedded in her frames.

NAME:	Vere
TYPE:	Pinnace
LENGTH:	40ft
BEAM:	10ft
DISPLACEMENT:	22 tons
DRAFT:	4ft 6ins
ENGINES:	90 h.p. Gray + A Craig 40 h.p.
HULL CONSTR.:	Teak
BUILT BY:	The Admiralty
YEAR BUILT:	1905

Ramparts in Southampton were one of the best known and respected builders of motor yachts in the 1930s and many of the Dunkirk Little Ships had been built there.

Lady Lou originally had twin 20/40 h.p. Morris Commodore petrol engines but these have now been replaced by Perkins diesels. She was owned after the war by Charles Mansell, a yacht chandler, who was at one time Commodore of the London River Yacht Club.

Later she belonged to the chef of a Henley hotel, who lived aboard. Now she is owned by Mr G. Borsboom who previously had boats on the river Arun in Sussex, moored on the Duke of Norfolk's estate.

Mr Borsboom has largely restored *Lady Lou*, fitted new diesel engines and faithfully restored the wheelhouse. He keeps the veteran boat beside his home at Shepperton and plans to take her to France in 1990.

NAME:	Lady Lou
TYPE:	Motor Yacht
LENGTH:	40ft
BEAM:	9ft
DISPLACEMENT:	Approx. 10 tons
DRAFT:	4ft 3ins
ENGINES:	Perkins x 2
HULL CONSTR.:	Pitch pine on oak
BUILT BY:	Rampart
YEAR BUILT:	1937

Motor Yacht Lurline of Ipswich

When Liz Devas, a night sister at Kingston hospital, heard that the nurses' home was to be demolished in 1970 she decided to take to the water and bought an old ketch-rigged wooden cabin cruiser from the TV producer Mark Stuart. Soon she found herself caught up in a legend. Only a few months later, totally ignorant of the art of navigation, she was invited to take her new home from its safe mooring at Ash Island, Hampton Court, down river to the channel to join the 30th anniversary cruise of the Little Ships to Dunkirk.

Thirty years earlier, on 25th May 1940,, according to Tough Bros.' records, *Lurline*, crewed by H.L. Bayle of London and A.C. Buckle of Richmond, was despatched by them on the same journey down the Thames to join the flotilla which went to Sheerness and on to Dunkirk. Bob Tough has his father's notebook which records that *Lurline* returned relatively unscathed but minus her dinghy which was replaced, at a cost of £8.

At the 1970 reunion, unfamiliar until then with the detailed story of Dunkirk, Liz was deeply moved by the ceremony of the lone Shackleton circling the little fleet and dropping a wreath in memory of those who did not come back from Dunkirk in 1940. Like all new owners of the Little Ships she could not help but be touched by the comradeship which exists between these caretakers of a part of British history.

Now *Lurline of Ipswich* belongs to Michael Simcock, who took part in the 1985 return to Dunkirk and had to be rescued by Margate lifeboat when strong N.E.winds drove *Lurline* aground at Botany Bay, Kingsgate. He has done much to improve the ship and is now working hard to get her ready to cross the channel in May 1990

NAME: Lurline of Ipswich	
TYPE:	Motor Yacht
LENGTH:	37ft
BEAM:	9ft
DISPLACEMENT:	11.58 tons
DRAFT:	3ft 4ins
ENGINES:	Perkins P60
HULL CONSTR.:	Pitch pine on oak
BUILT BY:	Howard, Maldon, Essex
YEAR BUILT:	1914

for the 50th anniversary of Dunkirk. Her original 6-cylinder Gleniffer paraffin engine has long been replaced by a Perkins P 60 diesel and her hull and paintwork will be restored to compete with the best in the fleet.

Fireboat Massey Shaw

When the London Fireboat *Massey Shaw* first left her river mooring for Dunkirk, she had only been to sea once before, on her delivery trip to the Thames in 1935 from John Samuel White's boatyard on the Isle of Wight. She was not intended to be a sea-going vessel but, until the time of Dunkirk, had been moored at Blackfriars Bridge in London. Her two massive 8 cylinder 160 h.p. Gleniffer diesels had more than enough power to propel her through the water at 12 knots, but were principally intended to operate her 3,000 gallon-per-minute centrifugal pumps to put out fires along London's river. She was named after Sir Eyre

Massey Shaw (1861 - 1891) who, at the age of thirty, founded the Metropolitan Fire Brigade.

On 29th and 30th May 1940, from her mooring at Blackfriars, the *Massey Shaw's* crew had seen tugs coming down the river towing strings of small boats, yachts, lifeboats and even dinghies. Then they heard that the destination was Dunkirk, and *Massey Shaw* was to follow them. A volunteer crew of 13 was chosen. This was more than her normal complement because they expected to spend several days fighting fires off the French coast, without relief. A pilot took them to Greenwich and another to Ramsgate. Her sparkling brasswork and fittings were covered with grey paint on the way. A young Sub-Lieut. RN came aboard to take command, carrying nothing more than a steel helmet and a chart to show him how to navigate through the minefields across the channel from North Goodwin Light-ship to Bray Dunes, the beach where they were to pick up Allied troops.

The *Massey Shaw* did not even possess a compass, but they had bought one hastily from a chandler's in Blackfriars. There was no time to swing and correct it, which made it rather unreliable since the large steel hull of the fireboat caused a massive deviation. As a result, despite the excellent landmark of smoke from Dunkirk's burning oil tanks, they were well outside the swept channel when they got to the French coast. But their shallow draft enabled them to cross the hazardous sandbanks without grounding.

The fires ashore were what the *Massey Shaw's* crew were used to, but the bursts of shells, bombs and anti-aircraft fire were a new experience. As they steamed parallel to the beach, they saw columns of men wading out

Massey Shaw returning to a hero's welcome at Lambeth pontoon, 1940

NAME:	M a s s e y S h a w
TYPE:	Fireboat
LENGTH:	78ft
BEAM:	13ft 6ins
DISPLACEMENT:	50.54 tons
DRAFT:	3ft 9ins
ENGINES:	2 x 8 cyl.Gleniffer dies.
HULL CONSTR.:	Steel
BUILT BY:	J S White, Cowes
YEAR BUILT:	1935

in the shallows, waiting to be picked up by a host of small boats. Late that afternoon, they anchored off Bray Dunes.

They used a light skiff, picked up at Ramsgate Harbour, to go ashore and collect the first of the men. Most of the soldiers were non-swimmers and at first, too many of them tried to get aboard so that they swamped and sank the skiff. There were many other small boats operating from the beach, but each of them already had its own ship to fill. After many attempts to find a suitable way of ferrying soldiers to the

Massey Shaw, a line was made fast to a derelict lorry and a small boat was used to ferry altogether 40 of a company of Royal Engineers aboard the fire float. The young Naval officer who had spent most of the day in the water between the fire float and the beach, then safely navigated her back to Ramsgate where they arrived next morning. They escaped major damage, despite an attack by a German bomber which had spotted the *Massey Shaw's* phosphorescent wake, but whose bombs missed by a boat length.

The crew of the *Massey Shaw* re-fuelled hastily, got some food and left for another trip. Some of the exhausted firemen were replaced by naval ratings and they brought a Lewis gun on board as a defence against air attack, but this was never used. Another RNVR Lieutenant came aboard to command the ship and they brought two stokers to take care of the engines and a beach party commanded by a second young naval officer to handle the embarkation on the other side.

They also took a 30ft. ship's lifeboat in tow as a tender. At 2300 they arrived and anchored off Bray Dunes in 10ft. of water with their head towards the shore. The fires of Dunkirk gave them enough light to work by and the thick blanket of smoke provided some cover from air attack. But the shelling from German guns was relentless. The two to overcome, stretcher cases began to arrive and these were hard to handle and transfer to the troopship. They made about five journeys from the beach to a paddle steamer and it was estimated that they embarked 500 men in this way. As dawn broke, the troopship was full and left for England. *Massey Shaw* returned to the

Naval officers set a splendid example of calm and the beach party rowed ashore, fixing a line to maintain contact with the float. After four or five journeys, the *Massey Shaw* was full once more with troops pressed together in the cabin and standing shoulder-to-shoulder on deck. Her load of nearly 100 men was transferred to a troopship at anchor in the channel and she returned to be re-loaded.

After some engine trouble which the naval stokers, unused to the *Massey Shaw's* machinery, eventually managed

beach and started loading again. At this point, on a falling tide, they began to bump on the sands and were in danger of damaging their propellers but, with their engines throbbing at full power, they just managed to get back into deep water. At 0330 they were the last boat to leave that part of the beach. Halfway across the channel, the naval skipper began to have doubts about the compass, but then, to his relief, came across a drifter towing two small boats packed with troops and they followed them into Ramsgate where they arrived at 0800 on Sunday 2nd June, landing 30 or 40 more soldiers.

The *Massey Shaw* returned to Dunkirk again the next evening with a Fire Service crew. This time they went to the jetty of Dunkirk harbour. It was difficult for soldiers to board her from the towering jetty and she came away empty. After returning to Ramsgate, she was ordered back to London. Off Margate, the *Emile Deschamps*, a French ship which had sailed to England from Dunkirk laden with troops the previous night, was passing her at a distance of 200 yards when it struck a mine and sank almost immediately. The *Massey Shaw* picked up 40 men, all severely injured and took them back to Ramsgate. Early on Wednesday 5th, she finally returned to London and as she came up the river she was cheered as she passed each fire station. Finally the wives and mothers of all on board were fetched from their homes and gave the crew a splendid reception. Sub-Officer A.J. May was awarded the Navy's Distinguished Service Medal, a rare honour for a civilian. Two of her firemen, Henry Ray and Edmond Wright, were mentioned in despatches.

The *Massey Shaw* continued with her fire-fighting work on the river and was not retired until 1971. During the next eleven years she fell into neglect until she was discovered by the man who planned to restore her, Phil Wray, of the London Fire Brigade's training school at Lambeth. With help from the Maritime Trust, Tailor Woodrow Ltd. and the GLC, the *Massey Shaw and Maritime Vessels Preservation Society* was formed in 1980. Both the London Fire Brigade and many of its individual members have given generously of their time and resources not only to restore the vessel, but to make her available at public functions such as the Lord Mayor's Show, the opening by the Queen and Prince Philip of the Thames Barrier, and for displays and celebrations up and down the River Thames as far as Oxford. She has twice attended returns of the fleet of Little Ships to Dunkirk and plans to be there again for the 50th anniversary in 1990.

Massey Shaw in action, fighting a fire at the tea warehouse, Colonial Wharf, Wapping in 1935

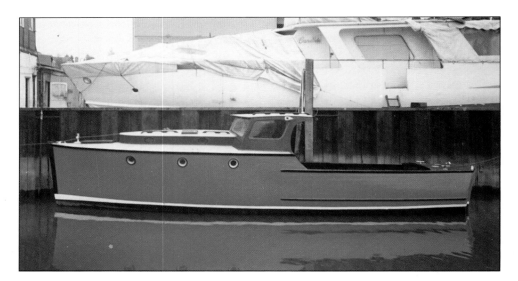

William Osbourne's long established yard in Little-hampton had been famous for strongly built and well designed motor cruisers in the 1920s and '30s and it still exists today.

Inspiration II was built there in 1931 and at 30ft. was one of the smallest of the Little Ships to set out across the channel during the first days of the evacuation.

Like so many of the smaller craft, she was towed across to save fuel, and to increase her speed. No one knows quite what happened on the way. Perhaps she broke her tow or had her lines severed in an aerial attack but she was found drifting on the tide by the tug *Kenia* who picked her up and as with many other damaged vessels, helped her back to the port of Dover.

In 1988, *Inspiration II* was sold to Dennis Wells who also owns *Warrior*.

Inspiration II is a pretty boat, whose brightly painted red hull has now been painted in the original white to be preserved just as she was built nearly sixty years ago.

NAME:	Inspiration II
TYPE:	Motor Yacht
LENGTH:	30ft 9ins
BEAM:	9ft
DISPLACEMENT:	Not known
DRAFT:	2ft 6ins
ENGINES:	2 x BMC Comm. diesel
HULL CONSTR.:	Pitch pine on oak
BUILT BY:	Osborne
YEAR BUILT:	1931

Paddle Steamer Medway Queen

NAME:	Medway Queen	
TYPE:	Paddle Steamer	
LENGTH:	180ft	
BEAM:	24ft	
DISPLACEMENT:	316 tons	
DRAFT:	5ft 6ins	
ENGINES:	Compound diagonal	
HULL CONSTR.:	Steel	
BUILT BY:	Ailsa Yard, Troon	
YEAR BUILT:	1924	

Few ships associated with Dunkirk have fought so hard and escaped destruction so tenaciously and for so long as the *Medway Queen*. Even today, she is still far from secure and is in need of all the help that her many admirers and well-wishers can muster.

She started life in 1924 at Ailsa's Yard in Troon, Scotland and was one of the finest and most luxurious paddle steamers built - to provide excursions in the Thames and Medway Estuaries. She was much loved by the thousands who sailed in her until, in 1939, she was called up to serve with the Navy as part of the 10th Minesweeping Flotilla. She was originally designed to carry almost a thousand passengers at 15 knots.

H.M.S. Medway Queen's naval service started in the bitter winter of 1939, yet her new crew came to love her and were soon welded into an efficient fighting force as part of the Dover Patrol. On 28th May 1940, they were anchored on the south coast spotting enemy aircraft laying mines when she was ordered to proceed to the beaches of Dunkirk. She was thus one of the first ships to arrive there and she quickly filled up with men to her full capacity. By 0700 hours, she was on her way back to Dover when she was attacked by German planes and her machine-guns accounted for one German fighter. The *Brighton Belle*, which was nearby, was less fortunate. She drifted over a submerged wreck, tore open her bottom and sank. So the *Medway Queen* picked up as many of her survivors as she could and added them to her own load. On the second day, by 1700 hours the *Medway Queen* was once again steaming for Dunkirk from Dover under her Captain, Lieut. A.T. Cook RNR with J.D. Graves RNR as her First Lieutenant. They entered the harbour of Dunkirk amid heavy gunfire. The oil tanks were ablaze by

then and there was wreckage everywhere. Scaling ladders were used to enable troops to come down to the ship from the mole high above them and she was soon full again. Lieut. Jolly, her navigator thoughout the operation, quickly got her under way. They slipped over the minefields to save time, relying on their shallow draught to avoid destruction. As night fell, her crew devised ingenious ways to subdue the phosphorescence in the water with oil, to escape enemy detection. This time they returned to Ramsgate and arrived between 1000

and 1100 hours. Once more, they refuelled and took on all the stores that they could carry. Now they went back alternately to the harbour and the beaches of Dunkirk. On the beaches, they had to use their motorised dinghy to bring the troops out. Once aboard, the men were taken care of by the *Medway Queen's* extraordinary cook, Thomas Russell who, with his assistant 'Sec' (his full name is not recorded), took pride in caring for every one of the soldiers with meals and hot drinks.

Engineer Davis was in charge of the *Medway Queen's* engines and kept them running, never leaving his post,

from 27th May until 4th June when they made the last of their seven runs to Dunkirk. In all, the *Medway Queen* is credited with saving 7,000 men and some of them still remember their rescue with great emotion. John Howarth from Rochester recalls how he was in the middle of the Channel surrounded by bodies and almost resigned to death when, over the horizon, came the *Medway Queen* on her way back to England, crammed with troops. He could hardly believe his luck when the ship stopped long enough to pick him up!

A French soldier, Paul Dervilers who, in 1989 is 87 years old, also recalled his rescue.

"I was on the beach walking up the coast towards Belgium when I saw some Englishmen getting into a dinghy and I joined ten of them who tried to get aboard. But the dinghy became waterlogged. We all began bailing hopelessly with our helmets. Fortunately, half-way to an off-lying ship, we picked up an abandoned little skiff in good shape and we got into it. It was 2300 when we climbed up the ladder of the *Medway Queen*."

After Dunkirk, the *Medway Queen* was refitted in Chatham Dockyard and continued her service in the Navy until the end of the war. In 1947 she was refitted at Thornycrofts at Southampton and became a pleasure steamer once more. In 1953 she followed the *Royal Yacht Britannia* through the lines of assembled ships at the Spithead Coronation Review.

In 1963 the *Medway Queen* was laid up in Rotherhythe Dry Dock. The surveyor's report was ominous. With all the work required, it was clearly not economic to repair her and she was sold to a Belgian ship-breaker. At this time her many admirers let out an anguished cry for her preservation. Eventually, the *Medway Queen Trust* was formed and several national newspapers publicised her desperate fate. Three young businessmen in the Isle of Wight, led by Alan Ridett, bought the *Medway Queen* and transferred her to the Mill Pond on the River Medina where she became the club house for a new marina. There, she was much appreciated until, in 1963, her success in her new role was her undoing; she became too small for the task and was replaced by a larger paddle steamer. Still, there were people wanting to preserve her and one group moved her from the club house mooring, only to hit an underwater obstruction and see her sink in the Medina.

Eventually in 1983 a group of business men who now owned her, brought her back to her home river, the Medway. Hundreds of tons of silt were removed from the ship. In 1987 she was raised from her semi-sunken state. Then, she was towed down river to her new berth at Dam-Head Creek, Kingsnorth-by-Medway. Eventually *Medway Queen* became the property of the *Medway Queen Preservation Society* and they are still struggling to keep her alive and restore her once more.

Heroism in time of war is recognised but briefly. Her skipper, Lieut.. Thomas Cook RNR and her First Officer, Sub-Lieut. Graves RNR received the DSC. Two of her Petty Officers, Crossley and MacAlister and Seaman Olly received the DSM. Two of her crew were mentioned in despatches, but the ship which rescued 7,000 soldiers now barely survives through the private charity and dedication of the *Medway Queen Preservation Society.*

Motor Yacht Lady Anita

Another Osbourne boat is *Lady Anita* originally called *My Babe II* when she was built at Littlehampton in 1939 for Gerald Marcuse of Bosham. Her records, like those of so many Dunkirk Little Ships, were themselves casualties of the war but we know that she was taken over by the Admiralty in 1940 for service in Dunkirk.

After the war her new owner A.C. Draycott changed her name to *Alliance* and she then had no less than eight owners and in 1980 D.B. Stewart, her latest owner, finally changed her name to *Lady Anita*

NAME:	Lady Anita
TYPE:	Motor Yacht
LENGTH:	32ft
BEAM:	8ft 3ins
DISPLACEMENT:	7.56 tons
DRAFT:	3ft
ENGINES:	Twin Gray Petrol
HULL CONSTR.:	Carvel
BUILT BY:	Osborne, Littlehampton
YEAR BUILT:	1939

As early as 14th May 1940 the BBC announced that "the Admiralty requests all owners of self-propelled craft between 30ft. and 100ft. to send all particulars within fourteen days" so that they could be requisitioned. This was more an order than a request and by 26th May most of them were called into service. The *Nydia* had only just been completed by Thornycrofts for Harold Turner, who had commissioned her, when the Admiralty took her over. They kept her throughout the war and she was only returned to Harold Turner for a short time and was then sold to C.J. Deal, the young Naval officer who had commanded her briefly in the war.

At Dunkirk she ferried troops from the beach to the larger vessels lying off and she finally returned full of British and French soldiers. For the rest of the war, she was stationed in Chatham Dockyard. *Nydia* is one of the fortunate ones. She never fell into disrepair and has gradually been restored and improved - first by Percy Bartlett who found her in Faversham and took her on the Medway, the Thames and later to France for long river holidays. Then Judith and Geoff Simpson lived aboard and explored the Seine, visiting Paris. They spent six months following the French canals

NAME:	Nydia
TYPE:	Motor Yacht
LENGTH:	30ft
BEAM:	9ft
DISPLACEMENT:	8 tons
DRAFT:	3ft
ENGINES:	1 x 2.2 BMC
HULL CONSTR.:	Carvel
BUILT BY:	Thornycroft
YEAR BUILT:	1939

and river Rhone to the south of France. Now *Nydia* is owned by Peter Cherry, who has a boat hire business in the south of France. He hopes to return with her to Dunkirk in 1990 and in his ownership her future seems assured.

Ketch Wairakei

Wairakei is a 42ft. ketch-rigged motor sailor built by James Silver at Rosneath, on the Clyde in Scotland in 1928. She is a handsome boat with a canoe stern and is comfortably fitted out for cruising.

In her time, the Brown Owl class to which she belongs, was a popular design costing £1,650 new, which was not cheap in 1928. But the famous O.M. Watts himself navigated one of the first of these cruisers all the way from Scotland, through the Forth and Clyde Canal and down the east coast to Chelsea, on the Thames. He paid compliments to the seakeeping qualities of the John Bain design in *Motor Boat* magazine. Strangely, the only record of her participation in Dunkirk is a list of her crew which consisted of I.Hassall, P.Mansfield and J.Galway. With a 5ft. draft, her navigator must have been extremely skilful to bring her home undamaged. After the war, her original petrol engines were replaced by two powerful Perkins 4107s which give her

NAME:	Wairakei
TYPE:	Ketch
LENGTH:	42ft
BEAM:	10.85ft
DISPLACEMENT:	20 tons
DRAFT:	5ft
ENGINES:	2 x Perkins 4107
HULL CONSTR.:	Pitch pine on oak
BUILT BY:	J A Silver Ltd. Rosneath
YEAR BUILT:	1928

a good speed and generous margin for safety when under power, with the added comfort of having three sails to propel her when there is a reasonable breeze.

When she left His Majesty's Service in 1948, she was re-named *Vivanti* and registered in London. Her present owner, R.V. Harris keeps her at Ramsgate.

Old Sailing Clipper Falcon II

When she was built and named *Xebec* in 1898, she was an ocean-going sailing clipper designed to carry casks of wine from Portugal to England. Only 58ft. long, she was unusually small for sailing regularly across the notorious Bay of Biscay.

In 1935 she was converted into a private motor yacht, re-named *Falcon II* and given a 4 cylinder MacLaren Benz engine. She did 5 trips and took on 90 men on each occasion, bringing them back to Ramsgate. Her total score was 450 and she survived unscathed.

Wing Commander Leonard Lambert DFC, AFC found her in 1975 moored on the river bank at Thames Ditton. He had himself been rescued from Dunkirk by a Little Ship after 5 sleepless nights when he lay wounded on the beach. After his rescue, he spent many months in hospital. It was therefore especially significant for him to be the owner of a Dunkirk Little Ship. At this point, *Falcon II* was re-named *Alabama*.

In 1988 the gallant old vessel nearly met her end when at Cadogan Pier, Chelsea, in the heart of London, she was struck by a hit-and-run ship and sank at her moorings. The culprit was never identified. The insurance company pronounced her a write-off and gave instructions for her to be broken up. However, Michael Hamby who has a special interest in Dunkirk Little Ships and who also owns *Count Dracula*, heard about it and offered £1 for her, undertaking to have her re-floated and taken to Toughs Boatyard at Teddington for repairs. He made a video film of the raising of the

NAME:	Falcon II
TYPE:	Old Sailing Clipper
LENGTH:	58ft
BEAM:	15ft
DISPLACEMENT:	50 tons
DRAFT:	5ft 6ins
ENGINES:	75 h.p.+ 2 x 50 h.p diesel
HULL CONSTR.:	Mahogany on oak
BUILT BY:	Vosper, Portsmouth
YEAR BUILT:	1898

Alabama which was done with great skill and care by Tough's boatmen. The Yard was formerly owned by Douglas Tough who assembled the flotilla of Little Ships for Dunkirk on the upper Thames. Michael Hamby has taken on an onerous task to bring *Alabama* back to life, but this is the kind of dedication that the Little Ships inspire.

White Orchid (originally *Aquila*) was built by James A. Silver at Rosneath, Scotland, in 1932. She was a Dunkirk Little Ship which had led a distinguished and eventful life, grew old gracefully and finally died with dignity.

White Orchid got used to being in the limelight when, in 1935, she led the Thames Silver Jubilee procession in honour of King George V and Queen Mary up the Thames from Teddington Lock. After seven years as a gentleman's motor yacht, she was commandeered by the Royal Navy and went to Dunkirk with the rest of them, operating off the beaches of La Panne.

Following her return from Dunkirk, she was compulsorily acquired by the Admiralty and used as a torpedo recovery vessel on the south coast until 1949. It is strange to find, from the records of so many of the Little Ships, that they did not pass into the ownership of the Admiralty until *after* their Dunkirk service. The reason is

NAME:	White Orchid
TYPE:	Motor Yacht
LENGTH:	36ft
BEAM:	9ft
DISPLACEMENT:	12 tons
DRAFT:	3ft 6ins
ENGINES:	2 x Morris petrol
HULL CONSTR.:	Carvel
BUILT BY:	J. Silver, Rosneath
YEAR BUILT:	1932

simply that there was no time to go through such formalities when the emergency arose. The acquisition was regularised later when the extreme usefulness of these craft was recognised, their naval crews had got used to them and it was assumed that they might well be needed again.

After the war, *White Orchid* returned to her original function and her name was changed to *Doutelle*. She was owned in partnership by Ben and Norman Cannell and participated in the very first return to Dunkirk on the

25th anniversary of Operation Dynamo in 1965. Both Ben Cannell, who became Commodore of the Association of Dunkirk Little Ships in 1975 and his son, Norman, have been leading members of the Association since its inception. Norman, as Vice-Commodore of the Association in 1989, is preparing to attend the 50th anniversary return to Dunkirk in 1990 in his Little Ship *Janthea (Reda*, at Dunkirk.)

In 1967, *Doutelle* was part of the ADLS Guard of Honour at the Tower of London to welcome Sir Francis Chichester on his return from his single-handed circumnavigation of the world. Then, in 1975, *Doutelle* returned to Dunkirk once more for the 35th anniversary celebrations. Later she played an active part in all the pageants and celebrations which are enacted against the romantic background of the River Thames each summer and are at the heart of English life. For a quarter of a century, *Doutelle* graced the banks of the Thames at Fawley Meadows during Henley Royal Regatta where the Upper Thames Motor Yacht Club was founded.

In 1986, it was discovered that *Doutelle* had extensive dry rot in her main frame and beams which, in a boat, is like terminal cancer in one of us. An international marine surveyor and two reputable boat builders, like eminent physicians, pronounced her irreparable and she was put to rest at Thames Ditton in October 1986 - destroyed physically, but not in spirit.

A fitting epitaph to *White Orchid* and her kind is a poignant poem by John Masefield, the Poet Laureate, who was also a war historian at the time of Dunkirk:

To the Seamen - *by John Masefield*

You seamen, I have eaten your hard bread
And drunken from your tin, and known your ways;
I understand the qualities I praise
Though lacking all, with only words instead,

I tell you this, that in the future time
When landsmen mention sailors, such, or such,
Someone will say "Those fellows were sublime
Who brought the Armies from the Germans' clutch."

Through the long time the story will be told;
Long centuries of praise on English lips,
Of courage godlike and of hearts of gold
Off Dunquerque beaches in the little ships.

And ships will dip their colours in salute
To you, henceforth, when passing Zuydecoote.

Motor Yacht Sundowner

Charles Herbert Lightoller, born in March 1874, started as an apprentice on a sailing barque in Liverpool at fourteen, was shipwrecked in the Indian Ocean in 1889 and was Second Officer on the *Titanic* when she sank in 1912. After diving from the stricken vessel, he reached a raft and was eventually saved by the *Carpathia*. In World War I, he earned the DSC hunting German U boats, one of which he rammed and sank.

NAME:	Sundowner
TYPE:	Motor Yacht
LENGTH:	52ft
BEAM:	12ft 6ins
DISPLACEMENT:	Not known
DRAFT:	5ft
ENGINES:	72 h.p. Gleniffer
HULL CONSTR.:	Teak
BUILT BY:	The Admiralty
YEAR BUILT:	1912

In 1929 Lightoller's wife, Sylvia discovered, lying in the mud at Conyer Creek, eight miles eastward from the River Medway, the hull of an old steam pinnace. They had been looking for a boat to convert into a cruising yacht. The hull was surveyed and pronounced sound, so they set about converting it. They had her ketch-rigged with jib, mainsail, mizzen and mizzen staysail. Because Sylvia was Australian, they called the ship *Sundowner*, - the Australian term for a tramp. She was finally launched on 28th June 1930 and after trials on the Thames, undertook her first voyage to France. During the next 10 years *Sundowner* cruised extensively along the north coast of Europe as far as the

Baltic, up the Somme and through the French canals taking part successfully in many international competitions. The strength of her hull and rigging were put to the test in 1932 when she encountered a force ten gale off Ostend. But Lightoller was no mean seaman and they survived 32 hours at sea, completing in that time a journey which would normally be done in 8 hours.

As the clouds of war began to gather in 1939, Lightoller was chosen to undertake a secret mission to survey the

European coast in very much the same area where the 'Riddle of the Sands' took place.

It was not surprising when, on 30th May 1940, the Admiralty announced that they were going to requisition *Sundowner* to go over to Dunkirk. The owner's reply was that if anyone was going to take her it was he, together with his eldest son Roger, and a Sea Scout called Gerald Ashcroft. On 1st June, in company with 5 other ships, they crossed the Channel. On their way, they met the motor cruiser *Westerly*, broken down and on fire. They went alongside and transferred her crew, taking them back to Dunkirk. By strange coincidence, Lightoller's second son, Trevor had been evacuated from Dunkirk 48 hours previously. *Sundowner* embarked 130 men and packed them in like sardines. On their way home, they avoided being hit by enemy aircraft through using evasive techniques of amazing skill. Deep in the water with their extraordinary load, their greatest danger was being swamped by the wash from fast-moving destroyers. On arrival at Ramsgate, they were nearly sunk by the weight of troops moving to one side of the ship to disembark until Roger shouted to them to lie down and not move until told to do so. The Lightollers were dying to return to Dunkirk, but by then only ships capable of doing 20 knots could go.

The *Sundowner* continued her war service as a coastal patrol vessel and took part in a number of spectacular rescues: once, when a Walrus flying boat crashed in the sea and, on another occasion, when a Spitfire belly-flopped in the mud in the Thames Estuary. She also became a film star when she was used to demonstrate for a newsreel documentary the role for her type of craft in coastal defence and rescue operations.

In June 1946, Charles Lightoller got his ship back and as early as July 1947 she was back in Dunkirk, this time to take part in the *Pavillon d'Or.*

Charles Lightoller died in 1952 aged 78 years and his wife Sylvia continued to cruise in *Sundowner,* taking part in many competitions. At the age of 80 she still took the helm of her husband's boat and she led the Armada of Little Ships on the 25th Anniversary return

to Dunkirk when she suffered a bad fall and had to be flown back to England. This was the end of her association with the great Little Ship, but *Sundowner's* travels had not ended. Under a new owner, she went to Spain and the Mediterranean and she returned from there 10 years later. In 1986 she was struck by a N.E. gale (the remains of Hurricane Charlie) off the North Foreland in Kent and suffered damage to her steering and planking. That autumn she was taken over by the East Kent Maritime Trust who now take care of her in their maritime museum at Ramsgate. The old girl still has many admirers who are determined to restore her yet again.

Her next assignation is the 50th Anniversary return to Dunkirk in May 1990 where she once more intends to be the star.

Motor Yacht **R e d a**

NAME:	R e d a
TYPE:	Motor Yacht
LENGTH:	45ft
BEAM:	12ft
DISPLACEMENT:	23.43 tons
DRAFT:	3ft 6ins
ENGINES:	Twin 4 cyl. BMC diesel
HULL CONSTR.:	Carvel
BUILT BY:	Whisstocks Ltd
YEAR BUILT:	1938

Among the pre-war owners of the Little Ships are many prosperous personalities of the 1930s. *Reda* was built for Mr Austin Reed, head of the successful clothing firm. He had his comfortable 45ft. yacht designed by Claude Whisstock at Woodbridge in Suffolk in 1938 - entirely without drawings - but never had a chance to sail in her. Ron Lenthall, who was Ron Tough's waterman at Teddington, brought her from Suffolk to the Thames on her maiden voyage.

Then in 1940 it was Ron Lenthal who was given the task of collecting the Little Ships. It had been a busy few days for Ron. For several weeks boats on nearby moorings had to be kept immobilised, without their batteries, for fear that they might be used by enemy agents. Then about ten days

before the start of the evacuation, the word was given to make all available boats ready in case they should be needed at short notice, and collect together others which might be used. "We knew where they were going, and what they would have to do," Ron recalled. "We had to take down the masts - as we knew most of the boats would be used for work off the beaches and not actually to bring men back - and take unnecessary gear out of them to make more space inside." He remembered taking down *Reda's* mast and painting the name on its heel. He also remembered how Austin Reed visited his boat at Tough's and remarked on the full drinks locker, "There's plenty of booze; leave it there, the chaps will have a greater need for it than I."

On 29th May 1940 *Reda* sailed from Ramsgate in company with five other motor yachts across the Channel, all manned by willing and eager crews, fired by the one common purpose of saving the British Expeditionary Force. After severe machine-gun attacks from the air off Gravelines they arrived at La Panne beach at 1500 and at once began towing whalers full of troops to off-lying ships. The *Reda* then returned to Ramsgate with 21 soldiers aboard. She braved a bombing raid as she left but survived unscathed. On 31st May she went back for more and after ferrying 50 Frenchmen to a larger transport, brought 23 more direct to

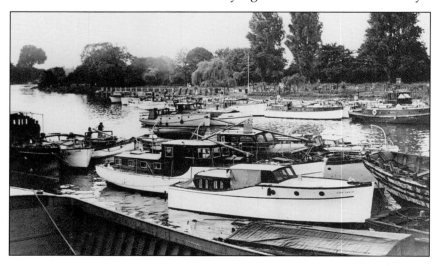

Ramsgate. After Dunkirk *Reda* continued as an auxiliary patrol vessel. A tetchy correspondence took place between Austin Reed and the boatbuilders in 1941 when the owner was billed for certain property removed from *Reda* prior to Dunkirk and still held in Tough's stores: a companion ladder and a cardboard box containing pyjamas and gloves were mentioned. Mr Reed also referred to a refrigerator, some stainless steel cutlery and kitchen utensils. Fortunately there was an inventory which, even in the heat of events, Ron Lenthall had kept meticulously.

Surviving members of Austin Reed's family remember the boat coming back to them after the war (when her name was changed to *Columbine)* for a brief time before she was sold to Leeds businessman Arthur Kaye who renamed her *Janthea*. He had her for thirty years and kept her at Hampton Court as a family motor yacht. Ron Lenthall took the Kayes' on her to Holland and through France.

Since 1984 she has been owned by Norman Cannell, Vice Commodore and founder member of the Association of Dunkirk Little Ships, and his wife Marion, and is moored at Marlow in Buckinghamshire.

R.N.L.I. Charles Cooper Henderson

Nineteen RNLI lifeboats from as far north as Great Yarmouth and east from Poole, were at Dunkirk while the RNLI still maintained its service along the English coast. Built and maintained entirely by voluntary contributions, many of the lifeboats were manned by dedicated volunteers, many of whom considered themselves to be more experienced seamen than the RNVR crews who took their place. The lifeboatmen had a very personal attachment to their boats and did not take kindly to the idea of beaching them at La Panne. Some with naval crews, some manned by civilian crews, all the lifeboats acquitted themselves well: ferrying troops, towing disabled ships and rescuing men from the wreck-strewn sea in the face of shore-based shelling and aerial attacks. The Dungeness-based *Charles Cooper* *Henderson*, Britain's longest-serving lifeboat, was first launched on 9th September 1933 and, with her twin 30 h.p. Weyburn petrol engines, was the first of the 'beach motor lifeboats' which took over from the pulling and sailing ones. During her forty-three years on active service, she took part in 171 rescues and saved sixty-three lives. No lifeboat-style log was kept to record her service at Dunkirk. But we know that, on 1st June, found damaged and drifting off Margate with her four naval ratings aboard, she was herself rescued and towed back to the English coast by Margate lifeboatmen.

After the necessary repairs, she resumed her duty at Dungeness. Her coxswain, George Tart, won the RNLI bronze medal for gallantry in the rescue of nine men from the collier *Teeswood* on 29th July 1956 in a rare

NAME:	Charles C Henderson
TYPE:	R.N.L.I. Lifeboat
LENGTH:	41ft
BEAM:	12ft 3ins
DISPLACEMENT:	15.66 tons
DRAFT:	3ft 8ins
ENGINES:	Twin Parsons diesel
HULL CONSTR.:	Mahogany on oak
BUILT BY:	Groves & Gutteridge
YEAR BUILT:	1933

force-12 storm. Between noon and midnight that day, the *Charles Cooper Henderson* was launched no less than three times. On each occasion, as her coxswain said afterwards, "it took her a long time to get back, pounding against wind and sea".

There is never a shortage of applicants when lifeboats go out of service and come up for sale. This is only partly due to the strength and stability of their hulls and their meticulous maintenance. Their life-saving history, the affection which stems from the fact that they were donated and manned by volunteers and generous donors, all contribute to their popularity. In 1977 Eileen and Philip Larkin re-built the *Charles Cooper Henderson* into a motor yacht with a sensitive and aesthetically

pleasing conversion which included a 20ft. wheelhouse and deck saloon with fore and aft cabins - enough space for eight people. They also replaced her petrol engines with two 47 h.p. Porbeagle diesels.

Re-named *Caresana*, she has been owned and beautifully maintained since 1986 by Jenny and Ron Wylie and is based at St. Peter Port, Guernsey where she is used for family cruising around the Channel Islands and French coastal waters.

R.N.L.I. Lucy Lavers

NAME:	Lucy Lavers
TYPE:	R.N.L.I. Lifeboat
LENGTH:	35ft 6ins
BEAM:	10ft 3ins
DISPLACEMENT:	6 tons
DRAFT:	2ft 3.5ins
ENGINES:	35 h.p. Weyburn petrol
HULL CONSTR.:	Mahogany
BUILT BY:	Groves & Gutteridge
YEAR BUILT:	1940

Aldeburgh lifeboat, *Lucy Lavers,* had only just arrived from Groves and Gutteridge on the Isle of Wight where she was built, when she was called to service at Dunkirk. Her exceptionally shallow draft of around 2ft. made her particularly suitable and she took her place alongside the other eighteen lifeboats which were at Dunkirk.

Lucy Lavers was the Aldeburgh number two lifeboat for nineteen years and during this time she was called out on thirty occasions and credited with saving seven lives before she joined the relief fleet. During this period, she went out fifty-two times and saved thirty seven souls.

In 1968 she retired from the RNLI and became the first pilot boat in the Channel Island port of St. Helier, Jersey. Subsequently she was a private fishing boat and in 1986, now called *L'Esperance,* she was bought by the Dive and Ski Club of St. Helier where she is cared for by Mike Gibson. During the tourist season, she provides around four-hundred trainees with practical experience on a training course from the bays of St. Aubyns, St. Brelade and Portlet as well as the Island of Sark.

R.N.L.I. Cyril & Lilian Bishop

Hastings lifeboat, the *Cyril and Lilian Bishop,* went into service in 1931 as a shallow-draft sailing lifeboat. Built at Cowes for the RNLI, she was a self-righter - and proved it, when she capsized during service in 1944.

In 1950 she was sold as a fishing vessel and went to the west coast of Scotland where Arra Fletcher bought her in 1976. He re-named her *Lindy Lou* after his daughter and brought her to the free port of Askaig on the Isle of Islay. There, she earned fame when her owner fought a battle against authority in 1980.

The Duke of Kent was due to visit the island and the powers that be wanted the old boat removed from the harbour because of complaints that her time and weather-worn appearance might offend the Royal eye. Arra Fletcher who had painted her and dressed her overall, and whose ancestors arrived in Islay centuries ago, occupied his ship to defend the islanders' right to free use of the harbour. He won the day when his case was taken up by press and T.V. after letters of protest to 10, Downing Street and Buckingham Palace and a flood of sympathetic messages from all over Britain. There,

NAME: Cyril & Lilian Bishop	
TYPE:	R.N.L.I. Lifeboat
LENGTH:	35ft 6ins
BEAM:	8ft 10ins
DISPLACEMENT:	9 tons
DRAFT:	2ft
ENGINES:	35 h.p. Weyburn Ford
HULL CONSTR.:	Double diagonal
BUILT BY:	J.S. White, Cowes, I.O.W.
YEAR BUILT:	1931

in Askaig harbour, *Lindy Lou* still lies, immobile but proud of her history. But perhaps her future would be more assured if Arra Fletcher could once more restore her and allow her to take to the sea rather than deteriorate from the effects of weather in Islay harbour.

R.N.L.I. Mary Scott

Launched in 1925 and getting on for middle age, in lifeboat terms, when she went to Dunkirk, the *Mary Scott* was towed there by the paddle steamer *Empress of India* together with two other small boats. Between them they took 160 men to their mother ship and when it returned fully laden to Dover, they made a journey with fifty men to another transport vessel.

When her engine broke down and could not be re-started, *Mary Scott* was beached and abandoned at La Panne. Then Sub.-Lieut. Stephen Dickenson, her Commander (a former RNLI Inspector of Lifeboats), together with her crew, came home to Dover in the *Louise Stephens*, the Great Yarmouth and Gorleston lifeboat.

Mary Scott was later re-floated and brought back to England where, during her last twenty-eight years in the service, she saved forty-seven lives. As the Southwold lifeboat, she was launched thirty

NAME:	Mary Scott
TYPE:	R.N.L.I. Lifeboat
LENGTH:	46ft 6ins
BEAM:	12ft 9ins
DISPLACEMENT:	17 tons
DRAFT:	3ft 3ins
ENGINES:	White 80 h.p. petrol
HULL CONSTR.:	Mahogany
BUILT BY:	J.S. White, Cowes, I.O.W.
YEAR BUILT:	1925

more times before the station closed in 1940. She then continued to serve in fifty-two more rescues as part of the RNLI relief fleet.

Sold out of the service in 1953, she was re-named *Atanua* and converted six years later by a jewellery manufacturer.

Her present owner is Bill Long, who has had her for ten years and keeps her at Gillingham Pier. He takes her to the Channel Islands and as far as the South of France on fishing and diving expeditions.

Intended to be the Clacton lifeboat, *Guide of Dunkirk* was still un-named and undelivered when she was called for, direct from her builders at Colchester, Essex on 1st June 1940 to take part in the Dunkirk evacuation. She was manned by a crew drawn from the towns of Walton and Frinton in Essex, under naval command. At Dunkirk she was badly damaged by machinegun fire and, during her work off the beaches, a rope got round her propeller. She was towed back to England stern first and when a naval party boarded her, they found her exhausted crew fast asleep down below.

On her second trip across the Channel, she was hit by shellfire and had to return to her builders, Rowhedge Iron Works in Colchester, for extensive repairs.

A self-righting lifeboat, of light construction for launching from the beach, she had been funded by the Girl Guides Association. Her name pays tribute both to her benefactors and to her heroic baptism. After Dunkirk, she served at Cadgwith Cove, Cornwall until John Moor bought her when she came out of service in 1963. Being a local man himself, he remembers the day she arrived and he had relatives who were among her crew. He changed her name to *Girl Guide*, but did not make any structural alterations. He now uses her at

NAME:	Guide of Dunkirk
TYPE:	R.N.L.I. Lifeboat
LENGTH:	35ft 6ins
BEAM:	9ft 8ins
DISPLACEMENT:	8 tons
DRAFT:	2ft 9ins
ENGINES:	72 h.p. diesel
HULL CONSTR.:	Double diagonal
BUILT BY:	Rowhedge Iron Works
YEAR BUILT:	1940

Mevagissey where she is a workboat and, with her handsome red and blue livery and her proud nameplate, a tourist attraction during the summer season.

R.N.L.I. Rosa Woodd & Phyllis Lunn

Rescuing people in severe conditions is every-day work for the lifeboats and it is not only at Dunkirk that they have earned their medals. The *Rosa Woodd and Phyllis Lunn* was launched in 1933 and was Shoreham's 5th lifeboat. The cost of £6,500 was met by a private legacy and other collections. But in order to accomodate the boat a new boathouse had to be built together with a slipway so that her launching was not dependent upon the state of the tide. She served for thirty years, during which time she was launched 244 times and saved 143 lives. She then spent another ten years on the reserve fleet of the RNLI. She made three trips from the beaches of Dunkirk back to Dover, but naval crews did not keep

detailed logs which are the rule in the RNLI. There is a story that the naval officer in charge protected his men from shrapnel and strafing by constructing a makeshift wheelhouse from steel plate.

On 16th November 1941 she was called out to the *President Briand*, a minesweeper, which was in danger of being driven ashore by a strong south wind off Shoreham. The lifeboat's coxswain was put aboard the *President Briand* and the *SS Goole*, a blockship, went out to tow her in. By then, the wind had increased to a gale and the *Goole* also got into difficulties. The lifeboat attempted to tow both ships, but the ropes parted. She had to go alongside six or seven times before taking off all

NAME:	Rosa Woodd & Phyllis Lunn
TYPE:	R.N.L.I. Lifeboat
LENGTH:	41ft
BEAM:	11ft 8ins
DISPLACEMENT:	15 tons
DRAFT:	3ft 6ins
ENGINES:	Parsons Porbeagles x 2
HULL CONSTR.:	Mahogany on oak
BUILT BY:	Groves & Guttridge
YEAR BUILT:	1932

twenty-one men including the lifeboat's own coxswain. She came back to harbour through heavy, breaking seas eleven hours after she had first gone out. The acting coxswain, James Upperton, in charge for the first time, earned a silver medal for gallantry and Henry Philcox, her motor mechanic, the bronze medal.

On 8th August 1948, the *Rosa Woodd and Phyllis Lunn* again hit the headlines when, in a strong southwesterly gale off the Sussex coast, she went out to rescue a yacht. The lifeboat used her sails to help her engines and pursued the yacht for fourteen miles to Newhaven where, only 500 yards offshore, heavy seas washed right over her. Yet despite the tremendous seas, the lifeboat, with unbelievable skill, went straight into the surf and plucked the three men, two women and a boy off the yacht to safety.

In 1973 T.B. Lawrence bought the *Rosa Woodd and Phyllis Lunn*, then lying at Bangor near Belfast. He re-named her *Dowager* and converted her into a cruising yacht.

O ne of only three RNLI lifeboats designed to be launched from the beach, she had just come into service at Great Yarmouth & Gorleston when *Louise Stephens* found herself off to Dunkirk on 30th May, 1940. During her career with the RNLI she was launched 311 times and saved 177 lives at sea. Sold out of service in 1974, she became for a while a fishing boat off the north-east coast of England. In 1984 she was re-engined with two four-cyliner 72 h.p. tractor engines and a large trawler wheelhouse was added.

NAME:	Louise Stephens
TYPE:	R.N.L.I. Lifeboat
LENGTH:	46ft
BEAM:	12ft 9ins
DISPLACEMENT:	9.84 tons
DRAFT:	3ft 6ins
ENGINES:	Twin ferry 40 h.p. VE4
HULL CONSTR.:	Mahogany
BUILT BY:	J.S. White, Cowes, I.O.W.
YEAR BUILT:	1939

Howard Fawsitt bought the lifeboat, now called *Tyne Star*, in 1986 when she had come down to Poole to be sold and he keeps her at Starcross in south Devon. She is a family pleasure boat, cruising the coastal waters of south-west England and the Isle of Wight.

The enjoyment of owning *Louise Stephens* has prompted its owner to buy *Duke of Cornwall*, the last Barnet class lifeboat to come out of service.

R.N.L.I. Michael Stephens

Few of us, living in peace time, when mariners meticulously obey the 'Rules for Avoiding Collisions at Sea', can visualise the chaos on 1st June 1940 around the harbour of Dunkirk, where the *Michael Stephens* rescued fifty-two soldiers. Ships of all sizes, often manned by exhausted unfamiliar crews were coming and going amid shellfire and dive-bombing through waters strewn with bodies and wreckage.

The *Michael Stephens* was twice rammed by motor-torpedo boats as she came and left the harbour, jostling with naval and civilian craft coaxing soldiers to climb to their decks from the shattered pier high above them.

This former Lowestoft lifeboat, was built by Samuel White at Cowes. She and her sister ship, Gorleston lifeboat *Louise Stephens,* was bought with the legacy of the family after whom they were named. *Michael Stephens* served at Lowestoft for 24 years, spent five more at Exmouth and then seven in the reserve fleet before she was sold out of service in 1975. In her time she was launched 182 times and saved 92 lives - apart from her Dunkirk involvement. Now she has been converted to a cruising boat with two Ferry Engine Co. diesels. C.J. Cave found her in 1976 at Crosshaven, County Cork in very good shape and has twice helped yachts in trouble at sea - once off the Bramble Bank in the Solent. She has cruised in Wales, Ireland and the Isles of Scilly.

NAME:	Michael Stephens
TYPE:	R.N.L.I. Lifeboat
LENGTH:	46ft
BEAM:	12ft
DISPLACEMENT:	23 tons
DRAFT:	4ft
ENGINES:	Twin ferry diesel
HULL CONSTR.:	Carvel
BUILT BY:	J.S. White, Cowes, I.O.W.
YEAR BUILT:	1939

NAME:	Cecil & Lilian Philpott
TYPE:	R.N.L.I. Lifeboat
LENGTH:	45ft 6ins
BEAM:	12ft 6ins
DISPLACEMENT:	25 tons
DRAFT:	4ft 6ins
ENGINES:	Ford 4D 72 h.p. x 2
HULL CONSTR.:	Carvel
BUILT BY:	J.S. White, Cowes, I.O.W.
YEAR BUILT:	1929

The Newhaven lifeboat saved 51 soldiers at Dunkirk, but the mission nearly ended in disaster when she was left high and dry for 4 hours before returning on 3rd June. *Cecil & Lilian Philpott* was in service at Newhaven from 1930 to 1959; apart from Dunkirk she was launched 159 times and saved 99 lives. In November 1940 she was rammed and nearly cut in half by HM trawler *Avanturine*, but she survived. Later she served in the RNLI's reserve fleet at various lifeboat stations around the coast increasing her score with a further 76 incidents, and saving 49 more lives.

Dr. Oliver Dansie bought her in 1969 as "a successful investment in family life". Then his children were growing up; now his grandchildren are enjoying her. Re-named *Stenoa* he ran her for a year on her two thirsty petrol engines which demanded 22 separate operations before they could be started up. Now he has two 4-cylinder Ford diesels, and considerably more space. When he bought her he was told that the open boat could take 136 people on deck before her stability began to be affected. The Dansie family have used *Stenoa* for two decades as a powerful, safe cruiser. She has taken them through inland Britain and around France, Belgium and the Channel Islands.

The Ramsgate lifeboat *Prudential* was one of the few which was taken to Dunkirk by her own crew. Howard Knight, the coxswain, with gas masks and steel helmets set out on Thursday 30th May 1940 towing seven wherries filled with supplies of water for the waiting troops. He also took in tow the punt *Carama* which belonged to the lifeboat's second coxswain, A. Moody. All the boats discharged their water and other supplies as soon as they arrived on the beaches. The lifeboat had to lay off because of her deeper draft and the naval ratings who manned the wherries had some difficulty handling them through the breaking seas. Members of the lifeboat crew therefore took their places and managed to establish communications with the officers in charge of the troops ashore.

The soldiers were ferried out in batches of eight, which was all the small boats could take, as far as the lifeboat which then took them out to transports. Eight hundred men were rescued in this way on the Thursday night. As the last three boatloads were being taken from the water, the officer called "I cannot see who you are; are you a naval party?" When he learned that it was the crew of the Ramsgate lifeboat he called "thank God for such men as you!" On the way home, the *Prudential* helped by putting her engineer aboard a 500-ton ship, the SS *Rian* whose engines were failing and this got her back to Ramsgate. The *Prudential* towed a string of small craft full of troops on the return journey, including the punt *Carama*. They were under constant enemy attack for forty hours and on their return found not only major damage from shrapnel, but a hole in their bottom. The coxswain was awarded the medal for gallantry for this service. In 1941 the *Prudential* was 'adopted' by Miss Violet Bonnings', Walton School for Girls at Aylesbury and she became the flagship of the Commodore, Lifeboat Division at the Spithead Naval Review in 1953. That same year she was sold out of service. Re-named the *Trimilia,* she belongs to Richard Rothery who keeps her in Suffolk and still proudly shows the patches on her hull where enemy shrapnel pierced her teak during the evacuation of Dunkirk.

NAME:	Prudential
TYPE:	R.N.L.I. Lifeboat
LENGTH:	48ft 6ins
BEAM:	13ft
DISPLACEMENT:	19 tons
DRAFT:	3ft 10ins
ENGINES:	Russell & Newberry
HULL CONSTR.:	Teak
BUILT BY:	Saunders, Cowes, I.O.W.
YEAR BUILT:	1925

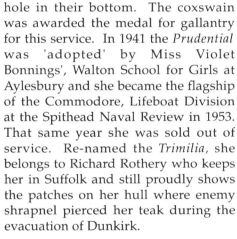

R.N.L.I. Thomas Kirk Wright

I deal for working off the beaches, the surf lifeboat *Thomas Kirk Wright*, with its two impellers instead of screws, draws only 2ft. 6ins. and was the first of the lifeboats to reach the beaches of Dunkirk on 30th May 1940. She was manned by naval ratings and was loaded with French soldiers when she came under fire from German troops. Miraculously no one was hit, but the boat was seriously damaged; one engine was burned out and there was a foot of water in her hold. She was saved by her tremendously strong construction with double-skin Honduras mahogany laid diagonally in opposite directions and a framework of Indian oak, Canadian rock elm and mahogany secured with brass fastenings. The boat is divided into five separate water-tight compartments, each of which has the whole available space filled with air cases - a total of seventy-one - with another twenty seven above deck. She was

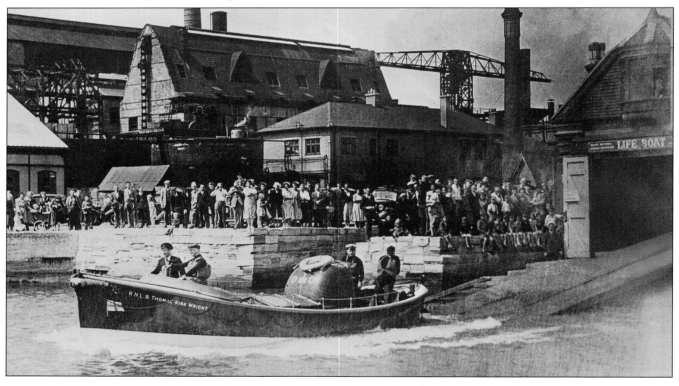

quickly repaired and returned to Dunkirk for a second trip on 2nd June when she was towed across by the tug *Foremost 87*, together with the RNLI lifeboat, *Cecil and Lilian Philpott*. When she left the lifeboat service in 1964, she was bought by Paul Neate of Poole who, together with his son Rupert, took good care of her for ten years. She was then acquired by the National Maritime Museum who restored her to museum standard. She is now housed as a static exhibit in the little boathouse at Poole and has not been back in the water since 1976.

NAME: Thomas Kirk Wright	
TYPE:	R.N.L.I. Lifeboat
LENGTH:	32ft
BEAM:	9ft 3ins
DISPLACEMENT:	4.5 tons
DRAFT:	2ft 6ins
ENGINES:	Weyburn 12 h.p. x 2
HULL CONSTR.:	Mahogany
BUILT BY:	Groves & Gutteridge
YEAR BUILT:	1938

Apart from the eleven lifeboats already described, eight more took part in the evacuation of Dunkirk but less is known about them - or they have disappeared.

Greater London, (below) the South-end-on-Sea lifeboat was large for its type: 48ft. 6ins. long with a 13ft. beam. Built by J. Samuel White in 1928, she was sold out of service in 1957, re-named *Adesi* and went to Montevideo in Uruguay. At Dunkirk, with just an hour to go before the final order to leave became effective, and with the block ships about to be sunk at the harbour entrance, the *Greater London,* fully loaded went to the aid of a trapped minesweeper full of French soldiers. *HMS Kellet,* embarking 200 men from the mole had one of her screws caught on an under-water obstacle, could not move, and was in danger of being left behind. *Greater London* hauled her stern away from the wall and both got away in the nick of time. It is thought that, despite her great age, she still operates as a lifeboat in South America.

E.M.E.D. The 1928 Walton & Frinton lifeboat built by J. Samuel White, went out of service to Chile in 1956. She was a large vessel of her type: 48ft. 6ins. long with a 13ft. beam. She went to Dunkirk twice in 1940 and survived three enemy air attacks off Gravelines which destroyed boats with which she was in tow. She came back with a rope around her propeller. The officer in charge was killed by a shell.

Viscountess Wakefield. When the coxswain of the Hythe boat arrived at Dover, he realised that he was being asked to run his vessel on to the beach at Dunkirk, load her with troops and ferry them out to the naval destroyers. *Viscountess Wakefield* weighed 14 tons, and the coxswain argued that, on a falling tide, they would be stranded without winches to get them off. The civilian crews of the Walmer and Dungeness boats agreed, having even heavier vessels. In addition there were arguments between the crews and the naval authorities concerning insurance for their dependents, culminating in the civilians refusing to go. The Navy immediately took over the lifeboats, manned them with their own less experienced personnel, and gave the lifeboatmen railway vouchers for their journey home. Later *Viscountess Wakefield's* coxswain and mechanic were dismissed the service following an RNLI enquiry which charged the coxswain with inducing his and other crews not to go to Dunkirk. But the RNLI had dismissed a brave man, a coxswain for more than two decades, who quite simply knew more about his boat and its capabilities than the Navy did, and who continued to rescue men in his own fishing boat. *Viscountess Wakefield* sailed on 30th May with the second fleet of the day; all the RNLI vessels from Great Yarmouth to Poole. Nothing was ever heard of her again.

Abdy Beauclerk . The Aldeburgh lifeboat was the first to leave its station, yet of its work at Dunkirk nothing is known. *Abdy Beauclerk* was built in 1931 by J. Samuel White, her length was 41ft. and her beam 12ft. 3ins. When sold out of service she became *St. Ita*, and after a time with the Cork Harbour Commissioners was last heard of in Southern Ireland.

Lord Southborough, the Margate life-boat, manned by her civilian crew, brought Cdr. H. du P. Richardson's exhausted beach party back from Dunkirk. For three days they had been in charge of a section of the evacuation. Before that, *Lord South-borough* transported troops from the beaches to a Dutch barge which had towed her from Margate, and then to an off-shore destroyer. She went a second time, taking over 500 men to the destroyer *HMS Icarus*. Built in 1924 by S.E. Saunders, *Lord Southborough* was 45ft. long with a 12ft. 6in. beam. She was sold out of service after thirty-one years to the Crown Agents for the Colonies and is believed to have gone to Benghazi.

Edward Z. Dresden. When the Clacton-on-Sea lifeboat came to the end of her service life after forty years in 1968, she was re-named *St. Peter* and was last heard of at Troon. Built in 1928 *Edward Z. Dresden* had a length of 45ft. 6ins. and a 12ft. beam. At Dunkirk, she took men from the wharfs and quays of the inner harbour to the outlying ships. She finally brought back a ship's lifeboat full of soldiers and, with *Greater London* was the last of the surviving RNLI lifeboats to return.

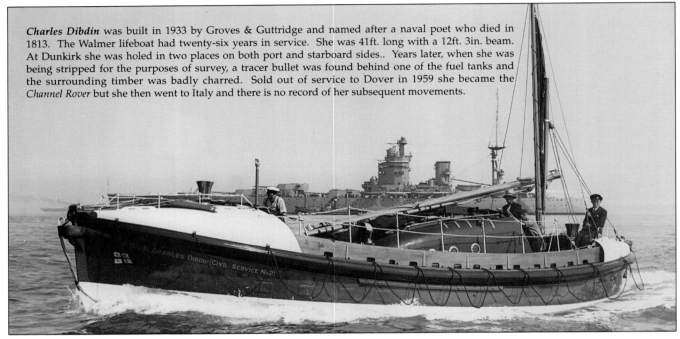

Charles Dibdin was built in 1933 by Groves & Guttridge and named after a naval poet who died in 1813. The Walmer lifeboat had twenty-six years in service. She was 41ft. long with a 12ft. 3in. beam. At Dunkirk she was holed in two places on both port and starboard sides.. Years later, when she was being stripped for the purposes of survey, a tracer bullet was found behind one of the fuel tanks and the surrounding timber was badly charred. Sold out of service to Dover in 1959 she became the *Channel Rover* but she then went to Italy and there is no record of her subsequent movements.

Jane Holland, (below) the Eastbourne lifeboat, just 40ft. long with a 10ft. 6in. beam, built by J. Samuel White, was the oldest of the RNLI fleet at Dunkirk, and the one to survive the greatest damage. She was hit forward by a French motor boat, and then aft by a British torpedo boat and strafed by enemy aircraft. Abandoned by her crew, a French destroyer tried to sink her by gunfire, as a hazard to navigation, but failed. She was found drifting full of water and towed home, with her fore-end box stove-in and riddled by more than 500 bullet holes. She was soon back in service and remained so for twelve years. She was last heard of as *Reporter* at Birkenhead.

Motor Yacht **Salvor**

The former Moelfre lifeboat *Charles and Eliza Laura* earned awards for gallantry before the men of Dunkirk were ever born. A 12-oar, 15-man pulling-and-sailing vessel, she saved her first lives on her delivery trip in 1910, after she left the river Mersey, when she was called to the yacht *Drake* sinking with two people on board. Rigged with a standing lug foresail, mizzen and jib, she proved her sailing qualities during her most dramatic rescue in 1927, when the ketch *Excel*, bound from Birkenhead to Ireland with a cargo of coal, started shipping water and was soon out of control in a heavy south-westerly gale. Second coxswain William Roberts commanded the lifeboat. The *Excel* had been in tow of the German tanker, when the tow rope parted. There was little time left to rescue the three men

NAME:	Salvor
TYPE:	Motor Yacht
LENGTH:	40ft
BEAM:	11ft
DISPLACEMENT:	9.6 tons
DRAFT:	3ft 6ins
ENGINES:	Perkins 432 diesel
HULL CONSTR.:	Mahogany on oak
BUILT BY:	Blackwell
YEAR BUILT:	1910

aboard her. Heavy seas made it impossible to go along-side, so the coxswain took the desperate measure of driving his ship over the crest of a big wave on top of the *Excel* where they stayed long enough to take off her crew before her stern dropped and they slipped off again. The gale was now approaching hurricane force and

the *Charles and Eliza Laura* was holed in five places, but they went on with rescuers and rescued holding on desperately, sailing through the sea more than on it. They brought the boat home safely after seventeen and a half hours on the storm-swept ocean. Her coxswain and one other, received the RNLI Gold Medal, the rest of the crew got the bronze. One died from his injuries. In 18 years, the ship went out on 35 similar occasions and saved the lives of 84 people and a dog. Then, on 11th February 1929, she broke from her moorings in heavy seas and was damaged too badly to be considered for repair to lifeboat standard. She therefore sold out of service.

Douglas Kirkaldy, famous coxswain of the Ramsgate lifeboat at the time, bought her and sailed her home from Anglesey in 1940. That is when her name was changed to *Salvor*, but she continued much as before, first in the Trinity House Lightship service and then as a stand-by lifeboat. At this time, she was commandeered by the Navy and became *HMS Salvor*. A naval crew took her to Dunkirk and she was

returned after the war to Douglas Kirkaldy who stipulated that she should be burned at his death - a request no-one was prepared to obey. Eventually, she was found rotting at her moorings at Richborough Kent, by Reg Cornwell, a timber preservation specialist who could not let this grand old servant of the sea die". He pulled her out and spent a year restoring her. He then took her back to Ramsgate harbour where a warm welcome awaited her. She goes out on fishing and pleasure trips but is treated with awe by those who know her history.

When Thanet boatmen Len C. Brockman and his assistant, John Titcombe built the open rowing boat *Tamzine* in 1937, they gave her their local peculiarity: a characteristic Viking-style straight stem. This enabled the Margate fishermen to identify and claim her as their own when, saturated with blood inside, but other-wise undamaged, she was towed back by a Belgian fishing smack after ferrying troops from the beaches of Dunkirk to off-lying ships. Though hundreds of similar small boats were used, few were recovered or could be traced back to their owners in the same way.

Named after the eighteen-year-old wife of a sailing skipper, who was drowned off the Isles of Scilly in an eighteenth century shipwreck and is said to be buried in the churchyard at St. Mary's, *Tamzine* is the smallest surviving open fishing boat to take part in Operation Dynamo. She is less than 15ft. long, clinker built, light yet strongly made and was designed for year-round fishing off the shore at Birchington in Kent. Her removable centre thwart - the oarsman's seat - allowed five people to stand upright in her at any one time and safely haul in the trawl net.

Tamzine is no longer at the mercy of the elements and will continue to be an evocative reminder of how much was done with such simple tools in 1940; for she was given to the Imperial War Museum where she remains an important and beautifully preserved exhibit in a fascinating and painstakingly maintained museum.

NAME:	Tamzine
TYPE:	Open Fishing Boat
LENGTH:	14ft 7.5ins
BEAM:	5ft 1.5ins
DISPLACEMENT:	—
DRAFT:	1ft.6ins
ENGINES:	None
HULL CONSTR.:	Canadian Spruce
BUILT BY:	Brockman & Titcombe
YEAR BUILT:	Margate, 1937

Motor Launch **Eothen**

Eothen was based on an original design by Irwin Chase, chief designer of the Electric Launch Company (formed 1892 for the purpose of building fifty-four 36ft. electric launches before the World's Fair in Chicago the next year) at Boyonne, New Jersey. From the outset of the first World War the British suffered heavy losses at the hands of German U-boats. Elco company head Henry R. Sutphen suggested to the British government that light, ocean-going motor launches powered by two 6-cylinder petrol engines might be effective against these as anti-submarine vessels. Chase came up with a design which included certain criteria stipulated by the British, and in April 1915 the Admiralty placed an order for fifty 'motor launches' through Canadian Vickers, acting as their agents. These were wooden-hull vessels, 75ft. long. With the United States still neutral, the boats went from New Jersey to Canada, euphemistically called 'yachts' with attractive names on their hulls.

The sinking of the *Lusitania* was the catalyst for a huge, additional order. In June, 1915 the Admiralty requested a further five hundred; they were to be 80ft. long, would cost over £12,000 each and the first twenty five were to be delivered by the last day of November. Two hundred more had to be in British hands by the end of May, 1916 and the remainder delivered at the rate of fifty per month thereafter. *Eothen* was part of the batch to be delivered in June 1916.

Her parts were prefabricated at Bayonne and sent by rail to Quebec (an Elco assembly plant was also opened at Montreal for the same purpose) to be put together. The British code name

NAME:	Eothen
TYPE:	Motor Launch
LENGTH:	80ft
BEAM:	12ft 3ins
DISPLACEMENT:	37 tons
DRAFT:	4ft
ENGINES:	Twin pet. 4 cyl. 22 h.p.
HULL CONSTR.:	Pitch pine on oak
BUILT BY:	Electric Launch Co.
YEAR BUILT:	Quebec, Canada, 1916

the Admiralty ordered a final thirty.

Eothen would have been sold off between late 1919 and 1924 when only eight of the MLs were still in military service. So popular were they and reasonably priced by the Admiralty, that the weekly *Motor Ship and Motor Boat* ran extensive articles thoughout July 1919 on the best ways of converting them to motor yachts in every detail 'to allow comfortable cruising at moderate cost'. *ML286* became *Cordon Rouge* in private hands, and then, in 1930, *Eothen* which was still her name at Dunkirk. Afterwards she was returned to Ramsgate and towed to Teddington by Toughs, from where she was requisitioned for service as an auxiliary patrol vessel in the Thames. Found to be unsuitable, however, she was returned to her owners in August 1940.

As recently as 1986 she was said to be in 1920s condition with her original bronze castings by Tiffanys, but deteriorating fast. All efforts to find sponsors, interest trusts and museums or set up a fund, have failed and she now lies at Isleworth, Middlesex in a sad state of neglect, awaiting the inevitable.

for the motor launches (MLs) was 'Sutphens', and the controversially high price paid by the Admiralty gave the MLs the nickname 'Money Losers'. They were not ocean-going and could not cross the Atlantic on their own, so they were shipped to Britain in fours as deck cargo. For most of the building period Elco was producing a complete boat each day, and in 1917

Motor Yacht **M i n n e h a h a**

he Teddington boatyard of Tough Brothers played a prominent part in the story of Dunkirk. Here some of the hastily requisitioned boats from the upper Thames were collected, and from Teddington they set out in convoy on the first part of their journey. Tough's files record, in Douglas Tough's handwritten notes, the civilian crew, - boatmen from around London - who were assigned to individual craft and whose names crop up again and again as they served on different boats under naval command. Afterwards, some of the vessels which survived Dunkirk were towed back by Tough's watermen from Ramsgate and Margate harbour and stored, pending either requisition by the Admiralty for auxiliary service or return to the owners - if they could be found! There were some angry owners, whose boats had been used

NAME:	M i n n e h a h a
TYPE:	Motor Yacht
LENGTH:	40ft 6ins
BEAM:	10ft 3ins
DISPLACEMENT:	15 tons
DRAFT:	4ft 6ins
ENGINES:	2 Thornycroft 60 h.p.
HULL CONSTR.:	Teak
BUILT BY:	J. S. White, Cowes, I.O.W.
YEAR BUILT:	1936

without their knowledge and they sometimes found them but could not take them back until the Admiralty decided on their future. In other cases, Tough's had the problem of tracing the owners of boats which were no longer required by the navy. And to cap it all, the Admiralty set a deadline, after which they would no longer be responsible for storage charges. The

128

owners of Mount's wharf, where the boats were stored on behalf of Tough's, had to employ a night watchman in case of fire, caused by incendiary bombs and this prompted them to increase their charges. It took months to sort it all out.

Tough's also had many damaged vessels to repair. Some of those very same boats, perhaps with changed names, are today looked after by Bob Tough and his men, and many of the surviving Dunkirk Little Ships in the area come regularly to Tough's for maintenance. Two which came back in 1940 for repair were *Tigris I* and the motor yacht *Minnehaha*, at one time called *Tigris III*, which now belongs to Bob Tough, re-named *Thamesa*.

Minnehaha was designed by William McMeek for J. E. Tanner and built at Cowes in 1936. It was a conservative, businesslike design; the report of the trials did not use the complimentary

Minnehaha

Minnehaha in 1936

adjectives like 'comfortable' and 'spacious', but instead conservative descriptions like 'obvious restraint' and 'sound common sense' and 'every comfort that is really seamanlike and reasonable is provided'. Her owner based her on the Solent and used her for summer cruising.

After Dunkirk, *Minnehaha* was found in Ramsgate harbour with her wheelhouse badly burnt and the charts used by her crew still in her chart drawer. They are reproduced on the endpapers inside the covers of this book. Tough's took off the cabin and used her as a tug until 1944, when Douglas Tough bought the boat and re-converted her to a motor cruiser. With the necessary naval clearance obtained and re-named *Tigris III*, she was one of the first yachts to visit Calais after the war. Just ten years after the evac-uation, she returned to Dunkirk for the first reunion ceremony in 1950. An extensive cruiser, powerboat racer competitor and trophy winner, *Thamesa* once helped 'The Beatles' to avoid the crowds at the height of their popularity by taking them to Thames Television studios on the river. She had a moment in politics, when she conveyed an anti-VAT petition to Parliament, and has been used in television programmes. Bob Tough was Commodore of the Association of Dunkirk Little Ships in 1986/87.

Matoya in the 1980s

D esigned by A.M. Coulson and built by J. Husk & Son, Wivenhoe, *Matoya* was on the upper Thames when Douglas Tough's watermen collected her for service at Dunkirk. Their record shows a crew of three: J. Jameson, L. Milson and A. Crump - presumably civilians, but no log survives of her exploits during the evacuation. She continued in war service on yacht patrol and was damaged while putting the crew aboard a drifter, which then struck a mine and blew up. The *Matoya* lost her propellers, her rudder and part of her keel. She was next heard of as an auxiliary fire float on the Thames.

After the war, almost derelict in Ramsgate harbour, a Mr. and Mrs. Dinniwiddie bought and rebuilt her, inside and out. In order to rebuild her transom while she was afloat, they moved two tons of ballast into her forepeak so that, duck-like, she raised her stern out of the water to be worked on.

Matoya had two more owners before Bill Finch, a dedicated member of the ADLS and formerly owner of *Ryegate II*, took charge of her and got her ready to

NAME:	M a t o y a
TYPE:	Motor Cruiser
LENGTH:	50ft
BEAM:	12ft 3ins
DISPLACEMENT:	26 tons
DRAFT:	4ft
ENGINES:	2 x 40/52 h.p. diesel
HULL CONSTR.:	Carvel, larch on oak
BUILT BY:	J. Husk & Son
YEAR BUILT:	Wivenhoe, 1930

join the 1985 return to Dunkirk. Then, in 1988 they had another setback when *Matoya*, on passage to Ostend, at the start of a trip through the Dutch canals, struck a submerged object and her seams opened up. The Dover lifeboat came to the rescue. Now she is once more receiving the kiss of life with every hope of recovery in time for the 50th Anniversary reunion at Dunkirk.

and pre-war

NAME:	Cachalot
TYPE:	Gaff Cutter
LENGTH:	41ft
BEAM:	9.8ft
DISPLACEMENT:	6.8 tons
DRAFT:	5ft
ENGINES:	Stuart Turner 6 h.p.
HULL CONSTR.:	Carvel
BUILT BY:	R. Saunders, Folkestone
YEAR BUILT:	1900

The advertisement in *The Yachtsman* of 14th October 1897, three years before she was commissioned, did not overstate the virtues of *Cachalot*. Locals say that she is the only sailing yacht ever to be built in Folkestone. It was not until 1936 that she first had a small Stuart Turner 6 h.p. auxiliary engine, so she almost certainly crossed the Channel to Dunkirk under sail.

FOR SALE - Handsome 6-Tons SAILING YACHT, now building and almost completed; exceedingly strong; partly copper-fastened; built of the best material; she cannot be beaten. Offers wanted. Apply, etc., ROBERT SANDERS, Timber Yard, Lower Sandgate Road, Folkestone.

She is a fine old gaffer, cutter-rigged with a long counter and bowsprit. Her owner in 1936 was Sir Lancelot Elphinstone, cousin of the Queen who, by a strange coincidence, was taken prisoner at Dunkirk while his former yacht cruised off the beaches taking off survivors.

Her skipper at Dunkirk was a civilian called Spurling. After the war she was variously owned by two stockbrokers, a parson and a Brigadier and cruised extensively round Britain, the Baltic, the Red Sea and the Mediterranean with many fast passages to her credit. But as the years went on, she fell on hard times and successive owners, in the name of modernisation, removed first her beautiful interior teak panelling, then her brass cabin lamps, copper running lights and unique square compass of which the only other example can be seen in the Science Museum. But, as often happens with boats, she has once more struck lucky in her present owners, Ian and Jen Kiloh, who are painstakingly re-fitting her as closely as they can to her original, beautiful state.

Deborah and Walter Raven bought a boat. Now, *Lazy Days*, moored at Cadogan Pier on the Thames at Chelsea, is known as their floating balcony. From there they can get a very privileged view of London: the Houses of Parliament and the city, up-river to Teddington, Windsor and even Oxford.

At the time of Dunkirk, *Lazy Days* was owned by M.V. Lazarus and she spent three days ferrying troops from East Beach amid fierce air attack. She returned to England with many of her ribs broken at the waterline. Most owners would have called it a day, but she was rebuilt as new in 1952 and had a wheelhouse added. After Dunkirk, while on parachute mine patrol, a mutiny occurred aboard *Lazy Days*. Her Petty Officer, who was a hard-bitten, yacht skipper, took exception to the green young Lieutenant who came aboard when she was duty boat. The P.O. had a pint too many at lunchtime and when the young Lieutenant nagged him about the course he was steering, he hit him. He was sentenced at a Chatham Court Martial to 90 days in the glasshouse. But while being escorted from Chatham to Bristol, he gave his escort the slip and disappeared. More recently, *Lazy Days* had another major re-fit with a new teak deck, and a ferro-cement

NAME:	Lazy Days
TYPE:	Motor Yacht
LENGTH:	34.2ft
BEAM:	8ft 8ins
DISPLACEMENT:	11.5 tons
DRAFT:	3ft 6ins
ENGINES:	British Leyland diesel
HULL CONSTR.:	Larch on oak
BUILT BY:	Cliff & Jones, Castleford
YEAR BUILT:	1930

sheath for her hull which should protect her from the rot which marks the end of many a wooden boat.

Ketch **Omega**

His Majesty's Yacht *Omega*, began life in naval service. She was built at the Admiralty's Devonport dockyard during World War I. When the war was over, she served as a patrol boat at the Spithead Schneider Trophy Races of 1929 - 1931 when British entries won every year and therefore became outright winners of the trophy.

Later, *Omega* was sold to Mr A.C. Foreman who owned her for twenty-three years. The Admiralty required her for the Dunkirk evacuation and she then continued in naval service on east coast patrol. Later, she became a barrage-balloon vessel and finally, an

NAME:	Omega
TYPE:	Ketch
LENGTH:	43ft
BEAM:	11ft 7ins
REG. TONNAGE	17.63 tons
DRAFT:	4ft 5ins
ENGINES:	4 cyl. Paraffin Gardner
HULL CONSTR.:	Teak
BUILT BY:	H.M. Dockyard
YEAR BUILT:	Devonport, 1917

accommodation vessel. Then, before she was returned to the previous owner, the Admiralty reconditioned her throughout.

Omega is a substantial ketch-rigged yacht. She has a straight stem and is carvel built with an elliptical stern. She is powered by a 68 h.p. Gardner diesel engine. Mr and Mrs Rouse, who bought her in 1985, keep her at the Severn Motor Yacht Club, Clerkenleap, at Worcester and she is a member of the Association of Dunkirk Little Ships.

Life has gone full circle for *Elsa II* which was built at Thornycroft's in 1929. Now she is owned by former Thornycroft apprentice, Fred Bourne together with his wife Sheila, who is the secretary of The Thames Vintage Boat Club.

Elsa II is one of the many ships whose presence at Dunkirk is well documented, but no detailed records of her achievements survive. However, she has one of the oldest brasss commemorative plaques given to Little Ships even before the A.D.L.S. came into being. She took part in the 1975 and 1980 returns to Dunkirk and, on the earlier occasion the owner, John Bailey and his wife rather cheekily asked the

NAME:	Elsa II
TYPE:	Motor Cruiser
LENGTH:	32ft
BEAM:	8ft 6ins
DISPLACEMENT:	9.5 tons
DRAFT:	3ft 9ins
ENGINES:	Petrol "Handy Billy"
HULL CONSTR.:	Carvel
BUILT BY:	Thornycroft
YEAR BUILT:	1929

Mayor of Dunkirk if he would come aboard for tea. When the Mayor arrived with his entire entourage, he found that *Elsa II* was only 32ft. long and there was hardly room for himself and the owners inside the cabin!

From 1967-1988 *Elsa II* was owned by a syndicate - all friends - who used their own efforts and skills to maintain her in perfect order without professional help. Many of those who own Dunkirk Little Ships have to rely on their own resources, otherwise maintenance and overhauls on classic wooden boats can run away with many thousands of pounds a year. *Elsa II* has survived particularly well and has hardly been changed since she was built. Of course there have been moments of peril, like the time when she got stuck on a sandbank eight miles off the Dutch coast. Everyone expected her to break up under the relentless pounding of the waves. Then, suddenly, she was lifted clear and floated away to safety.

During the next three years, she helped to conduct sea trials of new life-saving radio beacons in the Channel for Kelvin Hughes and International Marine Radio . Her Handy Billy petrol engines were converted to paraffin but paraffin is no longer freely available at marine filling stations. So they had to resort to pushing supermarket trolleys laden with 5-gallon drums across cobbled streets in Holland to where she lay in the harbour.

Under Fred Bourne's ownership at Weybridge, *Elsa II* is in good hands. He is a yacht chandler and keeps her at the bottom of his garden where he is getting ready for new adventures on the inland waterways of Europe.

Bob Hilton was commissioned into the army in 1936 but was badly injured soon after and medically discharged. When war began he volunteered again and was soon selected for officer training. But when he received his second commission they found out and discharged him once more. In May 1940 he volunteered to take any available ship to Dunkirk. But they insisted on crews of three and he only had one companion, a ginger-haired man by the name of Shaw. They overcame their difficulty by offering a drink or two, plus £1 in cash, to a longshoreman at Tilbury, just to sign on. After that, they told him, he could disappear, if he didn't feel like coming. They were given *Ryegate II* and found her laden with jerry cans, some, they were warned, containing water. The sealed ones, they found, had petrol in them.

On a lovely late May evening they reached Ramsgate where they went ashore to get some stores. The WVS had plenty of food but no implements. So they pinched some glasses from a pub and set out for Dunkirk. "It was just like Piccadilly Circus" Bob recalls:

"There were masses of ships going to-and-fro. There was no need to navigate, we just followed the others. We just got on with the job, which was to sail in as close as we could to the shore, pick up all we could carry and ferry them out to the off-lying ships."

"After some time, the engine seemed to be seizing up and the tide went out,so we tied up behind a ship called the *Horst* and used their lifeboat to row ashore to pick up soldiers. Several times we turned over when the men, who had waded out into the water up to their armpits, all grabbed our boat by the gunwales to climb aboard. In the end we were ordered home, packed like sardines, in a small steamer."

NAME:	Ryegate II
TYPE:	Motor Yacht
LENGTH:	40ft
BEAM:	10ft
DISPLACEMENT:	—
DRAFT:	3ft 6ins
ENGINES:	Perkins 4 - 236
HULL CONSTR.:	Pitch pine on oak
BUILT BY:	Gibbs of Teddington
YEAR BUILT:	1937

Ryegate was towed home and up-river at the end of a whole line of Little Ships by a tug - as shown in the picture above, After Dunkirk Bob Hilton joined up again, this time in the navy, received the King's commission for the third time and won the DSC as Lt. Commander RNVR.

Ryegate II now belongs to David and Elizabeth Pamment who live at Rochester and took her to the Commemorative return to Dunkirk in 1985.

Motor Yacht Sylvia

The harbour master at Ramsgate saw the horrors and the heroism of Dunkirk reflected in the ships that came home - in their crew and their passengers.

He never forgot the way the *Sylvia* returned, loaded with soldiers, many of them wounded. She had been machine-gunned, set on fire and on the port side above the waterline was a hole which the soldiers had plugged with their tunics to keep the water out. Even so, they had to take turns on the pump all the way back.

He congratulated the skipper who promptly announced that he was going back. The harbour master begged him not to, but the sailor looked him straight in the eyes and said: "I have seen the sea red with human blood, severed arms and legs, a sight I shall never forget. The Lord is with us, the sea is calm and if she goes down, I shall go down with her." So he went.

The following day, the harbour master recalled, "there was a lot of noise and a hooter blowing as ships from Dunkirk were waiting to unload. The noise came from the *Sylvia,* full of troops. We rushed her in to get the weight off her, as the water was right up to her engine. Had she gone another mile or had the sea been rough, she would have sunk. When she was moored, the skipper walked out of what was left of her wheelhouse and I never saw him again."

But he did see the *Sylvia* return, years later, fully restored and rushed out to tell her new owner the story and to

NAME:	Sylvia
TYPE:	Motor Yacht
LENGTH:	45ft
BEAM:	9ft 8ins
DISPLACEMENT:	14 tons
DRAFT:	4ft
ENGINES:	1 Gray 6 cyl. petrol
HULL CONSTR.:	Carvel
BUILT BY:	Launch & Boat Co.
YEAR BUILT:	Southampton, 1930

thank him for saving her. Then the harbour master's story was proudly entered into the log.

Now the *Sylvia,* which was originally built for A.J. Anstey, M.D. of B.M.C. Garages, is called *Wendy Ken* after the children of Bert Harpur another previous owner. Ian and Doreen Pearson, whose boat she is now, live aboard her in Cuxton Marina, Rochester, which Ian manages. The 50th anniversary of Dunkirk will coincide with *Wendy Ken's* sixtieth birthday.

L ong before annual holidays for all became the custom, a day by the sea and then a trip round the bay were a traditional form of amusement every summer for thousands of people along the coasts of Britain. There they rubbed shoulders with their seafaring countrymen and came home sunburnt and exhiliarated, with stories of seas a little rougher than expected and the occasional adventures with the elements and with each other.

The brightly painted open motor vessel *Brit II*, was built in Great Yarmouth in 1935 and licenced to carry 200 passengers. Until war began, she spent five summers working for Longfields, taking passengers to fill their lungs with sea air and see the seals basking on the sandbanks along the north sea coast of Norfolk.

But as soon as war began, she changed her occupation, her name and her colour. As HM Tender *Watchful*, she became a base ship for the fleet, and was repainted in battleship grey. She carried stores and torpedoes to the destroyers lying in Yarmouth roads. Her bar became the wardroom for her officers and she had a gun turret installed on her foredeck. On 29th May 1940 she was called to cross the Channel and help evacuate the troops from Dunkirk. She is reported to have rescued 900 troops. One naval officer from her base, the shore establishment *HMS Watchful*, Lieut. A.H. Turner received the D.S.C.

Her peacetime owners, the Longfield brothers, remained with her throughout the war. At the end of 1945 she was returned to them, repainted and given back her name *Brit*, to operate once more as a pleasure cruiser.

In 1950 she took part in the Festival of Britain in London - that great national act of faith in a post-war future for Britain, when the whole country gave thanks for deliverance from war and proudly exhibited the first fruits of rebuilding and new design in its

NAME:	Watchful
TYPE:	Passenger Yacht
LENGTH:	88ft
BEAM:	19ft
DISPLACEMENT:	72 tons
DRAFT:	3ft
ENGINES:	
HULL CONSTR.:	Pitch pine on oak
BUILT BY:	Fellows, Gt. Yarmouth
YEAR BUILT:	1935

ravaged capital. *Brit* then went north to Scarborough, renamed *Yorkshire Lady* and later *Coronia II*. After a refit in Scotland in 1975 she eventually sailed for Gibraltar in 1985. There she again provides trips around the bay, showing visitors the Rock and the marine life around the colony.

On most days a school of dolphins rides the bowwave of *Coronia* to the delight of visitors. There is a great variety of shipping in the harbour of this crossroads of the seas, where Lord Nelson set out for the battle of Trafalgar. After his death, Nelson's remains were preserved in a cask of brandy to be returned to England for ceremonial burial in St. Paul's cathedral.

To the thousands of day-trippers who come aboard *Coronia II* in Gibraltar her skipper tells this and many other stories which make history come to life and he explains the reason why *Coronia* flies the white ensign defaced with the arms of Dunkirk.

L atona, in Greek legend was the mother of Artemis and Apollo, fathered by Zeus, whose jealous wife Hera made Latona ceaselessly roam the earth.

The Dunkirk Little Ship *Latona* is a 29ft. single-engined motor boat built by Boats and Cars at Kingston-on-Thames in 1938. She had to change her name to *HMS Hamford* when she was requisitioned a year later, because the Navy already had a minesweeper *Latona* (sunk by Italian aircraft off Libya in 1940). Under her new name she served the navy well. Her 2.5ft. draft made her ideal for the beaches of Dunkirk and later she was a member of the Auxiliary River Patrol on the Thames looking out for parachute mines. After the war she resumed her peacetime occupation as a handy little pleasure cruiser in the west country, on the rivers Severn and Avon. In the 1950s she was owned by W.A. Waterman, chief test pilot of Gloster Aircraft, who is thought to have written his book *The Quick and the Dead* while living aboard. He disappeared mysteriously, leaving his boat by King John's Bridge, sinking and derelict, and his Rover car parked behind the Bear at Tewkesbury. *Latona's* name was changed to *Gay Goblin* while she worked as a hire craft

NAME:	L a t o n a
TYPE:	Motor Yacht
LENGTH:	30ft
BEAM:	9.5ft
DISPLACEMENT:	9 tons
DRAFT:	2.5ft
ENGINES:	Grays petrol
HULL CONSTR.:	Carvel
BUILT BY:	Sam Emms, Kingston
YEAR BUILT:	1938

in the 1960s and again in 1974 by her next owner who called her *Senang* (the Malay for "happiness") and cruised her up the Thames as far as Lechlade. She was given an aft cabin, increasing her berths from four to six, and her Grays petrol engine was exchanged for a safer BMC Captain diesel.

In 1978 she reverted to her old name of *Latona* and joined the ADLS, taking part in the celebration of the 40th anniversary of Dunkirk in 1980. Bill Williams, her present owner restored her but she then spent a long time out of the water in Plymouth and this tends to make the planks of carvel-built wooden boats open up and require a great deal of work before they can again be watertight. *Latona* is once more in need of major restoration if she is to survive.

N ames of ships derive from the stangest sources and are often changed when someone wants to make a vessel peculiarly his own. *Quisisana's* name has been unchanged since she was built by Thornycroft at Hampton in 1927. There is a district in Malta by that name which means "quiet place". Maybe Cecil Yates, her first owner, once served in Malta and wanted to be reminded of it. Being only 30ft. with a 2ft. 6ins. draft, Malta was certainly beyond her reach.

She was ideally suited to take the troops off the beach at La Panne in 1940 and with two Handy Billy engines was quite capable of making her own way across the Channel in the prevailing calm conditions. She returned without major damage. This she suffered later, ironically not from bombs, shells or machine-gun fire, but from the cause of many a wooden boat's decline: lack of use and storage on land. *Quisisana* spent ten years laid up ashore. Being a carvel-built boat, her planks parted and she then needed a major overhaul before she could once more take to the water. Fortunately Nicholas Lidiard, who now owns her, is a boat builder, with a real interest in *Quisisana* and her history. He intends to invest the time, care and resources necessary to bring this Dunkirk veteran back to life. Much of her hull

NAME:	Quisisana
TYPE:	Motor Cruiser
LENGTH:	30ft
BEAM:	8ft 5ins
DISPLACEMENT:	8.5 tons
DRAFT:	2ft 5ins
ENGINES:	2 x Thornycroft
HULL CONSTR.:	Mahogany on oak
BUILT BY:	J Thorneycroft,
YEAR BUILT:	Hampton, 1927

will need to be re-planked and she needs new engines. But her oak frames and keel will last another fifty years and she has on her bulkhead one of the early plaques to commemorate her service at Dunkirk. Nick Lidiard has also bought her into membership of the ADLS.

Motor Launch Lady Cable

In the years after the Great War, two rival firms stood next to each other on the sands at Teignmouth, Devon, offering boat trips to Torquay, Brixham and along the River Dart - some of the most beautiful river scenery in England. Bert Hockin was his great competitor in the tourist trade when, in 1924, Morgan Giles of Teignmouth designed and built *Lady Cable* for Alf Pittaway. According to Alf Broom, who was her skipper for a while when the two former rivals merged, *Lady Cable* was a typical Morgan Giles design; nothing more than an extended 18ft. jollyboat, which was one of their specialities.

Named after Lady Cable of Lindridge, Bishopsteignton, who launched her, the boat has been a passenger pleasure craft for most of her life. In 1926 she took thirty Scotland Yard detectives on a trip to Slapton Sands; a private hire on a mysterious mission. By 1936 *Lady Cable* had been sold to C. & N. Mott of Torquay, and was the only boat to go from there to Dunkirk. During the evacuation as recorded in A. D. Divine's book *Dunkirk*, she is said to have taken 550 men from the beaches out to the larger transport shiups in seven trips, and she finally returned full of troops to Dover.

Afterwards, *Lady Cable* continued to be a passenger-carrying pleasure craft during the holiday season, sometimes taking her passengers on fishing expeditions. Mrs Irene Bolus, who bought the boat in 1987, with John Bolus as skipper, has used her to earn her living on mackerel fishing trips and cruises around the bay.

NAME:	Lady Cable
TYPE:	Motor Launch
LENGTH:	40ft
BEAM:	9ft
DISPLACEMENT:	5 tons
DRAFT:	3ft 6ins
ENGINES:	
HULL CONSTR.:	Carvel pitch pine on oak
BUILT BY:	Morgan Gibbs Ltd
YEAR BUILT:	Teignmouth, 1924

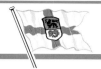

There can't be many private motor yachts which can claim - as the *Braymar* can - to have seen active service in two world wars. Built in 1910 by Courtney and Newhook in Lymington, to a design by Cox and King, she was named *Braemar* and it is not clear when the spelling of her name was changed. In 1914 she was owned and commanded by Lieut. George Paxton. On August 13th 1914, *Braemar* left for Le Havre, and helped with the landing of the Expeditionary Force. She then returned to England, had a week's refit, and subsequently went to Yarmouth on Coastal Patrol, where she and *Kiwi* were blown ashore in a howling gale in November, but were salved about a week later.

After World War One she had one or two more owners, but a Mr Bray completely rebuilt her when he came across her advertised in one of the yachting journals in 1936. He gave her a streamlined wheelhouse, concealed lockers, a Chrysler engine and sound insulated her throughout.

When World War II began, *Braymar,* who had also distinguished herself by winning the London to Cowes race no less than five times in six starts, joined up again. Her size, speed and sea-worthiness made it easy for her to cross the Channel laden with troops, but her 4ft. 6in. draft did not enable her to work from the beaches. Ironically she suffered major damage not from air attack, mines or shells at Dunkirk but from quite another hazard commonly faced by old wooden boats. She was laid up ashore for ten years after the war and competely dried out so that her planks and topsides parted and started to deteriorate.

Anthony Pay, her present owner is an engineer in the process of giving her new coachroof beams and beam shelves, new topsides, and a new laid

NAME:	B r a y m a r
TYPE:	Ketch
LENGTH:	49ft 3ins
BEAM:	10ft 6ins
DISPLACEMENT:	18 tons
DRAFT:	4ft 6ins
ENGINES:	Perkins P6M
HULL CONSTR.:	Carvel pitch pine on oak
BUILT BY:	Courtney & Newhook
YEAR BUILT:	1910

deck. He will need to replace some of her planks. Her 80-year old oak keel and ribs are still in good heart and her old Chrysler petrol engine was replaced by a Perkins P6M diesel, just after her war service.

Braymar is just another example of the charm which Dunkirk Little Ships exert on their owners causing them to make great sacrifices to ensure their survival.

Passenger Boat Seymour Castle

Exmouth and Lympstone and taken to Dartmouth, where they stayed overnight to be returned unused the next day! Not so with *Seymour Castle*; after Dunkirk the Admiralty kept her on in the Folkestone area for towing

NAME:	Seymour Castle
TYPE:	Passenger Boat
LENGTH:	60ft
BEAM:	14ft 8ins
DISPLACEMENT:	36.93 tons
DRAFT:	3ft 6ins
ENGINES:	2 x 6 cylinder Ford
HULL CONSTR.:	Pitch pine on oak
BUILT BY:	Ferris & Blank
YEAR BUILT:	Dartmouth, 1938

When she served at Dunkirk, the 60ft. Dartmouth excursion boat *Dartmothian* was called *Seymour Castle*. She was taken on her 200-mile journey to Ramsgate by Cyril Roper, one of the River Dart Steamboat Company's skippers. It was a company with a long tradition in a popular holiday area. Formed in 1834 to operate steam tugs and the local barges, they began a river passenger service to Totnes, Devon, in 1856 at the suggestion of the Duke of Clarence. Although the company closed in 1974, River Dart trips to Totnes have remained an enjoyable feature of holidays in the area since their mid-19th century origins. *Dartmothian* continues this tradition.

In 1940 she set sail for the Channel with the GWR's *The Mew* - an old railway ferry boat which operated between Kingsweir and Dartmouth, and whose job she occasionally took over. This was the longest sea voyage ever undertaken by the *Seymour Castle* since she was built by Ferris and Blank, Dartmouth, the previous year and no Dunkirk Little Ship came from further west. A whole fleet of boats was brought together from nearby

the portable Mulberry Harbours. This was the cover name for pre-fabricated floating harbours towed across the English Channel and placed off the Normandy beaches when allied troops returned to the continent of Europe in 1944. These would have saved many lives if they had been invented four years earlier.

Seymour Castle was built by Ferris and Blank at Old Mill Creek, Devon. One of a similar pair of passenger boats, she was the largest vessel these specialists in pulling boats and small motor yachts ever made. Victor Ashton, who worked for a rival firm of boatbuilders, designed her privately as a favour, and the builders made her frames from local oak trees, cut up on the pitsaw. (One man stood in the pit below, whilst another guided the long pitsaw to cut lengths of timber from above). She was built to take 210 passengers and crew - now reduced to 141 for reasons of safety and comfort - and given a Gleniffer engine.

In 1945 she came back to the River Dart as a passenger pleasure craft, and later took holidaymakers up and down the Tamar for a Plymouth operator.

For some years she was owned by the naturalist and writer Tony Soper who gave her a new wheelhouse, and equipped her saloon for lectures. As Wildlife Expedition Ltd's floating field centre, he used her for natural history tours out of Plymouth and later from Dartmouth. That is where she is now, again sailing on the Dart as one of the fleet of Red Cruisers of G.H. Ridalls & Sons.

A nother of Ridall's Red Cruisers at Dartmouth is *My Queen*, whose name was *Gondolier Queen* when she went to Dunkirk. At that time she was working as a passenger craft in the Poole and Swanage area in Dorset. She was built in 1929 by a small Essex boatbuilder, Husk & Son of Wivenhoe. *Goldolier Queen*, although intended for passenger carrying from the outset, was an almost open, single-deck vessel with a small wheelhouse amidships. For most of her life she remained that way. Her services were retained by the Navy after the evacuation, and she is next heard of as a pleasure boat at Southend where she remained until the early 1970s. George Wheeler Launches then brought her to the

wheelhouse. *My Queen* carries her passengers well, up to 169 of them at a time, for she has a very broad beam for her length. She has a shallow draft and John Ridalls, whose father started the family firm in 1930, says that *My Queen* "could float in a bucket."

During the season she carries boatloads of American visitors up the River Dart to Totnes. Many of them have come here, since the day in 1944 when 485 American landing craft went, out of the River Dart, bound for the D-Day landings four years after the Dunkirk evacuation. It is fitting that so many survivors re-kindle their memories on a boat that also went to war. Indeed, when France's President Mitterrand visited the area, it was on *My Queen* that he sailed up the Dart to look again at Brookhill House, wartime base of the Free French Forces, where he served with General de Gaulle. It is a strange coincidence that *Gondolier Queen* has come to work alongside her wartime companion at Dunkirk. Her present owners, who bought her two years ago, did not know much about her history then, but will now appreciate and preserve her all the more for that.

NAME: Gondolier Queen	
TYPE:	Passenger Vessel
LENGTH:	56ft 6ins
BEAM:	16ft 3ins
DISPLACEMENT:	36.76 tons
DRAFT:	3ft 9ins
ENGINES:	2 x Ford Watermotor
HULL CONSTR.:	Carvel
BUILT BY:	Husk & Son, Wivenhoe
YEAR BUILT:	1929

Thames, running a water bus service between Westminster Pier and Greenwich. From there she went to the west country and was given a new enclosed saloon, a top deck and an upper

Motor Yacht Fedalma II

Johh Knight who now owns *Fedalma II*, first became involved with the Little Ships of Dunkirk quite by chance, when he bought *Elizabeth Green* in 1964. He had no idea of her distinguished war record until the *Sunday Times* got in touch and told him about plans to take a flotilla of Little Ships back to Dunkirk for a celebration of the 25th anniversary of Operation Dynamo in 1965.

Then, in 1966 when the Association of Dunkirk Little Ships was formed, he became its Hon. Secretary. His interest grew as he began to search for information about his own Little Ship and to recruit new members. In 1972 he became Commodore of the A.D.L.S. and three years later, its Hon. Archivist. His patient and painstaking research, exhortation and encouragement to other owners was largely

NAME:	Fedalma II
TYPE:	Motor Yacht
LENGTH:	47ft
BEAM:	11ft
DISPLACEMENT:	17.82 tons
DRAFT:	4ft 9ins
ENGINES:	2 x 6 cyl. Gray petrol
HULL CONSTR.:	Carvel teak on oak
BUILT BY:	Charles Fox & Son
YEAR BUILT:	Ipswich, 1936

responsible for the growth of the Association and for the initiative which gave birth to this book. He conducted research at the Imperial War Museum, the Admiralty and the Ministry of War Transport. Much valuable information was also gleaned from A.D. Divine's book *Dunkirk* published by Faber & Faber in 1945 which contains the best and most comprehensive listing of the Little Ships. David Divine, who took his own boat *Little Anne* to Dunkirk and lost her there, was yachting correspondent of the *Sunday Times*. Though a civilian, he was awarded the Navy's Distinguished Service Medal for his part in the rescue.

The yachting press has contributed greatly to the quest for Dunkirk ships, partly by delving into pre-war issues of magazines published when the Little Ships were built and were the new stars of the popular yachting movement of the 1930s. But many of the member ships were spotted by John Knight and other enthusiasts on the Thames and in scores of harbours not only in England, but in the Mediterranean and the canals of France and the Netherlands.

John Knight was on holiday in Malta in early 1975 and decided to visit the owner of *Charlmaine*, a member of the A.D.L.S. whose ship was lying there. He gave him the news that *Fedalma II*,

another Dunkirk ship was also in Valetta harbour. Always delighted to rediscover more veterans and enrol them, John went to have a look, fell in love with her and decided to buy her, even though it meant parting with *Elizabeth Green*. The Knights then spent several more holidays in Malta, preparing *Fedalma* for the 1200-mile journey home to England. In 1977 they got as far as Port St. Louis on the Rhone and in 1978 they completed the voyage through the French canals - finishing the last 500 miles on one engine.

Fedalma II was built by Charles H. Fox in 1936 for Claud Scrutton who died during the war and had his ashes taken down river and committed to the sea from *Fedalma II*. She is a roomy 47-footer, ketch-rigged with well-stayed masts designed to carry 375 sq. ft. of sail, so that when she was built she was not entirely dependant on her two Gray petrol engines - replaced long ago by Perkins P6 354 diesels.

She is a handsome boat, with a great expanse of varnished teak above and below decks. Her 4ft. 9in. draft must have been an embarrassment when she lifted soldiers off the beach at Dunkirk in 1940.

Claud Scrutton recalled how he and his skipper, Dick Cook, were on the boat at Burnham-on-Crouch when war broke out and decided to take off her stores in case she should get bombed. A few days later she was requisitioned and after Dunkirk, taken into the Armed Patrol Service. No more is known about her involvement although she is specifically named as a participant in David Divine's book - where, strangely, her name is spelled *Fedelma II*.

John Knight is now looking forward to taking her back to Dunkirk for the half-century celebrations of Operation Dynamo.

Motor Yacht Elizabeth Green

Elizabeth Green was one of the first of the privately owned rescue ships to help in the evacuation of Dunkirk and on her second trip she was one of the last to leave. Her role is exceptionally well documented. Not many of the skippers - especially the young naval crews hastily detailed to command these unfamiliar and unarmed civilian vessels, kept a detailed log. But Sub-Lieutenant E.T. Garside, RNVR, compiled an hour-by-hour account of his first nine days of active service. Not that he was ever likely to forget it.

Sub-Lieut Garside, RNVR in 1940

It all started at 18.05 on 28th May 1940 when he left Sheerness Basin with a crew of one seaman and two stokers, towing a whaler and bound for Dover. He lost touch with his convoy when his engine failed but they were able to repair it. Next morning they refuelled and left for Dunkirk, where they arrived at 15.30 amid heavy enemy bombardment. They were sent on to La Panne beach where they began towing whalers full of troops to off-lying ships. At 16.00 they saw the paddle steamer *Crested Eagle* go down. At 18.00 the *Viewfinder* was dragged ashore by Belgian troops and she was

NAME:	Elizabeth Green
TYPE:	Motor Yacht
LENGTH:	43ft 6ins
BEAM:	12ft 6ins
DISPLACEMENT:	18.18 tons
DRAFT:	3ft 6ins
ENGINES:	2 x 4 cyl.Morris petrol
HULL CONSTR.:	Pitch pine on oak
BUILT BY:	H. Milland,
YEAR BUILT:	Twickenham

never refloated. At 19.00 the *Hanora* fouled her propeller and was abandoned. *Elizabeth Green* picked up her crew and transferred them to the minesweeper *Lydd*. Finally, at 21.20 they left La Panne with a full load in company with the motor yacht *Advance*.

They encountered thick fog on the way and anchored in Pegwell Bay before entering Ramsgate at 06.50 having spent thirty-six hours at sea and off the beaches without rest. Sub-Lieut. Garside then made another journey to Dunkirk in the RAF launch *Andover II*. But on 4th June he was again assigned to *Elizabeth Green* and, at 16.00, left Ramsgate with a crew of four seamen and an interpreter, sent to rescue some of the remaining French soldiers marooned at the end of Dunkirk jetty. The tug *Rania*, towed *Elizabeth Green* together with the Clacton lifeboat. By 21.50 the tow rope had parted and they proceeded under their own power.

This was the last night of the evacuation and conditions were appalling. Officers and men on the ships not only had the hazards of constant air attack, shelling and mines to contend with, but they went for days without sleep and proper food. Near the French coast the water was full of debris, stranded and sinking ships and bodies. Vessels of all sizes, some of them with their steering disabled, were coming and going,

often manoevering dangerously to evade attacks from the air, from German E-boats and each other. Collisions were frequent and were followed by a frantic scramble to pick up survivors.

Elizabeth Green got through to the Quai Jules Faure in Dunkirk harbour. She carried with her from England a 30-rung ladder which, as one of her crew, stoker D.R. Nichol reported, they placed from their deck to the sea wall to help twenty or so Frenchmen to climb down to them. On the way home their engine seized up but they succeeded in restarting it and shaped course for Ramsgate. The sea conditions deteriorated a little and the French officer in charge of the troops announced that they wished to be sick. "I handed them a plate each and hoped for the best. My hopes were ill-founded and I had a ghastly time clearing up the mess!" But their troubles were not yet over. Within an hour their engine died again off Broadstairs. They repaired it and finally arrived at Sheerness at 15.30, twenty four hours after they set out for Dunkirk, with virtually no food or sleep. Lieutenant Garside, whose third

trip this was, behaved with exemplary courage and coolness and was awarded the Distinguished Service Cross.

Elizabeth Green ended her war on mine-spotting duties and was often berthed in Sheerness at the same pier that was used by *HMS MMS 41,* a minesweeper commanded by Lt. Commander E.T. Garside DSC. After the war *Elizabeth Green* was bought by John Knight, Hon. Archivist and sometime Commodore of the A.D.L.S. and appeared in a T.V. programme about Dunkirk. She now belongs to Alan Jackson, the Events Secretary of the Association, who keeps her on the Thames at Teddington.

Motor Yacht Glala

When Sir Alan Cobham, famous aeronautical pioneer, needed to take a holiday from his exacting work in 1936, he decided to follow the example of many of his friends and buy a boat. He dreamed of crossing France by river and canal from the Channel to the Mediterranean. So, he sent his wife Gladys boat hunting - to Scotland which, he had been told, was the only place to get a good boat.

Soon he received a joyful telegram from Greenock, where she had found just what he wanted: a magnificent craft called *Cupid*, built in 1915 for exploring the Upper Amazon. A helpful Irishman called Sullivan beat down the price from £2,000 to a mere £900 and Sir Alan spent another £140 to fit her out. They renamed her *Glala*, combining part of both their Christian names, and began their journey south along the east coast of Britain. On the way, they experienced engine trouble and Sir Alan had to go on by train so as not to miss some important trials of Flight Refuelling Ltd., his pioneer company. They did not keep *Glala* long. Cobham was no great sailor and thought she rolled too much! So *Glala* was sold, - and had two more owners before she was requisitioned by the Admiralty in

NAME:	Glala
TYPE:	Motor Yacht
LENGTH:	77ft 6ins
BEAM:	13ft
DISPLACEMENT:	51 tons
DRAFT:	5ft
ENGINES:	Gardner 6L x B diesel
HULL CONSTR.:	Teak on oak and elm
BUILT BY:	Camper & Nicholson
YEAR BUILT:	1915

October 1939 from AEC, the commercial vehicle manufacturers. She then began the war as a Harbour Defence Patrol Craft at Sheerness.

Commanded by Sub-Lieut. J.A. Dow, RNVR, she set out for Dunkirk on 31st May, 1940 in company with the yachts *Amulree* and *Caleta*. She arrived in Dunkirk Roads $3^1/_2$ hours later and immediately towed two whalers full of troops to HMS *Golden Eagle*, a paddle steamer commissioned by the Navy as a Special Service Vessel, which was driving off German dive-bombers with her pom-pom gun. The *Glala* then towed boats for the destroyers *Venomous* and *Vivacious*. Again the dive bombers zeroed in on the small ships and Capt. Howson, in the yacht *Ankh*, gave the order to make for the open sea. *Glala*, who had sustained some damage, was ordered to return to Ramsgate for repairs and she arrived there on 2nd June at 18.45. From there she proceded to Sheerness with her port engine still out of action. In 1941, manned by a civilian crew, *Glala* became a hospital tender in Belfast and was later used by the Naval Fire Service in Liverpool for a time before she reverted to civilian ownership. Since then she has cruised along the French and Italian rivieras. Her present owners, P. Nachman and A.N. Wynter have now completely restored her and use her as a charter boat.

Passenger Vessel Queen Boadicea II

Built as a sturdy passenger boat, with a 65ft. all-steel hull, *Queen Boadicea II* was an ideal vessel to go to Dunkirk - providing always that the weather and the sea remained calm. Her 3ft. draft was ample for the river Thames, where she started her working life when Mrs. C.M. Smith, her first owner, used her to ply between Westminster and Greenwich in 1936, but hardly good enough for crossing the English Channel on a bad day.

On Friday, 31st May 1940, a fresh onshore breeze developed. *Queen Boadicea*, commanded by Lieutenant J.S. Seal, RNR, avoided the beaches in these conditions and made for Dunkirk harbour. There they met heavy shelling accompanied by enemy air attacks. They arrived just in time to see the motor boat *Janice*, working off Dunkirk pier, demolished by a direct hit from a bomb. Her skipper Sub-Lieut. Bell, RNVR, was killed, together with a stoker rating. The *Boadicea* managed to pick up three of her crew who were thrown into the water as she

went down. From then on, Lieut. Seal had no time to keep a log. But in the 1980s a holidaymaker told the present owner that she remembered caring for thirteen soldiers who returned from Dunkirk on *Queen Boadicea.*

After the war, she was acquired by George Wheeler Launches, to provide a Thames passenger service from Greenwich to Westminster and up-river as far as Kew and Richmond. Her next owners were Dart Pleasure Cruises, in Dartmouth, Devon, and she was finally sold to her present owners, Tamar Cruising, who use her to provide a ferry service in Plymouth. In 1988 *Queen Boadicea* hit the headlines when she carried travel writer Alison Payne and her one-ton shire horse *Mighty* from Admiral's Hard, Plymouth to Cremyll, Mount Edgecomb, in Cornwall as part of the writer's fund-raising effort for a charity.

NAME:	Queen Boadicea II
TYPE:	Passenger Vessel
LENGTH:	65ft
BEAM:	14ft 6ins
DISPLACEMENT:	45 tons
DRAFT:	3ft
ENGINES:	Gardner 6LX
HULL CONSTR.:	Steel
BUILT BY:	Thornycroft
YEAR BUILT:	1936

Ships, in their time, play many parts: humble, work-a-day, heroic and sometimes glamorous. In their various roles, they assume different names. *Our Lizzie*, at Dunkirk, where the details of her part were not recorded (save the fact that she went and was finally left lying at Newhaven) became *Freebooter* in the hands of Ray Barrett, who offers her for hire as a fishing boat in Dartmouth, Devon.

But these are just two of her occupations. She is a handsome, rugged, gaff-rigged ketch and looks her part: a sturdy, traditional working boat. This has qualified her to become a star of film and T.V. With her masts removed, a superstructure and funnel added, she has appeared in every series of BBC Television's popular *The Onedin Line*. And in her sailing rig she has starred in the film *The French Lieutenant's Woman* at Dartmouth. She appeared in *Dracula* at Mevagissey and in *The Apple Tree* just along the Devon coast at Sidmouth. To earn her keep, she will turn her hand to any

honourable task and she has performed, for some old mariners, their last request and taken their ashes to be scattered over the sea.

Her owner plans to take her on the pilgrimage to Dunkirk for the 50th anniversary in 1990, but then he intends to find for her a new owner who will appreciate her and keep her in the style that she deserves.

NAME:	Our Lizzie
TYPE:	Auxiliary Ketch
LENGTH:	46ft
BEAM:	14ft
DISPLACEMENT:	19.6 tons
DRAFT:	6ft
ENGINES:	Perkins 4236 diesel
HULL CONSTR.:	Pitch pine on oak
BUILT BY:	Porthleven, Cornwall
YEAR BUILT:	1920

Picturesque Brownsea Island, in Poole harbour, provided a refuge in 1940 for Dutch and Belgian refugees, who camped there after German armies began to invade their home-land. The Davis family owned a boatyard in Poole and used their 60-passenger ferry *Felicity* to take them food and blankets and to provide a link with the mainland.

Like many of her kind, the *Felicity* was an open fishing boat, used for catching sprats in winter, and in summer she took holiday makers for trips round the bay. Mr. Davis, the head of the well-known local family, recalls the day at the end of May 1940, when they received the call for all available boats to report to the Admiralty. He and his brother Jimmy took *Felicity* and another boat, the *Island Queen*, to Dover where they were told that naval crews would take over. They were not sorry, because they had enough to do at Brownsea Island. It was some time before they had any news of their boats, althouth they knew what was happening when banner headlines in

NAME:	Felicity
TYPE:	Passenger Launch
LENGTH:	35ft
BEAM:	9ft
DISPLACEMENT:	7.5 tons
DRAFT:	3ft
ENGINES:	Ford 72 h.p.
HULL CONSTR.:	Carvel pitch pine on oak
BUILT BY:	Davis Boatyard
YEAR BUILT:	1931

the press told the story of Dunkirk. In due course, *Felicity* came back to them, in need of a good clean-up but otherwise none the worse for her experience. *Island Queen* was never heard of again. The story was that she had been bombed. They were sorry to lose her, but proud that she had done her bit. After the war they sold *Felicity* and for a time lost touch. But now they know that she belongs to Sean Crane of Keyhaven and his company Hurst Castle & Cruises who run a passenger service in the Solent. He provided her with a new Ford 72 h.p. diesel and renamed her *Wight Rose*.

153

Motor Cruiser Dragonfly

During the fifty years since they earned their place in the history books, the Little Ships, like members of a large family, have been scattered widely and, like married daughters, sometimes assumed new names which make it difficult to identify them.

Our search for Dunkirk ships has taken us far and wide. Ontario, Canada is 3,000 miles from Dunkirk and far out of range for a little 8-knot motor yacht, yet that is where we found *L'Aventure* - not that this was her name when she took part in Operation Dynamo. At that time she was called *Dragonfly*. How she got to Canada is a strange story in itself. Built for Mr. J. D. Leech (*Sea Leech II* was her name then), she was on the Thames before the war when she was requisitioned and painted in battleship grey all over until, her war service completed, she went back into civilian ownership.

In 1962, a Canadian, General Allard, on a staff course in England, bought and renamed her *L'Aventure*. When he was posted to Germany to command a British brigade, he took her with him. Later, he cruised through the French canals to the Mediterranean and when he was recalled to Canada as Chief of the Defence Staff, he persuaded the Canadian aircraft carrier *Bonaventure*, which happened to be returning to Canada from NATO service in the Mediterranean, to carry her near-namesake, with the gallant military connection, back home for him.

An Ottawa architect, John Flanders bought her from Allard in 1965 and her present owners, Jocelyn and Cameron Graham became her proud owners a year later. During the next twenty-five years they lavished unimaginable amounts of time and resources on the Little Ship and have

NAME:	Dragonfly
TYPE:	Motor Cruiser
LENGTH:	35ft
BEAM:	9ft
DISPLACEMENT:	11.48 tons
DRAFT:	2ft 9ins
ENGINES:	2 Bukh oil 20 h.p.
HULL CONSTR.:	Mahogany on elm/oak
BUILT BY:	Thornycroft
YEAR BUILT:	1933

won six major prizes for craftsmanship and elegance at Clayton, New York and Ottawa shows for their back-breaking labour. Although they have installed some modern comforts and equipment, they have religiously maintained *L'Aventure's* original design and appearance.

But *L'Aventure* has not become just a museum exhibit. They enjoy her in the role for which she was created. Hundreds of hours of joyful cruising through the idyllic Canadian waters of the Rideau river and the Thousand Islands with their children and grand-children have repaid them for their dedication. There have been setbacks too, - especially, as happens with all owners of classic wooden boats, when earning one's living interferes with yachting. In 1979, *L'Aventure* was laid up for three destructive years and suffered from the ravages of the weather and sun on her tarnished metal parts, wooden hull and superstructure. In 1983 Graham, full of remorse, applied himself to make good the damage. He renewed ribs and bulkheads, gave her a new electrical system and a pair of new Bukh diesel engines. Now she is a proud and self-respecting lady again and they are considering the possibility of attending the 1990 return to Dunkirk. So, if the friendly captain of an aircraft carrier reads this book in time, please will he get in touch!

Motor Yacht Chalmondesleigh

In 1934 the Chrysler Marine Co. of Michigan, U.S.A. built a 29ft., 4-berth motor yacht for racehorse owner Dorothy Padgette. They installed one of their own 80 h.p. petrol engines, capable of pushing the boat to 20 knots, and in 1938 she was shipped to England to compete in speed trials off the Isle of Wight.

When comedian Tommy Trinder decided to buy her in 1939, the boat, an American Chriscraft, had recently been modified by a ferry operator at Shanklin, who used her for taking a dozen people at a time for trips around the bay. Brother Fred Trinder recalls: "Tommy sent me to pick up the boat at Shanklin and deliver it to him on the Thames. I didn't know how to get her there from the Isle of Wight. Tommy told me "just to follow the ferries, and

one of them would lead me up the Thames!" The boat was moored at Shoreham, Sussex when she was requisitioned by the Navy for Dunkirk. Trinder changed her name to *Chalmondesleigh* after the imaginary friend and confidant he frequently mentioned in his act - and had this name painted along the side of the vessel. "It took the signwriter about three days to complete," according to Fred. Pronounced *Chumley*, the name was shortened after the war to this spelling. Apart from the trip to Dunkirk, *Chumley* more or less stayed on the Thames apart from a few coastal trips. Fred lived on her for a while at Shoreham after he was demobbed, and they did once try to take her to France. However, Fred had no passport and his 'crew' was a three-man musical comedy act then appearing at the London Palladium, all wearing admiral's uniform. Such was their navigating skill, that they determined where they were by reading the names of the hotels on shore through binoculars, then looking them up in the guide books on board. "Just turn left at the Eddystone Light," said Trinder; but they never made it.

Tommy Trinder sold *Chumley* in 1949 and her whereabouts over the next decade are unknown. In 1959 Harry Roades found her in a boat sale at Wargrave-on-Thames. In the bilges were shell heads and half a ton of pig iron which had been used as ballast, and which he removed. In 1968 the boat was bought by Harry's two sons one of whom, Alan, is now the sole owner. She is, he says, in a sad state; the cabin which the Trinder brothers added has caved in and the hull is holed. She is on dry land near Aylesbury, Buckinghamshire, urgently in need of someone to save her.

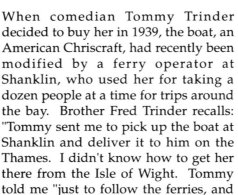

NAME: Chalmondesleigh	
TYPE:	Motor Yacht
LENGTH:	29ft
BEAM:	8ft 6ins
DISPLACEMENT:	5 tons
DRAFT:	3ft
ENGINES:	Chrysler petrol
HULL CONSTR.:	Pitch pine on oak
BUILT BY:	Chrysler Marine Co.
YEAR BUILT:	Michigan, 1934

Motor Yacht Lady Delft

Lady Delft is something of a mystery. A plaque on board gives full details of her service at Dunkirk. It says:

"Removed 491 men from the beaches of Dunkirk. She was taken from her mooring by four unknown Gentlemen. Later she was manned by two soldiers or ratings after her original crew had been killed. The ship herself sustained damage to her bow but was saved by her watertight bulkhead. The names of the four civilians and two servicemen have never been traced."

The name *Lady Delft* does not appear in any of the official records of Dunkirk, so it is likely that she sailed under a different name at that time, which explains why no other details are available.

What we do know is that she was built by Trimmer & Zoon in Holland in 1938, is a 50ft. ketch-rigged motor-sailer, with a steel hull, mahogany wheelhouse, twin screws driven by two Perkins 4236 diesel engines and is beautifully equipped for long-distance cruising. Her equipment includes a 240-v Petter diesel generator, radar,

NAME:	Lady Delft
TYPE:	Motor Yacht
LENGTH:	50ft
BEAM:	11ft 6ins
DISPLACEMENT:	10 tons
DRAFT:	5ft 3ins
ENGINES:	2 x Perkins 4236
HULL CONSTR.:	Steel
BUILT BY:	Trimmer & Zoon
YEAR BUILT:	1938

Satnav and autohelm with every comfort below and a beautifully renewed laid deck above.

She is at present lying in Gibraltar and has recently been bought by a Mr. Day, who lives in Derbyshire.

The only David Hillyard sailing yacht to take part in Operation Dynamo - and one of the very few pure sailboats, rather than motor sailers, *Windsong* was not ideal for the purpose. In the light airs prevailing on 1st June and with only a small Ailsa Craig auxiliary engine, she was not very fast or manoeuverable and took a great risk going near a lee shore amid bombing, shellfire and a host of every conceivable kind of ship, going in every direction.

She was taken to Dover by her owner, Mr G.L. Dalton, on the evening of 31st May, in response to the broadcast request for every kind of craft to be made available. Mr Dalton reported at 18.40 that he was "ready for sea and able to take thirty passengers" - which said more for his valour and patriotism than for the capacity of his vessel. In the event, she appears to have been towed across by the trawler *Kinder Star*, because she could not otherwise have completed the passage in the

time it took her to get there. Here her owner takes up the story:

We were on the point of making for the beach when we were heavily raided by dive-bombers, one large salvo just missing our trawler. We were ordered to cut adrift and make back; it was every man for himself."

Mr Dalton brought his yacht home safely and reported back to Dover at 21.15 on 2nd June. *Windsong* was retained by the Royal Navy, but Mr Dalton did not stay with her since one document refers to: 'T.H. Falkingham and A. Barden, both of *Windsong*, who volunteered and deserve a medal.'

After Operation Dynamo, she was taken to Brightlingsea where, in company with *Sundowner*, she was used as a patrol and mine-spotting vessel. There is no record to show when she was returned to Mr Dalton. She has had no less than eight owners since the war. At least one of these,

Lady Effie Millington-Drake, bears a famous name connected with World War II. Her husband, Sir John, was 'Our Man in Buenos Aires' at the time of the Battle on the River Plate. It was he who contrived to delay the departure of the German Battle Cruiser *Graf Spee* from Montevideo by a series of spurious radio messages, enabling the Royal Navy to reinforce what was left of Admiral Harewood's cruiser force waiting outside, so that they could successfully attack her when she left neutral waters. She was finally scurried to avoid falling into British hands.

Now *Windsong* belongs to Col. (Ret'd) M.N.V. Duddridge, OBE, who has her on the river Maas in Holland. He is a fine sailor who knows how to handle the 'old gaffer' well and cruises in her extensively. She looks in good shape and lends grace to the reunions of the Little Ships.

Often she demonstrates, even on the tidal River Thames, that she can keep pace with her motor-driven sister ships and turn the eyes of spectators with her handsome lines and well-trimmed sails.

NAME:	Windsong
TYPE:	Auxiliary Ketch
LENGTH:	44ft 6ins
BEAM:	10ft 9ins
DISPLACEMENT:	11.75 tons
DRAFT:	4ft
ENGINES:	Petter diesel
HULL CONSTR.:	Pitch pine on oak
BUILT BY:	David Hillyard
YEAR BUILT:	Southampton, 1931

F red Shoesmith of Glasgow had *Wairakei II* built at James A. Silver's famous yard in Rosneath, on the river Clyde in Scotland. It was 1932 and the Great Depression was at its height. One in four of all workers in Britain and the United States were out of work and in Germany the Weimar Republic had come to an end and Hitler's Nazi party began to assume power. Yet, strangely, this was a time when popular yachting and the building of small motor cruisers flourished and helped to provide new employment in Britain. Greater need for jobs can help to improve competitiveness and quality. *Wairakei*, designed by John Bain, was certainly a superbly built yacht and an improvement even on the owner's

NAME:	Wairakei II
TYPE:	Auxiliary Ketch
LENGTH:	52ft
BEAM:	11ft
DISPLACEMENT:	26.40 tons
DRAFT:	6ft
ENGINES:	BMC Commodore
HULL CONSTR.:	Pitch pine on oak
BUILT BY:	James Silver, Rosneath
YEAR BUILT:	1932

earlier ship *Brown Owl*. She was ketch-rigged and able to sail in a fair wind, but her main power came from her two Gleniffer petrol engines, which were in 1959 replaced by twin BMC Commodore diesels. With accommodation for seven (in three double and one single cabin), and ample deck space, the Ministry of War Transport requis-itioned her early in the war and she was commanded by a Lieut. Leyland. She had a machine-gun mounted on her foredeck and rifle racks all round her decks. David Devine includes her in his list of Little Ships used at Dunkirk and she is said to have saved 150 soldiers there. Lloyd's Register of Yachts shows her owner at the time as Mr F.G. Cox. After the war she had 8 owners, some of whom used her for holiday charter work.

By Saturday morning, 1st June 1940, the traffic of small craft on their way to Dunkirk was at its busiest when Lieut. H. Simouth Willing of the Twickenham Sea Cadet Corps arrived at Ramsgate from the Thames in *Rummy II*. He was left in command and was given a naval crew. They reached Dunkirk amid intensive shellfire towing two ships' lifeboats. They went in with these and brought back about 140 men during the night.

The pulling boats, though at times towed by power craft, had great difficulty in the strong tidal streams off the beaches and were instructed to take their full loads to the nearest transport they could find. Lieut. Willing proudly recorded: "We found the tug we were serving after a long row, under heavy fire and I am pleased to report my crew by name for steadiness under close fire."

In 1946 *Rummy II* was sold by the Admiralty to Jack Pritchard, who kept her at Lock Island, Marlow and in 1949 Dr. Charles Collins took a share in her and cruised with his family from Lechlade, near the source of the Thames, down to the sea. After 1956, *Rummy II* cruised in coastal waters from Faversham in Kent.

Eight years later, David Teare took a part share in the boat and he is the only remaining member of that group. But some years ago Leonard Walsh, who also owned a share, took the boat to Birkenhead in order to refurbish her, but died before work could begin. After his death, it appears, no-one was interested and even the ship's where-abouts could not be traced. So now *Rummy II* is officially lost and her owner is most anxious to have news of her...

NAME:	Rummy II
TYPE:	Motor Yacht
LENGTH:	30ft
BEAM:	8ft 5ins
DISPLACEMENT:	8 tons
DRAFT:	3ft
ENGINES:	2 x BMC Navigators
HULL CONSTR.:	Mahogany on Teak
BUILT BY:	Hyland and Woolf
YEAR BUILT:	1930

NAME:	M T B 1 0 2
TYPE:	Motor Torpedo Boat
LENGTH:	68ft
BEAM:	14ft 9ins
DISPLACEMENT:	33 tons
DRAFT:	3ft 6ins
ENGINES:	3 x Isotta Fraschini
HULL CONSTR.:	Mahogany
BUILT BY:	Vosper, Portsmouth
YEAR BUILT:	1937

Designed in 1936 by Commander Peter du Cane, CBE, the Vosper MTBs of which, in time, 300 were built, were originally a private venture, and the Admiralty still had to be persuaded of their worth. *MTB 102* was the prototype, built in 1937. She had a wooden hull, with double diagonal mahogany planking and was powered by three Italian Isotta Fraschini petrol engines, each of 1,000 h.p., which gave her an impressive maximum speed of 48 knots. In addition, for manoeuvring at slow speed, two Vosper V8 auxiliaries (adaptations of Ford V8 engines) were installed. She became the smallest and fastest warship of the Royal Navy.

Commander C.W.S. Dreyer, DSO, DSC, RN (Ret'd), remembers how, early in March 1940, then a Sub-Lieutenant aged 21, he was given command of *MTB 102*. His first Lieutenant was John Wilford and they had a crew of eight. During the next two months they learned all about their powerful ship and her equipment, which included the torpedo tube in her stem (later replaced by one on each side), machine-guns mounted on the fore deck, smoke-making equipment, echo sounder and an early form of radar. They also had to find time to train newly arrived MTB commanders and crews during their trials in the Solent. As targets for their practice attacks they used the somewhat startled Isle of Wight ferries. Their time of familiarisation was not free from mishaps. Once they ran aground on the Brambles Bank at 25 knots, but the ship came clear, none the worse for the experience. Then, on 26th May, things became more serious. They received their sailing orders from the Commander-in-Chief Portsmouth to proceed to Dover with all speed and report to the Flag Officer there. At that time they had no machine-gun mounted, so the First Lieutenant 'borrowed' a quadruple Vickers K O 303 from *HMS Vernon* and they rigged it between the torpedo tubes. At 07.00 on 27th May they reported to the SOO, Cdr. Boswell, who briefly introduced them to Admiral Sir Bertam Ramsey, in charge of 'Operation Dynamo'. They received orders to "nip over to Dunkirk and report to Captain William Tennant, the naval officer in charge

MTB 102 in 1940

Return to Dunkirk in 1985

there to see what they could do to help." It wasn't difficult to navigate to Dunkirk with the awe-inspiring pall of smoke, flames at its base, to guide them. On the way they encountered an oddly assorted fleet of every kind of ship going in the same direction.

They arrived at Dunkirk at noon on 28th May and found Capt. Tennant, who told them to go to La Panne, where Destroyers were working off the beach, and to see if they could be of help. As they opened up their powerful engines and cruised parallel to the beach, they were horrified to see the sands black with soldiers, like colonies of ants and suddenly there appeared splashes of water in the sea ahead. It took a moment or two to realise that these were shells landing - their first experience of being under fire. Amidst this bombardment there were small cruisers and rowing boats overfilled with exhausted soldiers trying to get free of the surf-washed sands.

They went onto their slower cruising engines and carefully approached the beach to help. Gradually they got the knack and by evening they had helped a few hundred to get away. Then they decided it was time to report to Capt. Tennant. He gave Dreyer a hand-written note and told him to take it

directly to Admiral Ramsey in Dover, taking with him as many soldiers off the pier as he could carry. They managed about thirty and reached Dover at midnight. Having delivered their message they fell into their bunks, totally exhausted.

Next morning at 06.00 they were called to return to Dunkirk and report to Admiral Wake-Walker who was now acting as Flag Officer off-shore in Dunkirk Roads, flying his flag in the destroyer *Keith.* They found his ship in the middle of a lively air raid and as they approached, she was hit by a bomb amidships. They received a signal to come alongside, which was quite tricky, since she was listing, her rudder was jammed and she was going rather rapidly in a circle. They managed it, by going on the inside of the circle and they took off the Rear-Admiral, his staff officers and some wounded men. The Admiral asked to be taken to Dunkirk and, weaving amid the traffic and the bombs at 30 knots, they took him there and were told to wait.

While they were waiting, lying alongside a mine recovery vessel, Dreyer recalled the sight of a sailor peeling spuds and the captain eating bread and marmalade, quite unmoved by the chaos around them. From them

Sea Cadet Kevin Smith polishing the ship's bell in 1979

they obtained morphia, a morning paper and a tin hat to replace one they had lost overboard. When they told him how grateful they were he explained that he didn't like wearing a tin hat anyway, because it gave him a headache! The morphia was a blessing for their wounded and helped them to last out until they got medical attention. The Admiral returned and asked to be taken to Dover and Dawkins, the torpedoman, hoisted the Admiral's flag he had made by painting a St. George's cross on a dishcloth.

In the course of the next few days, *MTB 102* made a total of eight crossings of the channel in her role as the Admiral's flagship. On the night of 3rd June they went over to bring off Captain Tennant and two Generals - one of them General Alexander, and landed them at Dover at 02.00. They went again the next day and then, for the final time, on 5th June, taking Admiral Wake-Walker to supervise the departure of the last of the transports and the blocking of the harbour by the scuttling of some old merchant ships, before *MTB 102* returned to England.

Lieutenant Dreyer was then given command of a brand-new MTB, but he did command the *MTB 102* once more, for a brief week or two, in September 1942 when the King came to Portsmouth and they performed a waterborne 'march-past' for him in the Solent. In 1943 the ship was transferred to the army's 615 Water Transport company, RASC, renamed *Vimy* and used for target towing duties. Then, the following year, she had another moment of glory, when she was chosen to take Winston Churchill and General Eisenhower on a secret outing in the Solent to review the armada of ships assembled for the 'D'-Day landings. After the war *MTB 102*, like all small craft, was sold and converted into a private cruising boat. Her first civilian owner loved her and, having installed some less thirsty Perkins P6 diesel engines, cruised in her along the east coast of England and to the continent. Her next owner had plans to convert her into a houseboat but she was saved from this indignity by a local scout group who raised the money to buy her, together with land and moorings, as a water activities training base in Brundall, Norfolk, with the ambition of bringing *MTB 102* back to life as closely as possible to her original state.

At this point, the powers that look after famous old ships took a hand and sent Kelso Films to rescue her in 1976. They wanted an MTB for the film *The Eagle Has Landed* and offered to refurbish *102* for their purpose and on completion of the film return her to the scout group as a fully operational sea-going vessel. In 1977 she went to Holland to feature in the Dutch film *Soldier of Orange* where she re-enacted the activities of the MTBs off the east coast in World War II. As a sea scout training ship she has not only been used to teach navigation and seamanship, but has also taken part in the Queen's Silver Jubilee celebrations, reunions of Dunkirk Little Ships and on Navy Days. In 1983, major work was carried out on her decks and hull by Fred Newson of Oulton Broad and two years later, Perkins of Peterborough generously provided a pair of turbo-charged V8 engines. Two new gearboxes and propellers have been fitted and untold hours of voluntary work and monetary contributions have ensured that this veteran does not die.

The need to raise funds for this worthy veteran will never end, but hopefully nor will the generosity of people who appreciate that she is a part of our history which deserves to be preserved.

Built by Staniland in Hull to a design by Hyland, for James Ebenezer Lambe, *Cordelia* belonged to R.J.F. Julian when she left for Dunkirk on 29th May 1940. She was commanded by Sub-Lieut. C. A. Thompson, RNVR, and followed three formerly Belgian ships: the *Yser*, *Sambre* and *Ambleve*, - all four towed by a drifter described in the records as *G.R. 1740*, together with a whaler.

By 05.30 on 30th May they arrived off the beach west of La Panne and, for a time, had a Commodore on board. During the next five hours, together with the whaler, they ferried 300 troops from the beach to off-lying ships. Their port engine had already seized up when, to their dismay, their starboard propeller was fouled by some of the mass of flotsam which made navigation so hazardous at that time. The *G.R. 1740* came to the rescue and took the *Cordelia* in tow, back to Dover, where they arrived at 20.30 that night.

The account, from the Naval Historical Branch of the Ministry of Defence, is brief, matter-of fact and laconic. But, clearly, Sub-Lieut. Thompson and his crew passed an anxious, dangerous and sleepless 26 hours feverishly working to save three hundred lives while under fire, on a little pleasure boat, and took it all in their stride.

After the war, *Cordelia* was bought by a Mr Slack, whose son David remembers how she arrived by road at Stanilands painted in battleship grey, to be refurbished. Her original Ford Hyland 24 h.p. 4-cyl. petrol engines were replaced by two BMC Commodores.

In 1952, Cordelia re-lived her part in the evacuation of Dunkirk in the film Operation Dynamo, starring Jack Hawkins, who played the part of her wartime skipper and took the helm in

NAME:	Cordelia
TYPE:	Motor Vessel
LENGTH:	34ft 6ins
BEAM:	9ft 6ins
DISPLACEMENT:	10.93 tons
DRAFT:	3ft 6ins
ENGINES:	2 x 2.5 BMC Commodore
HULL CONSTR.:	Pitch pine on oak
BUILT BY:	Staniland & Co., Hull
YEAR BUILT:	1934

one of the earliest returns to the beaches and harbour of Dunkirk. Some years later she became the property of Mr J.K. Fuller who is getting her ready for the 50th Anniversary return to Dunkirk in 1990.

Motor Yacht Blue Bird II

The last of the three yachts owned by Sir Malcolm Campbell, holder of the world land and water speed records before the war, was *Blue Bird II*. His previous two boats, also called *Blue Bird,* - as were his record breaking cars and power-boats - were the 29-tonner, now called *Chico* and the 16-tonner *Bluebird of Chelsea*, described later in this book. All three, as it happened, went to Dunkirk in 1940.

NAME:	Blue Bird II
TYPE:	Motor Yacht
LENGTH:	103ft 7ins
BEAM:	20ft
DISPLACEMENT:	175 tons
DRAFT:	9.8ft
ENGINES:	2 Baudoin DP12 400 h.p.
HULL CONSTR.:	Steel
BUILT BY:	Goole Shipbuilding Co.
YEAR BUILT:	1938

Built by the Goole shipbuilding and Repairing Company, and designed by G.L. Watsons, the Scottish Naval Architects, it was to be an ocean-going yacht, capable of crossing the Atlantic to fulfil his dream to go treasure hunting in the Cocos Islands in the Pacific, - Robert Louis Stevenson's Treasure Islands. But, only a year after he took delivery of his splendid yacht, with its five cabins, its dining saloon panelled in English oak and walnut-panelled smoking room, war broke out and *Blue Bird*, was requisitioned . Although her participation at Dunkirk is recorded in A.D. Divine's book, no

more details survive. A Royal Navy tele-graphist, has left an interesting first-hand account of some of her crew and her activities. At that time, she was engaged in the H.M. Customs Examination Service with a comp-lement of two R.N.R. officers and 16 crew.

It was spring 1941 and *Blue Bird's* Examination Station was west of the Bar Light Vessel, ob-serving the approaches to the Mersey Main Channel. They spent three days at a time at sea, during which the Examination Officer, assisted by the deck crew, checked on all traffic into the port of Liverpool. There were frequent air raids on Liverpool docks and the Birkenhead shipyards. As soon as the alert was sounded, *Blue Bird* would cast off from the river pontoon and take up station in mid-stream to look out for enemy mines dropped from the air, and for ships approaching by sea. Once she narrowly missed being blown up by a bomb which, had it not failed to explode, would have blown them sky-high.

In September 1941 *Blue Bird* was posted to Londonderry, N. Ireland to patrol the coast of Ulster and Eire to intercept 'neutral' cargo vessels and to identify coasters in the channel approaches. This left a fair time for fishing. Bob McKenzie, the coxswain, was a trawlerman in peace time and many of the lower ranks had been fishermen too. They soon rigged up an improvised trawl, a longline with 100 hooks at a time and hand lines to catch mackerel - all of which provided useful income, or currency for barter with the good people of Eire, when they passed in and out of Lough Foyle. A break in their routine was provided by their periodic visits to Belfast Lough for 'de-gaussing' - a process for making the ship less susceptible to magnetic mines. After the war, *Blue Bird* was de-commissioned, but by then Sir Malcolm Campbell was too ill to

realise his dream of going treasure hunting in her. In 1948 he died and five years later, *Blue Bird* was sold to Jean Louis Renault, the French car maker, who owned her for 25 years, changed her name to *Janick* and added crew's quarters on the foredeck. She cruised extensively in the Mediterranean and was eventually sold to Mr E. Colberg, who kept her at Long Beach, California.

This is where Bob Harvey-George and his wife Sheila heard she was for sale. They succeeded in buying her and sailed back to Cornwall, where they arrived in June 1986 after a five-week voyage, proving her seaworthiness whilst avoiding the first hurricane of the year in the Pacific. Since then, the ship has completed a major process of restoration. She has gone back to her old name: *Blue Bird*, and closer to her original design. Large areas of her deck have been covered with teak planking recovered from a ship which sank in the Bristol Channel in 1917. Her rigging, panelling and paintwork have all been restored and modern technology and comforts have been introduced discreetly without spoiling the charm of a more leisurely and elegant age.

She is based in Scotland and has revealed the beauty of the coasts, rivers and lochs of her environment to her passengers in a unique and delightful way. Her polished plaque with the inscription: "DUNKIRK 1940" displays the battle honour of her illustrious past to all who sail in her.

overboard by an accident in the heat of the evacuation, later identified *Thelmar* as the boat which picked him up.

The rest of *Thelmar's* war was spent as part of the floating garrison at Sheerness, and local fishermen recall her being moored just off the River Swale. The Navy stripped out her whole fore-section to give maximum space for carrying provisions, and the fixtures and fittings they removed were put into store. The idea was that after the war, owners should reclaim what was theirs. Millson was so incensed when his boat came back in such a dreadful condition that he did not bother, but sold her at once. Ten

T he Sittingbourne Shipbuilding Company of Rochester, Kent was more used to building barges when, in 1936, they made the motor yacht *Thelmar*. She may have been an apprentice piece, for her design was very basic. She was bought a year later, new and already named, by Claude E. Millson, a gentleman farmer of Goudhurst, Kent. He was a member of the Medway Yacht Club who enjoyed hunting for his dinner with a shotgun, from a punt in the marshes. He found *Thelmar* for sale at Harty Ferry on the river Swale. In the years before war broke out he had an aft cabin added, at Kirklands boatyard, because the ladies complained of getting wet in the bumpy Medway, and he only enjoyed one holiday aboard his ship, when he went to Burnham-on-Crouch.

Thelmar was at Rochester when war broke out. By then, Millson was a Paymaster Lieut., RNR, and he eventually finished his service as a Lieut. Commander. He used *Thelmar* to collect paysheets from other boats commandeered by the Navy, and she is listed as having been sent to Dunkirk. Indeed, one old fisherman, knocked

NAME:	Thelmar
TYPE:	Motor Yacht
LENGTH:	31ft
BEAM:	9ft
DISPLACEMENT:	6 tons
DRAFT:	3ft 6ins
ENGINES:	Twin BMC Vedette
HULL CONSTR.:	Carvel
BUILT BY:	Sittingbourne Ship-
YEAR BUILT:	building. Co.,1936

owners later, this decision caused problems for Stewart Sands who now owns her at Canvey Island, Essex, because he could not replace the missing pieces. Until 1989 she was out of the water for eight years, while she was painstakingly restored to her pre-war appearance. But exactly what did the fore-section look like? Not even her brief moment of fame when she appeared in the film *Dunkirk* was of help to him. But despite all obstacles he has restored her beautifully, and with the promise of some 1936 engines, which he will rebuild and install, *Thelmar* will become another time capsule in the A.D.L.S. fleet.

When we came to look into the part *Margo II* played at Dunkirk, we could not find her name in the official records, but then we saw a letter written to the Association by a yacht builder on the south coast who remembered her setting out at the time of Dunkirk, although no precise log was kept of her movements. She was once owned by Walter Young, the inventor of 'Young's Course Corrector', who installed in her the compass from the Wellington Bomber he flew during the war. He got her from a Harley Street physician together with a chest of Irish linen, hand-embroidered with the name : *Margo II*.

After he sold her, she fell into the hands of a company which encountered hard times. Richard Young heard about it and was able to buy back *Margo* from the Official Receiver in 1971. Though he sold her fifteen years ago, he clearly still has a soft spot for the Little Ship. He remembers the remarkable fact that every one of her deck planks ran unbroken, the whole length of the ship and, although she had no main frames, she was uncommonly strong. Her pitch pine was of the kind used in the decks of

NAME:	Margo II
TYPE:	Motor Yacht
LENGTH:	34ft
BEAM:	10ft
DISPLACEMENT:	7.30 tons
DRAFT:	3ft 6ins
ENGINES:	2 x 3.4 diesel
HULL CONSTR.:	Carvel pitch pine on oak
BUILT BY:	Royal Boat Bldg. Co.,
YEAR BUILT:	Poole, 1931

the old Thames sailing barges, matured in water for up to 40 years before it was used. Her next owner, from 1974, was Terry Holdaway, who kept her on the Thames at Putney in winter and cruised all over Europe in summer from her moorings at Rochester in Kent. He estimates that he made 30 trips to the Continent and once reached Putney from Calais in 9½ hours. In 1976, off Broadstairs, they rescued the crew of *Tamaroa II*, a converted ship's lifeboat, but were unable to save the sinking ship.

Margo II now belongs to Geoffrey and Duncan Prater, who have joined the A.D.L.S. and hope to join in the reunion at Dunkirk in 1990.

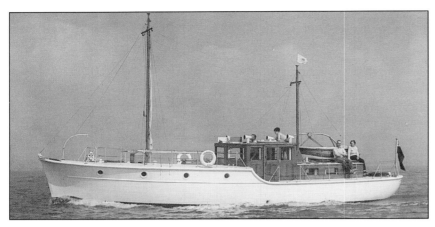

NAME:	Aberdonia
TYPE:	Motor Yacht
LENGTH:	48ft
BEAM:	11ft 3ins
DISPLACEMENT:	20 tons
DRAFT:	4ft 6ins
ENGINES:	2 Ford diesels
HULL CONSTR.:	Carvel Burma Teak
BUILT BY:	Thornycroft
YEAR BUILT:	1935

Ships, like people, seem to be divided into those who never budge from the place where they were born, and others, by contrast, which are only happy when they are on the move and sometimes end up at the other end of the world. The working barges of the east coast of England and the Medway have never gone far from the yards where they were built and the Thames passenger launches and Gentlemen's cruisers of the thirties still carry on in the tradition established in that leisurely age before the clouds of war gathered over Europe and, like their owners were called to serve their country.

Aberdonia is one of the many Thornycroft cruisers built at Hampton just before the war which went to Dunkirk where she is thought to have made four trips to the beaches even before they had time to repaint her in battleship grey. She was then requisitioned to work as a patrol boat in the Royal Navy. At that time they renamed her *Navigator* and she is known to have worked with the RN mine-sweepers and took sealed orders from the Admiralty to convoys lying off Shoeburyness and Deal.

Once, at this time, she narrowly escaped destruction when a German bomber was shot down and the pilot bravely attempted to crash into our ships as he went down into the sea. Wreckage hit the starboard side of *Aberdonia* and thirty years later Jack Cook, who then owned her, removed scorched timbers during her restoration.

Now, *Aberdonia*, after following owners to the south and north of England, has come back to Hampton, where she hailed from in 1935 and her graceful lines still draw admiring glances when Paul King, her owner sets out with his Dunkirk flag flying at her masthead.

Passenger Boat New Britannic

Nowadays the Bryher excursion ship *Commodore*, serving local residents and holidaymakers in the Isles of Scilly, is limited to carrying just 100 passengers. In a safety-minded age, that is the maximum for any passenger vessel around these tricky waters. But before World War II, when she operated in the Channel Islands and bore the name *New Britannic*, she was licensed to carry 117.

Not that they would have taken much notice of these limitations when coxswain W. Mathews of the Royal Navy took her over from her owner, Charlie Priddle of Ramsgate to go to Dunkirk. Built to carry a full load of passengers in safety, with easy access to her 54ft. open deck, a shallow 3ft. 6in. draft and a powerful 65 h.p. Lister engine to pull her clear of the sands, she was the ideal boat for the job. No wonder she is credited with lifting 3,000 men off the beaches. No doubt she ran a shuttle service from La Panne to the Destroyers and transport ships which had to stand off the treacherous sandbanks.

After the war she belonged to a Capt. Robinson, who had her working out of Ramsgate harbour and then sold her to a fisherman in Weymouth. At that time a 200 h.p. General Motors engine was installed. This is where Leonard Jenkins first saw her. His son Kenneth, of Bryher Boat Services, is her present owner. He took her to the Isles of Scilly, off the western tip of Cornwall and installed the two engines, which are a minimum requirement for any passenger vessel that ventures out into the Atlantic to Bishop's Rock Light.

All summer he takes holidaymakers around these beautiful islands to enjoy the scenery, the birdlife and the seals, which are still plentiful here. Each week there is some special event like the gig races, when hundred-year-old

NAME:	New Britannic
TYPE:	Passenger Boat
LENGTH:	54ft
BEAM:	15ft 6ins
DISPLACEMENT:	22 tons
DRAFT:	3ft 6ins
ENGINES:	Ford 4 cyl. + 6 cyl.
HULL CONSTR.:	Carvel Pitch pine on oak
BUILT BY:	Frank Maynard, Chiswick
YEAR BUILT:	1930

boats, propelled by just six paddles each, race against each other. They were originally built when this skill was a matter of survival - taking out a pilot to a ship, relieving the lighthouse or going to the aid of a shipwreck. Now they do it for entertainment, watched by visitors from a ship which once took part in a unique race for the survival of an army.

Motor Yacht Thame

Launched in October 1909, at the yard of Gill & Sons at Rochester in Kent, the month they laid the keel of the *Titanic*, the Port of London Authority's new survey launch was named *Jean*. They re-named her *Thame* and with her two powerful Bergius paraffin engines she became the maid of all work in the world's busiest port. When the call went out in May 1940 to collect every serviceable boat on the river Thames, *Thame* was already on war service, with a gun mounted on her foredeck, as an inshore minesweeper. She was detailed to collect the Little Ships at various points on the river and tow or escort them to Ramsgate and Dover.

Channel to France in her. As they passed through the Port of London, she was instantly recognized by her former friends and colleagues and the new *Thame* would dip her ensign in salute. There was some light-hearted banter from his old Royal Navy friends when John replaced the original wooden one-man box on her deck with a larger charthouse, which they referred to as 'the chicken coop'. Soon the Sharman-Courtneys began a family and, regretfully, had to sell *Thame II*.

This proved to be the beginning of the end for their much-loved old vessel. Many people are attracted by the idea of owning an old boat, - just like a dog,

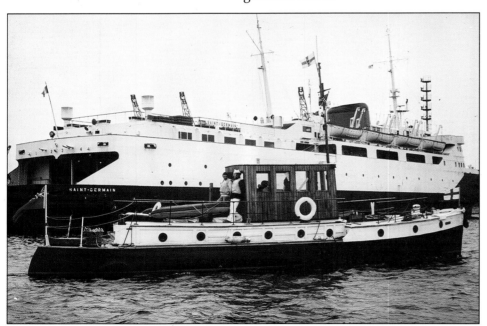

Thame, setting out for the wreath-laying ceremony at Dunkirk in 1975

NAME:	Thame
TYPE:	Motor Yacht
LENGTH:	52ft
BEAM:	10ft
DISPLACEMENT:	unknown
DRAFT:	4ft 6ins
ENGINES:	52 h.p. diesel
HULL CONSTR.:	Carvel Pitch pine on oak
BUILT BY:	Gill & Sons
YEAR BUILT:	1909

After the war, in 1952, she was replaced and sold out of service. So she had to relinquish her name to her successor and assume the name *Thame II*. For twenty years she served as a house boat until, in 1972, Lieut.Cmdr. John Sharman-Courtney found her at Teddington and spent a large sum of money to rebuild her into a very comfortable home for himself and his wife. They enjoyed her for five years and frequently sailed across the

or a cat. At the time they don't realize that this involves responsibilities as well as pleasures. So, when they find it isn't all fun, they become neglectful. For old boats, this can be fatal. Soon water gets in. At the very least, they start to decay. At the worst, one stormy night in winter, they sink. This is what happened to *Thame II*. Eventually, the Thames Water Authority, which is not unfamiliar with this problem, had to raise her, because she became a hazard to navigation. For two years, she sat on a barge at Sunbury and she was finally taken away and broken up.

Not a pleasant end for a ship with plenty of life left in her. Now this record is her only memorial.

The shapely hull of Walton Yacht and Launch Co.'s latest 40-ft. cruiser, designed by C.W. Burnard, AINA, was first seen at the Motor Boat Exhibition at Olympia in 1933. With her black-enamelled topsides, graceful bow, counter stern and well-rounded transom she looked business-like and very handsome. The hull was of mahogany on oak frames and she was rigged as a staysail schooner, powered by an Ailsa Craig engine. Her price? - £950 . . and there was no Value Added Tax to spoil it in those days! But then, her first owner, who called her *Betty*, wasn't allowed to enjoy her for very long. Like parents who raised children to maturity just before the war, only to lose them into the forces - and maybe for ever - it must have broken his heart when she went.

Betty was on the Thames in May, 1940 and was gathered up with all her kind to go to Dunkirk. Later, she was equipped with an Oerlikon gun on her foredeck and served as a patrol boat on the east coast of England.

After the war she became a civilian again and changed her name to *Nimrod*. For many years, her home port was Waldringfield, but later she moved to Woodbridge in Suffolk where she became sadly neglected.

Happily she was rescued by the well-known boatbuilder Ian Brown of Rowhedge, near Colchester in Essex, who restored her, with loving care, for his own enjoyment. At that time, she also underwent her third change of name, this time to *Nyula*.

NAME:	Betty
TYPE:	Motor yacht
LENGTH:	40ft
BEAM:	9ft 6ins
DISPLACEMENT:	12 tons
DRAFT:	3ft 6ins
ENGINES:	Mercedez Benz 42 h.p.
HULL CONSTR.:	Mahogany on oak
BUILT BY:	Walton Yacht & Launch Wks.
YEAR BUILT:	Shepperton 1933

In 1976, *Nyula* was sold and taken to Chichester, on the south coast. This is where P.M.A. Packard bought her, unaware of her Dunkirk history. This was only established when papers from the Admiralty were released in 1985, which made it possible to identify her as *Betty*.. Now she belongs to the Association of Dunkirk Little Ships and attends all their reunions.

Paddle Steamer **Princess Elizabeth**

On the Thames in London, in 1971

NAME:	Princess Elizabeth
TYPE:	Paddle Steamer
LENGTH:	195ft
BEAM:	24ft
DISPLACEMENT:	388 tons
DRAFT:	not known
ENGINES:	Oil-burning
HULL CONSTR.:	Pitch pine/oak
BUILT BY:	Day, Summers, Northam
YEAR BUILT:	1927

Built in 1927, for the Red Funnel Line, as a ferry between Southampton and the Isle of Wight, *Princess Elizabeth*, named to commemorate the birth of our present Queen, was the successor to the paddle steamer *Queen Mary*, which was lost in 1919, after serving in the Royal Navy throughout World War I, and finally in Malta, as a minesweeper.

After twelve years as a ferry and excursion steamer in Bournemouth and the Solent area, at the outset of World War II, *Princess Elizabeth* was taken over by the Admiralty and converted into a minesweeper (No. J111). A year later, she was on her way to Dunkirk where her first task was to clear the mines from the narrow channel off the beaches, which was the only escape route. Only then could the work of embarking the waiting troops begin. Many of her sister ships, including the *Brighton Belle*, the *Devonia* and *Gracie Fields* were sunk at that time.

On her first journey, on 29th May 1940, she and her fellow minesweepers embarked, in all, 3,415 troops. One of them, the paddle-minesweeper *Oriole*, had deliberately beached herself early that morning, to allow 2,500 troops to pass over her decks to other ships, before she refloated on the next high tide that evening. When *Princess Elizabeth* came again, on Saturday, 1st

June, she arrived in the middle of a furious air attack when, among others, the destroyers *Keith* and *Baselisk* and the minesweepers *Skipjack* and *Brighton Queen* were sunk. By evening, the fog

174

came down and *Princess Elizabeth* had to return to Dover. She made a third trip in the night of 3rd/4th June, joining in the last desperate effort to rescue some of the remaining troops. Among others, she brought back to Dover 500 Frenchmen that day. Before the end of the war, she served as an anti-aircraft vessel. Then, in 1946, she returned to her civilian occupation

When she was superceded as an excursion boat by more modern vessels, like many old timers, she enjoyed brief fame as a film star, and appeared in the Walt Disney film *The Castaways*. In 1966, another plan to keep her gainfully employed was to turn her into a casino, but this did not materialise. But in 1970, she was moored just up-stream of London Bridge as a restaurant. Finally, in January 1988, it was reported that she had been bought by the French typographical group ADAT to be moored on the Seine just outside Paris as the first museum of typographical art. Part of the ship was to be reserved for exhibiting details of her own remarkable history.

But when we went to Paris to see her, no-one knew of her whereabouts and we just hope that she will, one day, emerge to demonstrate, once more, her remarkable talent for survival.

Princess Elizabeth in the Solent, in 1927

Built by J. White & Son on the Isle of Wight during the early months of World War I, with a steam engine, the naval pinnace *MB 278* was delivered to Harland & Wolff, Belfast, to join her first mother ship, *HMS Sir John Moore*, in 1915. Her next ship, *HMS Raglan*, was sunk off the coast of Imbros, but *MB 278* survived and after five years in Malta, joined the battleship *Iron Duke* in the Mediterranean. Then she went to *HMS Barnham* and later to *HMS Resolution*, in the Atlantic. In 1929, she had her first major refit in Malta and received a new 22hp Farry engine before joining the battleship *HMS Queen Elizabeth* in 1930.

Just before World War II, she was assigned to *HMS Erebus* and she nearly missed Dunkirk when she was crushed in an accident in Portsmouth dockyard and sank, in March 1940. When hauled to the surface, her hull was badly damaged but she was quickly repaired and received a new engine. She has the scars to prove her Dunkirk service: a row of bullet holes made by a German machine gun in her hull, visible until her recent refit.

When the Admiralty disposed of *MB 278* in 1948, Thomas Duffy bought her for £125 and when he died in 1983, his son took over. She has been renamed *Susan K.*, much time and effort has been spent restoring her and she is worth it. When the Admiralty sold the ship, her description did not do her justice: ' *round bilge ex-Naval hull of double-skin mahogany with mahogany shelter aft. Fair condition. No engine.*' - In fact, she is of double-skin teak on rock elm and oak frames, with a third skin fitted internally athwartships. She has five steel bulkheads and when her present refit is complete, should last another hundred years - with a lot of love and care, as is due to a boat with such a history.

NAME:	M B 2 7 8
TYPE:	Naval Pinnace
LENGTH:	30ft
BEAM:	8ft 3ins
DISPLACEMENT:	8.85 tons
DRAFT:	3ft 6ins
ENGINES:	Perkins diesel 4.108
HULL CONSTR.:	Teak on Rock elm and oak
BUILT BY:	J. White & Son, Cowes, I.O.W.
YEAR BUILT:	1914

Motor Yacht **Firefly**

Just twenty-six feet overall and with a 2ft 10in draft and a minimum-sized single engine supplemented by a couple of sails, *Firefly* is one of the tiniest and one of the loveliest of the Little Ships. No wonder the Greens, her present owners, love her dearly.

They keep her in immaculate order at Walton-on-Naze and rarely go further than 15 miles, to Woodbridge, on the beautiful river Deben, "to get a few oysters and see the birdlife and seals."

Yet, *Firefly* got to Dunkirk in the midst of fierce enemy attack, by bombs, machinegun fire and artillery shelling, through minefields and tide-swept sandbanks. Lumps of shrapnel were found in her port side during recent renovation to prove it. When her old varnish was removed, they also found

NAME:	Firefly
TYPE:	Motor Yacht
LENGTH:	26ft
BEAM:	7ft 9ins
DISPLACEMENT:	5.71 tons
DRAFT:	2ft 10ins
ENGINES:	1.5 diesel
HULL CONSTR.:	Carvel
BUILT BY:	Cole Wiggins Ltd
YEAR BUILT:	1923

a whole lot of signatures, which were thought to be of her wartime crew, or the soldiers they rescued - like those of prisoners in an ancient dungeon, determined to leave their mark, in case they never come out alive. But Firefly's story has a happy ending: she is in an idyllic place and in good hands, with a history to be proud of.

Admirals Barge Count Dracula

Re-launching Count Dracula
after her restoration in 1986

NAME:	Count Dracula
TYPE:	Admiral's Barge
LENGTH:	50ft
BEAM:	9ft 6ins
DISPLACEMENT:	27 tons
DRAFT:	3ft 6ins
ENGINES:	Perkins diesel
HULL CONSTR.:	Teak on oak
BUILT BY:	German Imperial Navy
YEAR BUILT:	1913

Getting out of tight corners was nothing new to the *Count Dracula* when Cmdr. Ewart Brookes, DSC,RNVR, took her to Dunkirk. She started life in 1913, powered by a steam engine, in the Imperial German Navy. Kaiser Wilhelm II gave her to Admiral von Hipper who took her as his admiral's barge to every ship he sailed in. He used her when he left the *Lutzow*, just before she sank in the battle of Jutland in 1916, to transfer to the battleship *Moeltke*. Later he took her with him to the Grand Battle Cruiser *Hindenburg* and that could have been her end, when the German fleet, having surrendered, was scuppered at Scapa Flow in 1918. But a young German sailor could not bear to see the beautiful boat go down, so he released her from her davit winches and as the *Hindenburg* sank, she floated free and was salvaged by the Royal Navy.

She was a private yacht until her owner, Carl Greiner, sent his son Alan to take her to Ramsgate, where Cmdr. Brookes took charge. He had already spent two days and a night at the

beaches and his previous ship was sunk under him.

He was delighted at the speed and power of *Count Dracula* and he took two 35ft lifeboats in tow. They were loaded to the gunwales with troops and *Count Dracula* lifted 702 British as well as 10 Belgian soldiers. She ended up quite well armed, having collected, with her troops, three Brens and one French Hochkiss machine gun, which enabled them to have a shot or two at the Stuka dive bombers.

In Cmdr. Brookes' own words, "I finally brought her back to Ramsgate with 38 soldiers on board, Royal Engineers, who had spent all the week on the beach by the Casino, building a temporary pier of Thames barges."

"I felt rather pleased at the last little jab because at midnight on June 1st, the order was passed: 'all small boats back to England under escort.' - German 'E-Boats' had come down the coast. The intention was to abandon the Royal Engineers and to allow them to get into the town of Dunkirk as best they could - *if* they could. A difficult job then, because the Germans were close to the beach and had it under machine gun fire."

"A Mr. Jeffries from Brighton (a garage owner, I believe) and myself decided to take a chance and see if we could get the Royal Engineers off. We did. All of

The German battle cruiser
Hindenburg, *27,000 tons, 213 m*
in 1915. Scuttled: 21st June, 1919

them. And as they came away, they were exchanging fire with German troops in lorries or armoured cars. A close thing. I received a reprimand for leaving the convoy of small ships, but as it was one of many reprimands I had during the war for doing odd things, I didn't worry a great deal."

After the war, *Count Dracula* went back to the Greiner family, who eventually sold her and lost touch over the next 20 years until, one day, Mrs Greiner rediscovered her being used as a houseboat on the Upper Thames. This is how the boat came into membership of the ADLS. She joined the 1980 return to Dunkirk and was then sold to Richard Huggett who spent five years getting her into shape for the return in 1985. He received an inscribed tankard from Vice-Admiral Sir John Roxborough KCB, CBE, DSO,. DSC, for saving the old lady. But the yard had left out some keel bolts and a few days later, *Count Dracula* sank. But she was soon lifted and is now in excellent shape, owned by Mike Hamby.

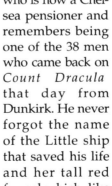

The plaque presented to Count Dracula *by the Royal Engineers*

There was a strange misunderstanding about *Count Dracula's* connection with the Royal Engineers. When Lt.Col. Davies, commanding 38 Engineer Regiment was told that there was a ship which was reported to have gallantly rescued '38 Royal Engineers under fire', he thought that this referred to his unit. In fact, of course, they meant *38 men* of the Royal Engineers. To compound the confusion, the 38 men rescued were also members of 38 Field Company, Royal Engineers! By this time, Col. Davies' interest and admiration had been aroused and he was determined for his Unit to honour the Little Ship.

So, 46 years after the event, *Count Dracula* received a plaque, now displayed on the bulkhead of her admiral's saloon, commemorating her valiant deeds. Present at the ceremony when the plaque was presented, was Sgt. Chalmers, of the Royal Engineers who is now a Chelsea pensioner and remembers being one of the 38 men who came back on *Count Dracula* that day from Dunkirk. He never forgot the name of the Little ship that saved his life and her tall red funnel which, like much of her timbers and deck gear remains unchanged since the day she was launched at Wilhelmshaven, on the North Sea coast of Germany, by the Kaiser in 1913.

The service to rededicate Count Dracula *with Sgt. Chalmers on board of the ship that rescued him*

Being an island race, the British have always been seafarers - for trade, exploration, conquest, defence and, during the last 150 years, for pleasure. Many types of yacht derive from working boats. *Frances,* or *Lady Frances* as she is now, is a barge yacht. Barges were developed to carry freight on inland waterways; of strong construction and shallow draft, they can sit comfortably on sand or mud when the tide goes out. This made them ideal vessels for the beaches of Dunkirk. One post-war owner of *Lady Frances* was at

Dunkirk, but not aboard her. He was protecting her from above. Cmdr. Charles Lamb, DSO, DSC, RN, whose wartime exploits are quite as remarkable as the story of Dunkirk, describes in his book: *War in a String Bag* what it was like to fly in his Fleet Air Arm Swordfish above the stream of ships plying between Dunkirk and the British ports of Dover and Ramsgate. "..from the air it looked as though it would be possible to use them as stepping stones to cross the Channel."

The out-dated 90mph Swordfish bi-plane carried a formidable armament, including an aerial torpedo capable of sinking a battleship. At Dunkirk, Charles Lamb, flying from Detling airfield in Kent, helped to protect the evacuation fleet from German E-boats, which came down the coast from the north to attack them. Together with fighters of the RAF he helped to drive off German bombers which came in waves, sometimes 100 strong, to destroy our army on the beaches and at sea. The part played by the RAF and Fleet Air Arm at this time has been greatly underestimated. Outgunned and outnumbered, they inflicted on the enemy losses of 4:1. On 1st June alone, they shot down 78 German bombers on their way to attack the embarking army on the beach and at sea.

After Dunkirk, Charles Lamb became one of the first Pathfinders, dropping flares to guide our bombers onto their targets. Then, in the Mediterranean, he took part in the most famous Fleet Air Arm action, the Battle of Taranto, when twenty of our Swordfish virtually destroyed the Italian fleet. He later flew from a secret base in the Albanian mountains, dropping and picking up our agents behind enemy lines, and from an airfield in Malta to

NAME:	Frances
TYPE:	Barge Yacht
LENGTH:	48ft
BEAM:	12ft 6ins
DISPLACEMENT:	15 tons
DRAFT:	3ft 6ins
ENGINES:	Twin BMC 2.2 diesels
HULL CONSTR.:	Oak on oak
BUILT BY:	J. Howard, Maldon
YEAR BUILT:	1909

attack ships supplying Rommel's Afrika Korps. After a year as a POW of the Vichy French, he served in the Far East. On his aircraft-carrier's flight deck, while preparing to take off to intercept a Kamikaze aircraft, a propeller severed his right leg. Despite this dreadful injury, he went back to flying with a permanent commission in the Royal Navy. His connection with Dunkirk was re-established when he bought *Lady Frances* after the war. He

was delighted to own one of the Little Ships of Dunkirk, having last seen them in action from the air and he became the first Hon. Admiral of the ADLS when it was formed. He helped to obtain for it the privilege of flying the Cross of St. George from the Jackstaff and, defaced by the arms of Dunkirk, from the cross-trees. Together, they went back to Dunkirk for the first time on the 25th anniversary in 1965 to pay tribute to those who gave their lives there, to the City of Dunkirk rebuilt after its dreadful destruction and to the Little Ships which earned their place in history during those nine amazing days in 1940.

Since his death in May 1981 *Lady Frances* belongs to Charles Lamb's son Jeremy, whose mother Jo hopes to sail with him among the fleet of Little Ships which will return to Dunkirk for the fiftieth anniversary in 1990.

John Lamb, hoisting the Cross of St. George on the Jackstaff

Cmdr. C. Lamb, DSO, DSC, RN watching a fly-past in his honour of a Royal Navy Swordfish, to celebrate the publication of his book: War in a String Bag

Motor Yacht Dab II

Colonel Hardy was incensed when the Royal Navy simply informed him by telephone that they had taken his motor yacht *Dab II* from the canal basin at Heybridge, on the river Blackwater in Essex, to take part in Operation Dynamo. His anger did not stem from a lack of patriotic fervour, but from the understandable feeling that he should have been given a chance to go with her. In fact, few of the owners went with the Little Ships.

NAME:	D a b I I
TYPE:	Motor Yacht
LENGTH:	52ft
BEAM:	12ft 7ins
DISPLACEMENT:	31.94 tons
DRAFT:	3ft 4ins
ENGINES:	2 x 100 h.p. Perkins SM6
HULL CONSTR.:	Carvel Pitch pine on oak
BUILT BY:	J.W. Brooke & Co. Ltd.
YEAR BUILT:	Lowestoft, 1931

Most were commanded and manned by the Royal Navy. *Dab II* was taken to Dunkirk by Lieut. R. W. Thompson, RNVR, who crossed the Channel no less than three times in six days. On his last return journey, he brought back a load of Dutch soldiers, who came from Breda in Holland and had fought a gallant rearguard action westward to Dunkirk, driven by the weight of the German advance. Painted battleship grey, *Dab II* served as a patrol boat until she was returned to Col. Hardy, who then decided that her name was unsuitable for a ship of her size and distinguished war record. But he thought it might be unlucky to change a ship's name altogether. So he called her *Breda*, which ingeniously retained all the letters in her original name and commemorated the Dutch soldiers she had rescued.

Since then, *Breda* has had a number of owners in Wales, Norfolk and Surrey and has cruised extensively, through the French canals to the Mediterranean. Peter and Lesley Farrant have used her as their home since 1974 and have taken her to France, Belgium, Holland and the Channel Islands. In 1988 *Breda* had another major refit with new beams and decks. The saloon and galley have also been entirely renovated by Mr Bowley, a boatbuilder at Twickenham. She is ready now for the return to Dunkirk in 1990.

Dab II, in centre of picture, lying in Ramsgate harbour after her return from Dunkirk

The Little Ships came in all shapes and sizes, from pleasure steamers to rowing boats. The most unlikely rescue ship to cross the Channel was the 30ft Thames motor launch *Lady Isabelle*. With her hull and deck of polished mahogany and her cockpit furnished with cane chairs, she turned many an envious eye when their chauffeur took her owners in style along the river to the shops in Staines. If the sun was too fierce for their fair complexions, or if it began to rain, he would simply erect the awning on her chrome-plated stanchions.

The battle-weary soldiers must have cheered as *Lady Isabelle* arrived on La Panne beach amidst heavy shellfire. Driven by her powerful 6-cylinder Gray engine she could cut through calm water at 12 knots but had the Channel been rough, she would not have got beyond Ramsgate breakwater. Her owners never forgave the boatyard which maintained her for letting her be taken away. When she came back, they changed their yard.

It is strange how quickly ships deteriorate and how soon dedicated owners can restore them. In 1960, after she was left lying in a field, George Bailey bought *Lady Isabelle's* hull for just £25. He re-named her *Geba* (the first two letters of his first and second name) and added a cabin - which some would think a desecration. To keep the water out of her leaking hull, he sheathed it in fibreglass. Her next two owners modified her further and changed her name twice before Dr. Robert Cowley bought her in 1960 for £600. Her fibreglass was peeling off and she was leaking so badly that he had to keep an automatic bilge pump going permanently while he cruised the inland waterways over the next eight years. A much travelled boat, winning prizes for 'adventurous cruising', she bumped her keel on the

NAME:	Lady Isabelle
TYPE:	Motor Launch
LENGTH:	30ft
BEAM:	6ft 6ins
DISPLACEMENT:	3.5 tons
DRAFT:	18ins
ENGINES:	Gray six
HULL CONSTR.:	Carvel
BUILT BY:	H Gibbs, Teddington
YEAR BUILT:	1930

stones of the Severn above Stourport, beached in the shallows on the Thames above Lechlade and went down to the sea to roll on the tideway. She even ventured down the river Trent and on the Leeds and Liverpool Canal. In 1981, began a restoration programme, completed by Peter Freebody back on the Thames, to bring her faithfully back to her original appearance. The fibreglass was removed, as was the unsightly cabin. An original 1934 Gray six engine was fitted. Now, since 1988, John and Rosemary Richards proudly keep her at Shepperton, looking every bit a Lady and as new.

Motor Yacht Surrey

Raymond Baxter, fighter pilot, author and famous broadcaster, had a dream in 1963. He wanted to own a gentleman's motor yacht for cruising the River Thames between Lechlade and the estuary - with, perhaps an occasional venture up the Medway. After a frustrated love affair with a boat called *Nomad*, which was too far gone for him to undertake her restoration, he found a boat which changed his life. But let him tell his own story:

'I was driving back, early one evening, from a broadcasting job in the West Country. My route took me through Staines. Whenever I drove along Packhorse Road towards the centre of town, I always looked left across the river, in the direction of Stanley Timms' boatyard and moorings which, in those days, one could glimpse briefly from the road, between the buildings and the railway bridge. And there, framed as in a snap-shot, I saw something which quite literally took my breath away. It was 'my' *Nomad*, riding elegantly to her mooring, pristine and immaculate, the evening sun glinting on her white hull and green deck and picking out the glow of burnished brass. To have restored to such splendour the drab hull to which I had so recently bid a sad farewell would have been nothing short of a miracle. I immediately abandoned my homeward journey, turned left over Staines Bridge and sought the approach road to the yard which I had previously always visited by water.'

'As luck would have it, Mr Timms himself was still at work or, to be more precise, I found him quietly contemplating his domain, meerschaum pipe as ever clenched firmly between his teeth. Feeling by now slightly foolish, I babbled out my tale to which he listened politely."

"Oh, you mean *L'Orage*", he said, "yes - lovely, isn't she. Belongs to a bank manager over at Strawberry Hill. His pride and joy. She went to Dunkirk, you know. Would you like to have a look at her? I'm sure he wouldn't mind".

'Sure enough, there in the cockpit was the highly polished brass plate bearing the legend 'Dunkirk 1940'. I had found my dream boat. To learn that she was also one of the heroic Little Ships was

NAME:	Surrey
TYPE:	Motor Yacht
LENGTH:	29.5ft
BEAM:	8.5ft
DISPLACEMENT:	5.73 tons
DRAFT:	3ft
ENGINES:	Petrol BMC Navigator 37 h.p.
HULL CONSTR.:	Carvel Mahogany on oak
BUILT BY:	Boats&Cars, Kingston Ltd
YEAR BUILT:	1938/9

almost beyond belief. But she belonged to another! I left Stanley Timms my telephone number. "If ever she comes on to the market you will let me know?" I said forlornly. And within a month she was mine! The agreed price was £1,150 including her sturdy copper-cleated clinker-built dinghy.'

'At the time, how could I have guessed that *L'Orage* would become such an important factor in the lives of my family and myself for more than a quarter of a century and that, because of her, we would become closely involved with people and events beyond my wildest flights of fantasy?'

What happened then has already been told in the Introduction to this book. Raymond Baxter, together with Commander Charles Lamb and John Knight, founded the Association of Dunkirk Little Ships, whose Commodore he became. They organised the 25th Anniversary Return to Dunkirk and became responsible for the encouragement which has kept so many of these wonderful craft alive.

Surrey had been re-named *L'Orage* by her first post-war owner and *in* common with other owners of Dunkirk ships, Raymond has made every effort to keep *L'Orage* in perfect

L'Orage, returning from Dunkirk in 1980, flying her Admiral's flag.

Two pictures, showing the restoration work carried out on L'Orage

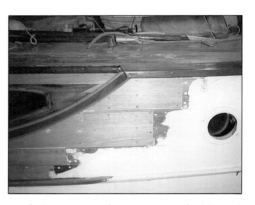

order. Like many an old lady who, despite honourable wrinkles, takes pride in her appearance, she looks more attractive than she did when young - as befits the Admiral's flagship: - since Charles Lamb died, Raymond has become the Hon. Admiral of the ADLS.

Wooden boats, unlike modern fibreglass ones, are made of a material which is subject to the elements. Out of the water, the wood soon shrinks and parts at the seams which then let in the water and eventually the wood tends to rot. Kept afloat, wood deteriorates more gradually and, from time to time, needs to be renewed. So the work on an old-timer never ends

and, in a way, the owners of old and historic boats would not wish it to. Mucking about in their boats is half the fun and they often prefer it to the idea of actually going somewhere. In this way, a very personal relationship develops between the owner and the boat - which then truly becomes his -or hers, because the owner constantly cares for it. Raymond Baxter calls it "the running battle we all wage to keep the old ladies afloat". Only this year, he found the starboard beam shelf had 'gone' on *L'Orage*, together with the beam ends from the wheelhouse bulkhead to the foc'sle.

The work was done by two young chaps called Stanley and Thomas who had recently set up on their own at Egham. The survival of the Little Ships depends on such dedicated men as these. All along our rivers and coasts there are still boatbuilders who practise and enjoy the traditional crafts of joinery and caulking and of laying decks in the time-honoured way: which allows the wood to expand and contract under different weather conditions and still keep out the rain and the sea... more or less. The irony is that once taken out of the water and left on shore, to protect them from the danger of sinking, wooden boats soon die. Allowed to remain in their natural element and used - with loving care - they will survive for a good long time.

Raymond Baxter on L'Orage, *passing through Richmond lock on the River Thames*

Motor Yacht Kitty

Listening to the stories of those who own Dunkirk Little Ships, again and again you find that they did not know of their involvement in 'Operation Dynamo' when they first bought their ship. When Simon Jones's father saw a lovely 1936 Ramparts cruiser advertised for sale in Exchange & Mart, he bought her just to potter about on the Thames with occasional brief excursions round the coast. When he died it became the joint property of Simon and his mother. The ship's original name was *Aureol* when a Mr Beech had her built in 1936

NAME:	Kitty
TYPE:	Motor Yacht
LENGTH:	30ft
BEAM:	9ft 6ins
DISPLACEMENT:	10 tons
DRAFT:	2ft 9ins
ENGINES:	Perkins 4-107
HULL CONSTR.:	Pitch pine on oak
BUILT BY:	Rampart, Southampton
YEAR BUILT:	1936

and she had already passed on to a Mr Wilkinson when she went to Dunkirk to lift troops from the beaches and take them to the transport ships off-shore.

After the war her name was changed again to *Zena* and she had a number of owners one of whom, Leonard Fierstone, restored her extensively in the 60s. He replaced her two petrol engines with a 47 h.p. Perkins and a 7 h.p. Volvo diesel when he went through the French and Dutch canals to the south of France. There he opened a boat-building yard and chandlery business.

He always brought her back to the Thames and it was there that Mr and Mrs P. E. Caspari bought her in very good condition in 1975. They never went further than the Thames and had her kept in immaculate condition.

When the Jones family bought her, they met, at Harlingford marina, the owner of the Dunkirk ship *Latona* who identified *Aureol* as a boat called *Kitty*, which also took part in 'Operation Dynamo'. They were thrilled and got in touch with John Knight, the Hon. Archivist of the ADLS. to get the story verified.

John Knight takes immense trouble to double-check the history of every boat against all information available in Naval and MOD records, the files in the Imperial War Museum and his own extensive library of war books. Only when he is convinced of their authenticity are ships allowed to join the Association. *Aureol* was admitted and Jean Jones and her son Simon now attend all ADLS rallies and events. Sadly, when they were on their way to Dunkirk for the 45th Anniversary Rally, *Lady Aureol* threw a tantrum and her engines broke down just outside Dover. Nevertheless she was given her brass commemorative plaque for effort!

Malcolm Campbell at Daytona in March 1935

Buying a pleasure boat is rarely the outcome of logical thought. More often it is a sudden impulse; certainly it is a love affair, indulged in even by men of otherwise strong character and sound judgement. No wonder we attribute to boats the feminine gender.

Malcolm Campbell, world land-speed record holder in 1924, was knighted in the year he commissioned his new boat *Blue Bird*. He added the world water-speed record to his others just six years later. The name *Blue Bird*, was taken from Maeterlink's play *L'Oiseau Bleu*, and given to all his record-breaking cars and boats and the three successive yachts he owned. *Bluebird of Chelsea* (her present name) was Malcolm Campbell's second yacht. He sold her after only three years when he felt uncomfortable about her petrol engines which he considered dangerous. A gypsy had warned him once that "his death would come from the water". *Bluebird* had three more owners before the war and, like others of her kind, was requisitioned by the Admiralty. She made two false starts in getting to Dunkirk. The first time she developed engine trouble. Then, when she got as far as Sheerness, there were too many volunteers and she was left behind.

Finally, she set out, commanded by a yachtsman, Lt. Col. Barnard, with a crew of naval ratings. At 4ft. 6ins., her draft was too great to let her work comfortably off the beaches, so she must have ferried troops from the harbour. She suffered no major damage, but it was recorded that her fuel tanks were accidentally re-filled with water. *Bluebird's* twin screws were fouled by debris and her engines stopped. She may have picked up one of the many army greatcoats discarded by soldiers to make it easier for them to swim to the rescuing ships.

Bluebird was finally towed back to England by HM skoot *Rika*. After Dunkirk, *Bluebird* continued to serve the Navy as a radar decoy ship operating between Gosport and Weymouth. At this point, the trail goes cold. Then, in 1984, she made another conquest. A new admirer took up with her, aware of the illustrious past and dormant beauty, but apparently blind to the enormity of what he was taking on!

Martin Summers, a dealer in impressionist paintings living in Chelsea, took his daughter along the embankment to Cadogan Pier when she asked him why *they* could not have a boat. Though no sailor himself, the idea appealed to him and he discussed it with his friend, Scott Beadle, an art director and experienced mariner. This was just the kind of assignment Scott enjoys and it was not long before he found the very thing. An advertisement in *Yachting Monthly* described "a beautiful yacht originally built for Sir Malcolm Campbell, lying in the South of France" and she appeared to be going cheap. Martin Summers became enthusiastic and within a few days, he and Scott Beadle were on the way to Grau du Roi in the Camargue to see the lady. What they found made their hearts sink. She was clearly in a very poor state and Scott, from his knowledge of boats, realised that the cost of restoring her would be

Blue Bird undergoing trials on the Thames, 1931

prohibitive. But before they could abandon their idea, fate intervened. While they were aboard, their hire car had been broken into and all their money and possessions taken. They appealed for help to *Bluebird's* owner who consoled them so well that their optimism returned. In the middle of the night they went back to have another look at their dream. By the light of their head-lamps, the ship looked far more romantic. They found a hatch open and climbed aboard and as the battery of their car began to run out, the depressing aspect of rotting wood faded and they saw a vision of what might be. By now they had talked themselves into it.

Back in London, they appointed a surveyor who explained that the ship had been well built and its hull was sound, but that restoring her would not only be expensive, but would require skills which are no longer common. Martin Summers decided to buy *Bluebird* and found a delivery

NAME: Bluebird of Chelsea	
TYPE:	Motor Yacht
LENGTH:	52ft
BEAM:	11ft 4ins
DISPLACEMENT:	23.42 tons
DRAFT:	4ft 6ins
ENGINES:	2 x Perkins 6.354 diesel
HULL CONSTR.:	Dbl. Mah. on Can. Elm
BUILT BY:	Thornycroft
YEAR BUILT:	Hampton Wick, 1931

skipper, 'Ginge' Sargeant who, with only one engine working, started out for England. She leaked, she listed but she limped home. Martin and Scott flew out several times to check on her progress. Finally, there only remained the English Channel which she had crossed so gallantly in 1940. As on that memorable occasion, she needed to be towed home again this time, when her second engine stopped.

At Poole, H & T Marine (Hiscock and Titterington) together with a team of superb craftsmen, took over. Her entire wheelhouse was decayed and there was serious rot in her stern. Little of the original interior panelling was intact and her electrics were dangerous. It was difficult to decide where to begin and where it would end, but Martin Summers is a perfectionist and he was determined. New plans were drawn up based on the original ones from a 1931 copy of *Motorboat*. The entire wheelhouse was rebuilt and a new transom was constructed. The large sliding sun-roof was improved to keep the water out and the after-deck was carefully redesigned to provide a large and elegant dining area with a folding table and varnished lockers which double as seats. A new clinker-built dinghy of traditional design was added

Restored in 1984

Martin Summers with Malcolm Campbell's granddaughter Gina Campbell

The new wheelhouse after restoration

and swung from derricks at the stern. The hull was carefully shored up to preserve its elegant shape while the deck and beams were removed. New planks were fitted to the hull, the ribs were doubled up and strengthened and an entirely new teak deck was laid.

Martin Summers was now able to indulge his love of beautiful interiors. Helped by Scott Beadle's girlfriend Gaynor Hill, an interior designer, they started on the galley, the saloon, the cabins and the bathroom. In the master cabin a ribbon-and-rose cotton chintz was used for both walls and bedding. The saloon sofa cushions and seats were covered in Peruvian fabrics from the High Andes.

A bath was constructed of mahogany panels made leak-proof by polyurethane varnish and they fitted brass taps to match the bronze portholes and gleaming door knobs. In the galley, the varnished mahogany cabinets were supplemented by a modern kitchen worktop and a 240-volt domestic cooker as well as a micro-wave and freezer.

Scott Beadle took charge of the machinery and Graham Parker of the electrics. Her two Perkins diesels were entirely over-hauled and a 10kVA 240-volt generator was added to supply the domestic equipment and charge her over-size batteries. The latest radio and navigation equipment was installed in the mahogany-panelled wheel-house, along-side the old

The chintz-covered owner's cabin

brass compass and wooden wheel. Every hand-hold and window catch, every light fitting, hatch and porthole is in period and in impeccable taste. The floor throughout is covered in Persian rugs. When *Bluebird* was first built, it took Thornycroft's less than two months. Her restoration in 1984 took a whole year and cost fifty times as much but then, when men of vision fall in love, they rarely count the cost!

Bluebird of Chelsea, as she was named when they re-launched her on 19th April 1986, like any wise and well-loved mistress, has re-paid Martin Summers amply for his generosity and care. Lying at Cadogan Pier, in the heart of London and only a few hundred yards from his beautiful Chelsea home, *Bluebird* has opened a new dimension in his life. The world looks quite different from a small boat than from land or from an ocean liner. Strangely, she spent much of her time at Cadogan Pier in Malcolm Campbell's day. Martin Summers has cruised the Dutch and French canals and has taken her to Paris and to the lochs of Scotland.

Bluebird has given Martin Summers access to more than just the world of cruising. Through her, he has become one of a very exclusive circle far removed from his world of modern art. The Association of Dunkirk Little Ships is quite different from any

The new dining area on Bluebird of Chelsea's afterdeck where the dinghy used to be stored.

ordinary yacht club. It is the ship which qualifies you for membership and only owners of authentic Dunkirk Little Ships can join. But that is the only qualification. Wealth, connections and social class are considered totally irrelevant.

Among the members are cockle fishermen, Thames firemen, shipwrights and garage mechanics. There is a spirit among members of the Association which makes it quite unique. They treat their ships with a kind of reverence and all of the owners make great sacrifices for them, in time and money. They all share the belief that the Little Ships of Dunkirk should never be allowed to die and yet few would wish them to become museum pieces like vintage cars or sought-after rarities to be auctioned at Sothebys.

They prefer to keep them active, to live real lives, as close as can be to their original purpose. More people are desperately needed with the vision and the enthusiasm of Martin Summers, and the practical skills of Scott Beadle to take pity on some seemingly doomed Dunkirk Little Ships, sunk and derelict on our rivers and shores, with not much time before they are broken up. The legend itself will never die, but wooden boats are vulnerable to the elements and need people to cherish and preserve them.

The restored saloon with Peruvian furnishing fabrics

Motor Cruiser Jong

NAME:	Jong
TYPE:	Motor Cruiser
LENGTH:	40ft
BEAM:	9ft
DISPLACEMENT:	13 tons
DRAFT:	3ft 6ins
ENGINES:	2 x Fiat
HULL CONSTR.:	Carvel Mahogany on oak
BUILT BY:	Thornycroft
YEAR BUILT:	1931

Friday, 31st May, was the sixth day of 'Operation Dynamo' and by first light that morning, an estimated 150,000 British soldiers had already been evacuated. This was good news, but left less troops to defend the perimeter of Dunkirk and La Panne beach could no longer be held. Evacuation from Bray-Dunes and Malo-les Bains continued under severe artillery fire. A further hazard was a fresh northerly on-shore breeze which created a dangerous surf and broke up the improvised lorry-piers.

The Thornycroft cabin cruiser *Jong*, commanded by Sub-Lieut. I.F. Smith, RNVR, was there, in company with *Marsayru*, loading s.s. *Foam Queen* and s.s. *Jaba* with French and British troops from the beaches. She had been collected by Tough's from her owner, Donald Aldington, a motor engineer, while she was lying on the Thames. A crew of three, entered in Douglas Tough's notebook as: G.Allendale, G. Thomas and H.Morte, took her down to Sheerness, where the Royal Navy took over. Douglas

Tough received her back with only minor damage to her stanchions and guardrail a week later.

After the war, in 1951, she was re-named Gentle Ladye. In 1960, owned by Wig Cdr. Tom Jefferson, DSO, AFC, AE, she was one of the founder members of the ADLS. She attended the first Return and cruised extensively along the south coast as far as Dartmouth.

She was always looked after with great care. Imagine then the horror, when one day a guest rushed on deck asking: "should there be water coming out of the wardrobe?" - Apparently, when she had recently been lifted out of the water, the hoist's chains had squeezed her too tightly and had cracked her ribs. By the time they arrived in A. E. Rogers' boatyard, the water was up to the top of her batteries and she was almost beyond repair. Although four ADLS members offered to have her lashed to their boats to keep her afloat, the Port of London Authority was not keen to have her left in the water.

She was rescued and changed owners several times, being seen along the Kent coast and at Allington Lock, on the Medway, stripped and unused. Now Paul Rainbow has restored her and keeps her at Platt's Eyot at Hampton, near the very place where she was built by Thornycrofts nearly sixty years ago.

Motor Yacht Dianthus

A good name for *Dianthus* would be 'Never say Die'. She has had plenty of cause to give up, but is now about to receive another life as an example to other Dunkirk Little Ships.

On 1st June 1940, Sub-Lieut. F. N. Dann set out from Ramsgate but *Dianthus'* 5.6l Chrysler petrol engine gave trouble and he was towed back by the motor-boat *Thark*. On the second attempt, an injury to the helmsman forced him to return and when he tried for the third time, the engine died on him again. In the early hours of 3rd June, adrift in the Channel, he sighted one of the last returning convoys and accepted a tow home.

Released from war service, *Dianthus* seemed to have equally bad luck. Various people made half-hearted attempts to restore her. After all, she was built by Timms of Staines, a famous Thames boatyard, of mahogany on oak. But when Clive Anderson, a 33-year old 'mature student' of yacht building at Cornwall College in Falmouth, saw her lying ashore, in the shadow of the s.s *Great Britain* in Bristol, her planks were rotten and she had lost her foredeck. The owner nearly snatched his arm off when he offered him all he had, which was a meagre £280.

'I bought her because she needed saving and was an ideal first restoration project. At first I used her as an office - the part of her that was habitable. Then I found a shed little bigger than the boat itself and two fellow students, Ant Crawford and Ben Barnett, did a great job, stripping her out and renewing the bottom planking. Colin Chase is overhauling the Chrysler engine. I'm going to pull the boat out of her shed and bring her back to Falmouth so that she's nearer and I can get more work done.' He is now talking to

NAME:	Dianthus
TYPE:	Motor Yacht
LENGTH:	30ft
BEAM:	9ft
DISPLACEMENT:	approx. 7.5 tons
DRAFT:	2ft
ENGINES:	Chrysler Crown
HULL CONSTR.:	Mahogany on oak
BUILT BY:	Timms, Staines
YEAR BUILT:	1938

Christian Brann, the author of this book who is looking for a Dunkirk Little Ship and wants to finance a perfect restoration.

Clive Anderson used to be a freelance architectural designer and worked on the Chelsea Harbour, where the Little Ships have often held their rallies. Then he worked on a design for a British Aerospace hanger. He wanted to change to work which is more functional and requires real ingenuity and creative talent. Boat-building, and especially restoring a worthwhile old boat like *Dianthus*, seems to give him the kind of inspiration he has been looking for. So, perhaps, they need each other and *Dianthus* will cease to be a loser after all those years.

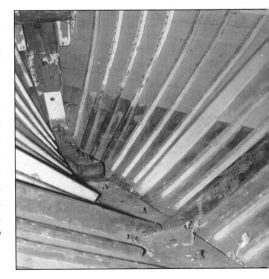

NAME:	Princess Freda
TYPE:	Passenger Vessel
LENGTH:	63ft
BEAM:	13ft
DISPLACEMENT:	38 tons
DRAFT:	3ft 9ins
ENGINES:	Leyland/Thornycroft 402
HULL CONSTR.:	Steel
BUILT BY:	Letchers, Cowes, I.O.W.
YEAR BUILT:	1926

Any day you care to go to Westminster Pier, a hundred yards downstream from the Houses of Parliament along the river Thames, you can take a ride up to Kew on the *Princess Freda*, one of the prettiest passenger vessels that went to Dunkirk. In passing, you'll get a fine view of members of both Houses on the terrace overlooking the river. *Princess Freda* was built in 1926 by T.C. Letcher on the Isle of Wight for Whatfords who had operated river boats on the Thames since before the turn of the century - but theirs were smaller than the rival steamers.

The *Princess Freda* was elegantly designed and substantially built. Her topsides were made of one continuous sheet of metal 150ft long, bent round

the stern and joined at the bows. The whole structure was then fitted to her bottom. Her hull has hardly changed since then, but when you board her now, you will have an awning and lee-rail dodgers to protect you from the weather and the spray.

Apart from the low profile and the modest freeboard, *Princess Freda* was the ideal ship for lifting troops off the beaches. The seamanship of Sub-Lieut. E.S. Foreman, who commanded her, must be admired when you consider that he manoeuvred this 65ft launch with a fast tide running close to shallow beaches on a lee shore under fire, filled her to capacity with troops and ferried them all day to an off-lying destroyer until flotsam fouled his propeller and he was towed home by the Dutch tug *Betje*.

Princess Freda went back to Whatfords until the business was sold in 1978 and the new owners had no need of her. She was then acquired by Thames Passenger Services, a co-operative of up-river operators who kept her for a while as a spare boat. Then, in 1982, Cliff Phillips bought her for a daily passenger service from Westminster to Kew. She proudly displays a plaque to prove she is a Dunkirk Little Ship, together with three others which operate from the same pier, but their appearance has changed dramatically over the years, while *Princess Freda* remains almost the same as ever.

Thereare some half-dozen firms which have been associated with the passenger service on the River Thames since the turn of the century. Joseph T. Mears began in 1907 and he was 37 years old when, the following year, the Port of London Authority was formed and the steel-hulled *Viscount* was built for him by another famous River Thames name: Salter's of Oxford. The *Viscount*, now owned by Thompsons, is the oldest passenger boat still in service among the Dunkirk Ships. Roland Hastings has been her skipper, on and off for thirty years. His father Harry went to Dunkirk in *Tigris I.*

Until the great drought of 1976, which lowered the water level of the Thames, *Viscount* used to go up to Hampton Court, but her 4ft 6in draft put her in danger of running aground and she now operates from Westminster to Greenwich. All the Thames launches were called up for Dunkirk and went down the river in 1940, but some would have it that the steamers could not have survived on sea water. After 50 years it's hard to tell!

In 1956 Thames Launches converted *Viscount* to diesel and they re-built her in 1964. They removed the wooden deck, undulating like waves from years of footfalls, planed it off and replaced it on top of a steel one. They gutted her aft of the engine room and added a steel saloon and a new funnel. In 1965 the wheelhouse was moved forward to about 15ft from the bows, a steel foredeck was laid and two entrances now lead to the saloon. A corrugated plastic awning over the foredeck and a canvas one on the top deck protect passengers from the elements.

Today, *Viscount* bears little resemblance to the original ship, but she has had to move with the times to make sure of earning her living in a competitive

Roland Hastings on Viscount

NAME:	Viscount
TYPE:	Motor Ship
LENGTH:	106ft
BEAM:	16ft 6ins
DISPLACEMENT:	74.98 tons
DRAFT:	4ft 6ins
ENGINES:	Gardner 8LX
HULL CONSTR.:	Steel
BUILT BY:	Salter Brothers Ltd., Oxford
YEAR BUILT:	1908

world. In 1977, Thompsons put the wheelhouse back to amidships and fitted a new Gardner 8LX engine. They now expect to get good value from the old *Viscount* for many years.

Motor Vessel Hurlingham

Another passenger boat built by Salter Brothers of Oxford seven years after the *Viscount* is the *Hurlingham*. In Edwardian times, gentlemen in white flannels, striped blazers and straw boaters would take their ladies for a cruise on the Thames on *Hurlingham*'s open top deck or under the canvas awning, which covered the foredeck. Rows of life-buoys lined the guardrails and bulk-heads and there was a saloon down below for the less adventurous.

Hurlingham was a tunnel-stern steamship, powered by a W. Sisson compound engine which was not replaced by a diesel until the 1950s. She was called up for Dunkirk and then spent most of the war in the River Emergency Service as a supply tender. After the war she was acquired by Thames Launches and thirty-one years later, for a season, by Marine Transit Ltd.

Like her sister ships, she was gradually up-graded and modernised, providing safe, enclosed accommodation, giving access to the fresh air only through her sliding sunroof and her covered foredeck. Down below, there is a bar and when she isn't taking passengers down-river to

NAME:	Hurlingham
TYPE:	Motor Vessel
LENGTH:	101ft
BEAM:	16ft
DISPLACEMENT:	87.65 tons
DRAFT:	4ft
ENGINES:	Leyland Thornycroft 760
HULL CONSTR.:	Steel
BUILT BY:	Salter Bros., Oxford
YEAR BUILT:	1915

Greenwich, she is available as a floating discotheque, or can accommodate a pop group or a jazz band.

Since 1979 she has been operated by Tidal Cruises Limited and her large, rebuilt accommodation can take 200 sightseers, 180 guests for a dance or a wedding, or 132 for a sit-down dinner.

As London's road traffic becomes more and more congested, passenger boats are coming into their own, giving visitors a varied and delightful view of the capital, along an historic highway, used since before the Romans by kings and commoners and still accessible on board passenger ships which took part in the Dunkirk evacuation in 1940.

Motor Vessel **Marchioness**

Eight years after *Hurlingham* was launched, *Marchioness* followed her from the yard of Salter Brothers in Oxford. She was 20ft shorter and had a little less freeboard which caused her trouble in the 1970s, when they planned to increase her weight by enclosing her upper deck.

Either the weather was better before the war (and the happy memories of the carefree twenties make it seem like that), or people who went on the river to see and be seen insisted on enjoying the fresh air, come what may! Certainly, *Marchioness* was an open boat apart from the small amount of shelter offered by her awning and the enclosed lower deck. Joe Mears was the proud owner from the day she was launched in 1923 until 1945 and throughout this time she was propelled by her powerful steam engine, which was not replaced by a diesel until 1950.

Apart from her Dunkirk involvement, *Marchioness*, together with *Kingwood* and *Hurlingham*, was part of the 13-strong Thames Hospital Emergency Transport Service, which was formed when war began. Only the largest of the river passenger vessels were chosen for this, which suggests that the government feared mass casualties and congestion in the streets, which would make evacuation along the river the best solution.

In 1946, *Marchioness* was bought by Thames Launches and stayed with them for thirty-one years. Though some modifications were made to her layout, she kept her open top deck for another twenty years. In 1978 she was briefly owned by Thames Party Boats, but became part of the Tidal Cruisers fleet in 1979. She was entirely enclosed with decks on three levels. Her bar, reception deck, saloon and dance decks, could accommodate 130 sightseers, 120 for a buffet or 70 for dining.

NAME:	Marchioness
TYPE:	Motor Vessel
LENGTH:	85ft
BEAM:	14ft
DISPLACEMENT:	33.46 tons
DRAFT:	4ft
ENGINES:	Ford Thornycroft 360
HULL CONSTR.:	Steel
BUILT BY:	Salter Bros., Oxford
YEAR BUILT:	1923

Sadly, on 19th August 1989, she was booked for a birthday party and in the early hours next morning was in collision with a dredger which ran over her and she sank with heavy loss of life.

Kingwood

Being one of a traditional family of River Thames boatmen, Roland Hastings learned to make himself useful early in life. He remembers taking out his first passenger boat at the age of twelve, during the war years, and recalls how busy they were in the Thames holiday passenger trade, at a time when the seaside was strewn with mines and out of bounds to civilians. So dense was the traffic on the river, that he often had to push boats aside with his boathook before he could bring his passenger boat alongside.

The *Kingwood* was another Salters-built passenger craft which enjoyed the boom in river traffic. She was built in 1915 as a sister ship to the *Hurlingham*. After her return from war service, Joe Mears owned the steamer until 1945, when he sold her to London Launches, who operated *Kingwood* for the next thirty years, after converting her to diesel in 1948.

In 1975 a fire broke out on board at Eel Pie Island in Middlesex. It destroyed much of *Kingwood's* after end and the following season she operated

NAME:	Kingwood
TYPE:	Motor Vessel
LENGTH:	106ft
BEAM:	20ft
DISPLACEMENT:	70.73 tons
DRAFT:	2ft 6ins
ENGINES:	760 Leyland Thornycroft
HULL CONSTR.:	Steel
BUILT BY:	Salter Bros., Oxford
YEAR BUILT:	1915

virtually as an open boat, without her saloon or top deck, or even a bar to slake the thirst of her summer trippers. Then, Albert Ellis bought *Kingwood*, took her to Robin's Lock at Limehouse and made her the modern-looking boat she is today. In 1985, Charles Wyatt took her over to provide a passenger service from Westminster Pier.

A small display on the forward bulkhead of *Kingwood's* saloon remembers the owner's father - then a sapper in the Royal Engineers- who was rescued from Dunkirk and whose medals and photograph are displayed beside the brass plaque which honours the *Kingwood* as a Dunkirk Ship.

Joe Mears was at the height of his success as a passenger boat operator on the Thames. His garage at Richmond looked after the coaches which brought holidaymakers to the river and he needed suitable vessels for smaller parties. So, in 1922 and 1923 he built two sister boats: *Mutt* and *Jeff*. They were named after two internationally popular cartoon characters created by Bud Fisher, a journalist on the San Francisco Chronicle. Jeff was the shorter of the pair, who always lost out in their encounters. Both launches were small, open craft of under 40ft and were the first of Mears' boats to be powered by internal combustion engines. *Mutt* ran from Westminster to London Bridge and *Jeff* from Westminster to Old Swan Pier. In the days when Joe Watson was skipper and Bert Wheeler her engineer, the return trip in *Jeff* cost just one shilling. Both launches went to Dunkirk and both survived the war but Mutt is now no more.

After 23 years, *Jeff* was sold to Thames Launches. Arthur Jacobs of Windsor took her over in 1952. He had a series of boats called *Windsor* and *Jeff* was renamed *Windsor IV*. She ran trips to Boveney Lock and when *Windsor II* was scrapped, she took over her name.

Whatford & Sons of Hampton Court were her next owners and when their business was sold in 1981, Turks Launches took her on as their spare boat. *Jeff* is rare among the Dunkirk Ships still operating, because she remains very close to her original appearance and a trip in her, perhaps more than in any other, is instantly evocative of the period of the lively young things whom she served to entertain in the boisterous nineteen-twenties. Little did some of them guess that she would be there to rescue them from the beach at La Panne, to get them back to England in 1940.

NAME:	Jeff
TYPE:	Motor Launch
LENGTH:	39ft 9ins
BEAM:	9ft 9ins
DISPLACEMENT:	12.5 tons
DRAFT:	2ft 9ins
ENGINES:	Ford diesel
HULL CONSTR.:	Carvel
BUILT BY:	J. Mears
YEAR BUILT:	1923

Motor Vessel Skylark X

Bolson's of Poole built a whole series of passenger launches called *Skylark*. Eleven of that name went to Dunkirk. *Skylark X* is one of these. She started life in 1926 as a Poole harbour ferry but was soon sold on to P.J. & R.F. Jackson of Hammersmith, who ran a service from Westminster to the Tower of London.

It was here in London that she was commandeered to serve in the Small Boats Service and then went to Sheerness. From there she was taken to Ramsgate in 1940 and on to Dunkirk, commanded by a Sub-Lieut. RNVR, with a Petty Officer and two Naval pensioners as crew.

After her return, *Skylark X* continued as a passenger boat on her old route until 1974, when she was laid up under Charing Cross railway bridge. In 1978 she was bought by Bob and Marian Balcomb who used her as a popular pleasure boat at Kingston and discovered that she had a disconcerting, but friendly ghost whom they named 'Fred Bloggs'.

'We first became aware of him in the summer of 1978, while we were moored to a buoy in the middle of the river, dismantling the starter engine. We heard someone walking on deck but when we went to look, we found no-one there. Then a chair was being moved in the wheelhouse and suddenly it was thrown out onto the deck. We made a rapid retreat home! A fortnight later, after an evening party, two ladies asked us: "do you know you have 'a prescence' on board?" We looked amazed and they went on: "No need to be scared, he's only looking after the boat. We felt he was there as soon as we stepped aboard". A fortnight later, I was taking the boat from Hampton Court to Kingston when *Skylark* started to veer to starboard and however much I corrected the wheel, she wouldn't come round until we nearly ran aground and then she suddenly answered the helm. I'm told that Fred still walks the deck! . .'

When *Skylark X* was no longer economical in 1980 she was sold, ghost and all, for a houseboat, first to Kingston Bridge Boatyard and then to Ian Scott Taylor who lived on her very happily for three years. Then, when he planned to sell her, he met strong opposition from Thames Water, who seem determined to reduce the number of houseboats on the river. Ian Taylor is afraid that this might endanger the ultimate survival of this Dunkirk veteran.

NAME:	Skylark X
TYPE:	Motor Vessel
LENGTH:	50ft
BEAM:	16ft
DISPLACEMENT:	47 tons
DRAFT:	3.25ft
ENGINES:	Gardner diesel
HULL CONSTR.:	Pitch pine on oak
BUILT BY:	J. Bolson & Son, Poole
YEAR BUILT:	1936

Motor Vessel Skylark IX

Many of the Dunkirk ships have moved far from the scene of their wartime exploits, but none farther north than Skylark IX, who began life in 1928 at Bolson's yard, in Poole, Dorset. Her precise part in 'Operation Dynamo' was unrecorded until, one day in 1987, Charles Fairman, touring in Scotland saw a notice advertising cruises on Loch Lomond in a boat called *Skylark IX*. He became interested and recognised her as the ship he commanded in Poole when he was a Petty Officer, RNVR, in 1941. He had first seen her the previous year, first at Dunkirk and later in Ramsgate harbour, whilst ferrying a yacht round to Felixstowe.

At Poole, *Skylark* served as a shallow water minesweeper and was engaged in placing anti-invasion obstacles around the harbour. At one time she erected decoys on Brownsea Island, consisting of wooden sheds filled with coal and sprayed with oil. They were set alight when German bombers flew over, looking for the Admiralty Armaments depot at Holton Heath.

After the war, *Skylark IX* gradually worked her way north, via Morecambe and Burntisland to Loch Lomond, where Sweeneys Cruises operate her now. She has been modernised and made a more comfortable little ship to

NAME:	Skylark IX
TYPE:	Motor Vessel
LENGTH:	50ft
BEAM:	14ft 6ins
DISPLACEMENT:	30 tons
DRAFT:	3ft
ENGINES:	Ulster HRWG
HULL CONSTR.:	Carvel Pitch pine on elm
BUILT BY:	J. Bolson, Poole
YEAR BUILT:	1927

cruise in, with an enclosed foredeck and covered rear saloon.

John Sweeney gives *Skylark IX*'s services free, to Dunkirk Veterans once a year, for their reunion on Loch Lomond.

In the presence of the Lord Lieutenant of Dunbartonshire, Brig. A.S. Pearson CB, DSO, OBE, MC, TD, reputedly the most highly decorated officer in World War II, wreaths are scattered on the loch. Veterans remember those who did not return from Dunkirk with *Skylark IX* and her fellow rescuers in 'Operation Dynamo' during those nine fateful days of 1940.

Motor Launch Folkestone Belle

NAME:	Folkestone Belle
TYPE:	Motor Launch
LENGTH:	50ft
BEAM:	12ft 8ins
DISPLACEMENT:	49.5 tons
DRAFT:	5ft
ENGINES:	6cc Ford Sabre
HULL CONSTR.:	Mah. on oak and elm
BUILT BY:	T.C. Letcher, Cowes, I.O.W.
YEAR BUILT:	1928

One day, forty years after Dunkirk, the passenger launch *Southsea Belle* was on her daily scheduled service, taking a load of visitors round Portsmouth harbour's heritage area, as she has been doing ever since Maurice Pearce bought her in 1972. She takes her trippers from *Warrior*, the first of the 'iron-clad' warships to the submarines of the modern Royal Navy, pointing out all the sights along the way.

One of her passengers that day was more interested in the *Southsea Belle* than in the historic sights they passed. He recognised her as the Little Ship that brought him back from Dunkirk in 1940. At that time she was called *Folkestone Belle*. She was carrying about 100 men and the crossing took 19 hours. He described certain features of the boat which had long been removed, but were known to have been there at that time.

This was the first her owners knew of her involvement in the evacuation and it sparked a painstaking investigation, which led to the Naval Historical Branch of the Ministry of Defence, the Public Record Office, the Imperial War Museum and to Rear Admiral T.O.K. Spraggs, CB, BSc., ACGI, FIEE, whose father had been one of the owners when *Folkestone Belle*, then a ferry at Hayling Island, was requisitioned to go

first to Ramsgate and then Dunkirk, in company with their other boat *Tarpon*. The last of the authorities to be consulted about the authenticity of *Folkestone Belle's* claim was John Knight, the ADLS Hon. Archivist. He found her mentioned by several of the authorities in his library and in one of the hand-written records of day-to-day movements of ships there was a note dated 2nd June 1940 recording that a destroyer dropped 5 drums of petrol on *Folkestone Belle*. This and other hastily scribbled mentions of her throughout the nine days amply corroborated the story that she was there and probably crossed more than once with the armada of rescuers.

Nowadays, *Southsea Belle* is an active member of the Association of Dunkirk Little Ships and often takes time off from earning her living to attend their reunions. Her sturdy construction of mahogany and elm on oak frames does not show her age. The old Gleniffer petrol engine, recalled by Rear Admiral Spraggs as "vicious to start", has long been replaced by a reliable Ford Sabre and her super-structure has been modified for easy access, comfortable seating and in her small wheelhouse she provides a little shelter for her skipper. Her new name may be a little confusing, but her Dunkirk flag now tells her story to all who sail in her.

NAME:	Fleury II
TYPE:	Motor Yacht
LENGTH:	33.5
BEAM:	9ft 1in
DISPLACEMENT:	12 tons
DRAFT:	3ft 5ins
ENGINES:	2 BMC Captains diesel
HULL CONSTR.:	Mahogany on oak
BUILT BY:	E.F Elkins Ltd., Christchurch
YEAR BUILT:	1936

When the Admiralty's Requisitioning Officer called at E.F. Elkins' boatyard at Christchurch in Hampshire, a wave of concern about his intentions swept over the owners of boats lying there. To some, their boat is their most precious possession, to others it is their living and no-one knew what he was looking for and the purpose for which the boats were wanted.

In fact, Christchurch was an ideal place for him to look because of its shallow waters, which meant that it contained ships of modest draft. The drawback was its distance from Dover and Ramsgate, where the Dunkirk evacuation fleet was assembled.

Reg Yebsley, who joined Elkins as a partner in 1930 and was there until the firm went out of business in 1976, recalls how they loaded some of their boats onto low-loaders, but then had to unload them again, when they heard that Dunkirk was over. He also remembers *Fleury II*, which was built in their yard. She had been designed by Eric French of Poole, from whose drawing board came most of the Elkins boats of 32ft - 36ft before the war. Her name was given to her by the Fleurets, her one-time owners. Later she was renamed *Mada*, by a later owner, Mr. Adam, who made up her name by reversing his own.

Her present owner, J.E. Loch-Lack, keeps her on the River Thames at Kingston-on-Thames. He took her to Dunkirk for the 45th Anniversary reunion in 1985.

Mada, *the former* Fleury II, *in sight of Dunkirk after crossing with the fleet from Ramsgate in 1985*

Lifeboat/Tender Patricia

The Corporation of Trinity House, London, operates a fleet of five Trinity House Vessels to service its aids to navigation in the North Sea and English Channel. During her 40 years as flagship of the Elder Brethren of Trinity House, *THV Patricia* helped to open the Iceland Naval base in 1940, acted as pathfinder for 'Route X' - the shortest 'safe' route to Dunkirk, was there to re-establish the Channel Islands' lights after the German surrender and, on numerous occasions, acted as Royal Escort, (a longstanding privilege of the Elder Brethren's flagship). She took the place of the Royal Yacht when Prince Philip went to the Olympic Games in Scandinavia in 1952 and attended many ceremonial occasions.

When she was retired in 1982 to become a restaurant in Sweden, her tender, also named *Patricia*, was sold into private ownership. At Dunkirk, *Patricia's* tender ferried troops off the beaches while her parent-ship, which was bombed soon afterwards, stood off to receive and repatriate them. After two previous owners, Kenneth and Phyllis Brewer bought her in 1986 and keep her near Boston in Lincolnshire. They are now trying to trace her sister ship, the second tender of *Patricia*, which was sold separately.

THV Patricia, tender on davits, seen from the Royal Yacht Britannia, dipping her Blue Ensign to the Queen and Prince Charles

NAME:	Patricia
TYPE:	Lifeboat/Tender
LENGTH:	27ft
BEAM:	9ft
DISPLACEMENT:	8 tons
DRAFT:	2ft 6ins
ENGINES:	Thornycroft
HULL CONSTR.:	Oak, Clinker
BUILT BY:	Smiths Dock Co. Ltd.
YEAR BUILT:	Middlesbrough, 1937

The part played by *Tom Tit* at Dunkirk is not on record because Ron Tomlinson and his brother Alan took her on impulse and without authority on 1st June 1940 from the end of Ramsgate Pier. Ron had been to Dunkirk the previous day as engineer of the trawler *Tankerton Towers* which was towed back full of French and British soldiers when her propeller had been fouled. When they disembarked their load at Ramsgate, Ron went home for a meal and a wash, but what he had seen over there did not let him rest.

With his brother Alan he went down to the Admiralty office in the harbour and volunteered to go again. They sent them off in a tiny boat with a young Sub-Lieut. who made them turn back when he found that they were taking him, safely they protested, the shortest route, straight across the Goodwin Sands. As they re-entered Ramsgate harbour, Ron saw *Tom Tit* tied up at the end of the breakwater and urged his brother to join him when he jumped across and took possession of her.

Their elder brother Fred, standing on the pier, saw what they were doing and warned them that one of the the ship's engines had been on fire, but before anyone could stop them, they had got under way and were again heading straight for the Goodwins. This was when they noticed a petrol leak - the cause of the previous fire. They quickly stopped the engine and repaired the leak, but lost precious time with the tide running out. They touched bottom a few times before they cleared the shallows, but reached Dunkirk safely.

They filled up with soldiers and took them out to the big ships, sixteen times, until a Sgt.-Major on the jetty told them not to come back because the Germans were on the pier. They told him they'd keep coming while he was there. On the last trip they persuaded him to join

them. When they arrived in Ramsgate next morning, they expected to be arrested for stealing *Tom Tit*, but the Senior Naval Officer congratulated them and said he wished he could have had more like them.

Forty-five years later, Ron was having a drink at the Mill House, Frogholt with the owner who showed him the picture of a boat his brother had just bought. Though her name was now *Melinda Margot*, Ron knew it was the ship he had taken to Dunkirk and proved it when they found signs of a fire in the starboard engine. Now Stephen Lucas has owned her since 1988

NAME:	Tom Tit
TYPE:	Motor Yacht
LENGTH:	39.5ft
BEAM:	10ft
DISPLACEMENT:	10.9 tons
DRAFT:	3ft 8ins
ENGINES:	2 x BMC 2.5 diesel
HULL CONSTR.:	Mahogany on pitch pine
BUILT BY:	K.R. Skentelberg, Plymouth
YEAR BUILT:	1938

When Lord Dunhill, the chairman of the tobacco company, wanted a motor cruiser in 1934, he gave the commission to Zabell Bros. of Westcliffe-on-Sea, Essex. They sub-contracted the job to E.G. King & Son and two local craftsmen, George Davis and his son Eric, designed and built it. Now in his eighties, Eric clearly recalls building Lady Gay, now called Mehatis.

"We didn't have a shed big enough to take her, so we set up a canvas shelter outside, which also saved us extra rates. We only had one 100-watt electric light bulb and no machinery. Every part of her was made by hand. I remember going to Maldon in Essex with templates of the woodwork to get the timber cut to size. Then we shaped it by hand. Three of us worked on her for nearly five months and my pay was under £3 a week. Every Saturday Lord Dunhill came to the yard in his chauffeur-driven car and handed out cigarettes and, on one occasion, pipes."

When she was finished, she had cost His Lordship £1,500. Having no slipway, George and Eric, with some helpers, dragged her through

the local carpark and manhandled her over the sea wall into the water. They went on board with the fuel, the twin Morris Commodores started first time and Lord Dunhill's boat was on its way!

When the war started, he handed over Lady Gay to the Royal Navy as a patrol boat. At that time she would have been given a Navy number, so her name does not appear in any of the lists of Dunkirk ships, but there is no doubt that she was there.

After the war she belonged to Cmdr. Clarke who was in charge of the Carshalton Sea Cadets. After several more owners, in 1969 she was re-named Mehatis and in 1972 her petrol/paraffin engines were replaced with Perkins diesels. During the ensuing years she cruised extensively on the waterways of France, Holland and Luxembourg. Now Mehatis belongs to Paul Richards, who plans to live aboard.

NAME:	Lady Gay
TYPE:	Motor Yacht
LENGTH:	36ft.2ins
BEAM:	10ft 10in
DISPLACEMENT:	13.84 tons
DRAFT:	3ft
ENGINES:	2 x Perkins 4108
HULL CONSTR.:	Carvel Pitch pine on oak
BUILT BY:	E.G. King & Son
YEAR BUILT:	Westcliff-on-Sea, 1934

Lieut. Commander Buchanan had been invalided out of the service when war began, but on 29th May 1940, he heard on the 9 o'clock news that the Admiralty wanted enginemen for yachts and he applied at once. Next day, he went to Robinson's yard at Oulton Broad and took charge of the engines in the estuary cruiser *Elvin*. Her two 25 h.p. Highlander petrol/paraffin motors needed all his skills! The crew, when they set out for Ramsgate, consisted of himself, a young Sub-Lieut. RNVR, a retired fisherman from Aberdeen, a Lowestoft longshoreman and Hackforth-Jones, a writer of yachting stories, who had served with Winston Churchill's battalion in the 1914-18 war.

They got to Ramsgate but, through some muddle, were sent back to Lowestoft, where they got fresh orders to set out for Ramsgate once more. At the second attempt they left for Dunkirk, though the authorities were very reluctant to let them go: "civilian crew, ship too slow, flying the red ensign " - but they lost patience and cut the mooring lines when they heard a CPO say: " they're going, Sir". The Commander on the dock shrugged his shoulders and there followed a shower of first aid kits into their cockpit. It was late in the evening on 2nd June and they arrived at Dunkirk at first light. They had no charts, but simply followed the traffic and steered for the glare of the fires and the shell-bursts. The starboard engine failed on the way, but Buchanan repaired it. As soon as they could see, they went alongside the eastern pier, where a column of soldiers was drawn up. A French officer called out "combien des soldats?", but since Buchanan could not remember the French for '25', he shouted "trente", which was more than they could comfortably hold! But another was admitted when one of the French pleaded: "mon ami!" They followed an open boat, grossly over-loaded, with a whaler in tow, making

NAME:	Elvin
TYPE:	Motor Yacht
LENGTH:	35ft
BEAM:	9ft
DISPLACEMENT:	14.5 tons
DRAFT:	6ft
ENGINES:	2 x 25 h.p. Ford
HULL CONSTR.:	Pitch pine on oak
BUILT BY:	Clapson & Son
YEAR BUILT:	Barton-on-Humber,

for a Destroyer. The *Elvin* was a bit top-heavy and they were worried about capsizing. By the time they had negotiated the wreckage which littered the approaches, the Destroyer had gone, so they chased some French minesweepers, but they were too fast for them. So, in the end they headed for Ramsgate. They did not know the swept channel but, with their shallow draft, they were less concerned with mines then with flotsam. They landed 25 French and 8 British troops on the north-east wall at Ramsgate.

After the war, *Elvin* went to Portugal. At one time, she belonged to the Marquis of Pombal and to the chairman of a cement firm in Lisbon. We are still looking for her present owners.

Motor Yacht **Irma**

NAME:	Irma
TYPE:	Motor Cruiser
LENGTH:	38ft 6ins
BEAM:	9ft 1in
DISPLACEMENT:	8.22 tons
DRAFT:	3ft 5ins
ENGINES:	diesel
HULL CONSTR.:	Carvel Mahogany on oak
BUILT BY:	Thornycroft & Co.
YEAR BUILT:	Hampton-on-Thames,

When the Thornycroft motor cruiser *Irma* was taken over by the Royal Navy in 1940, her owner, a Mr. Phillips, was in Madrid and, although she appears on several lists of ships that went to Dunkirk, there are no details of the part she played there.

After the war she was re-named *Nottac* and spent some time on the Clyde in Scotland. Then, in the '70s, she was used as a houseboat at Swan Island, Twickenham. Jerry Hulbert, who lived aboard, bought *Irma* from a couple who wanted to sail her to South Africa and fitted her out with all kinds of navigation equipment, an echo sounder and a set of signal flags, but at the last moment realised that a river cruising boat can't be adapted to cross an ocean. So she has remained on the Thames.

Keith Slaughter, her owner since 1981, lived aboard for a while, but now frequently has to travel abroad and only has time for occasional river trips on *Irma*. So work on her upkeep is falling behind and it may take him a while to get her into perfect order again.

Working boats are designed to suit their trade and the waters in which they earn their living. Our east coast rivers are muddy, tidal and tricky to navigate. But the oyster fishermen of the region know their waters like the back of their hands and their boats are designed to suit them, with a shallow draft, a low freeboard and wide decks to provide ideal working platforms. The Burnham Oyster Company had *Vanguard* purpose-built for dredging and she was designed to turn in her own length. Her deck allowed six men to work in comfort hauling in the nets. The deckhouse provided the minimum of shelter. *Vanguard* certainly was not intended for the open sea and would roll like a pig in anything above force 5.

Skipper Grimwade took her across to Dunkirk in 1940 with Joe Clough as his engineer. They went with another oyster dredger, the *Seasalter* which also survived and a ketch called *Ma Joie* which was abandoned and lost. They could not get into Dunkirk harbour, so they picked up the men from the beaches and 24 hours later, arrived back at Ramsgate loaded with troops.

At the end of the war, Keeble & Sons of Paglesham, Essex bought the *Vanguard* and put her back to oyster dredging which their family had done on the rivers Roach and Crouch for fifty years on thirty-four acres of rented oyster beds. But the bad winter of 1962 decimated the oyster population.

NAME:	Vanguard
TYPE:	Oyster Smack
LENGTH:	45ft
BEAM:	14ft 6ins
DISPLACEMENT:	11.5 tons
DRAFT:	4ft 6ins
ENGINES:	Kelvin 44
HULL CONSTR.:	Pitch pine on oak
BUILT BY:	R & J Prior, Burnham
YEAR BUILT:	1937

Those which survived the ice and the cold and succeeded in breeding since then, are now faced with the increasing hazards of pollution. So W. Keeble sold *Vanguard* to Ron Pipe, a fisherman at Burnham-on-Crouch, who used her for in-shore fishing for a while and sold her again. Ten years later, Doug Whiting bought her back from another owner in a sorry state. Now he has enlarged her wheelhouse, given up oyster fishing and has taken up shrimping on the Roach and Crouch.

J onathan Minns has spent his life restoring things, from water mills to beam engines and rarely meets the original designers who only leave the evidence of their skills in their artefacts. With *Providence*, it was different. When he first sailed her to Cornwall, he met a friend who said that her designer, Nigel Warington-Smyth was still alive and living in a beautiful cottage at the mouth of Frenchman's Creek. They decided to sail there and arrived on the designer's 75th birthday and the 50th anniversary of the launching of *Providence*. After some five hours of animated questions and answers, Jonathan said: "by the way, tell me about the *Providence* bell." To which Nigel replied:"What bell?" So Jonathan explained that he had found a bell hidden in the internal ballast tucked deep down by the dead wood aft. He had carefully removed and cleaned it and was struck by its beauty and the composition of its metal: bronze with a high silver content. It turned out to be late 18th or early 19th century Persian, perhaps brought back by a trading skipper as a souvenir. But when Nigel heard of it,

NAME:	Providence
TYPE:	Aux. Gaff Cutter
LENGTH:	38ft + 10ft
BEAM:	11ft 6ins
DISPLACEMENT:	11.08 tons
DRAFT:	7ft 2ins
ENGINES:	Perkins 4107 diesel 48 h.p.
HULL CONSTR.:	Carvel Pitch pine on oak
BUILT BY:	Gilbert & Pascoe, Porthleven
YEAR BUILT:	1934

tears came to his eyes and he explained the reason. *Providence* was built by Gilbert & Pascoe who used their family's oak trees from along the Helford River and were known to have hidden things in boats which they particularly enjoyed building. But nothing was ever found hidden in the

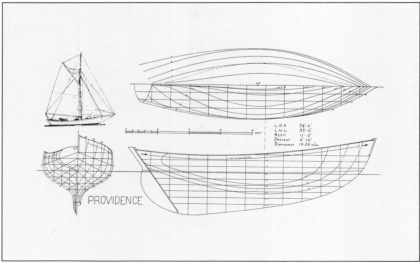

PROVIDENCE

Providence and Nigel feared that the builders had not thought much of her. Now, suddenly after all those years, he had learned the secret and his joy was a pleasure to witness. *Providence* is a ship anyone might lose his heart to. Lovingly restored by Jonathan Minns, she would make the owner of any modern luxury yacht green with envy. Few old gaffers have survived so close to their original form for half a century and who would wish to change her, with her polished brass compass binnacle and her shining, varnished wooden blocks! Her spars, deck and hull were painted, not varnished, to save expense and her interior is surprisingly roomy for four to cruise in. Her grown

The bronze bell found in the bilges of Providence

oak frames will easily survive a century. Since 1969 she has had a 42 h.p. Perkins diesel installed, but at Dunkirk she had no engines and must have been towed across. Had the weather turned nasty, it would not have

worried *Providence*. Her long 3½ ton iron keel and substantial ballast, together with her ample beam, make her a stiff boat and the reefing gear on her main enable the crew to reduce sail in minutes. Her pre-war owner reported how she once raced from Concarneau to Benodet - "We were home and stowed before the Bermuda rigs came in". After Dunkirk, she went to the east coast on barrage-balloon duty, moored in the River Crouch. When Nigel Warington-Smyth got her back she was in a sorry state and he could not afford to restore her. But she soon found enthusiasts who appreciated her qualities. In the hands of Jonathan Minns who keeps her on the Beaulieu river in Hampshire and often sails down to Falmouth in Cornwall, she has been restored to perfection and lends grace to all the rallies of the Association of Dunkirk Little Ships that she takes part in.

Daphne

Thornycrofts in 1932 built and supplied the R.H. 4 Pilot petrol engine which, 56 years later, still propels the motor yacht *Daphne*. Many other parts are stamped with their name, but she does not appear on the list of boats they built - a mystery which has never been solved.

Only 25ft long, with a 7ft beam, *Daphne* is one of the smallest boats that went to Dunkirk. She was requisitioned by the Admiralty in 1940, was towed across the Channel and ferried soldiers from tbe beaches to the destroyers and transport ships. On her return she probably seemed too small to serve as a patrol boat, as other larger motor yachts did, so she was left in a mud berth at Swale in Kent. Then she returned to private ownership and spent most of the intervening years on the south coast and the Medway. Derek Mills, the father of her present owner, found her in a builder's yard near Sevenoaks and bought her, in partnership with his brother and nephew. They worked hard to restore her, replaced her garboard strakes in the

NAME:	Daphne
TYPE:	Motor Yacht
LENGTH:	25ft
BEAM:	7ft
DISPLACEMENT:	Unknown
DRAFT:	3ft
ENGINES:	Thornycroft RH4 pilot
HULL CONSTR.:	Carvel Mahogany on oak
BUILT BY:	Thornycroft
YEAR BUILT:	1932

original elm, rebuilt her transom and rudder and removed the caked layers of accumulated paint, one eighth of an inch thick, before refurbishing her. Wherever possible, her original gear has been retained and overhauled and it is amazing how durable it has proved to be.

In 1978, Derek gave his share of *Daphne* to his son John who was then only 17 years old. John eventually bought out the others so that he now owns *Daphne* entirely. He has made few concessions to modern ideas of boat-building or propulsion and intends to keep her as a venerable classic boat.

Douglas Tough's notebook meticulously recorded the details of the ships he collected to go down the river to Sheerness and from there to Ramsgate and Dunkirk. *Tarifa* appears in his notes, together with the names of her crew: J.J. Jameson, L. Melsom, S. Brown and E.L. Peters, all civilians from London. This is the only record of her participation but many have left no more than that.

Built in the heyday of Thornycroft at Hampton-on-Thames at the beginning of 1932 for W.D. Wills, M.P. for

NAME:	Tarifa
TYPE:	Motor Yacht
LENGTH:	48ft
BEAM:	10ft 6ins
DISPLACEMENT:	15 tons
DRAFT:	4ft 6ins
ENGINES:	2 Perkins P4 diesel
HULL CONSTR.:	Carvel Mahogany on oak
BUILT BY:	Thornycroft
YEAR BUILT:	1931

Batley, Yorks, *Tarifa's* launching was reported with respect in the *Motor Boat*. Her crew's quarters forward gave access by an iron ladder to the foredeck and had their own toilet. The owner's suite aft boasted a bathroom with a full-sized tub and the mahogany panelled cabins offered wardrobes and dressing tables. For Mediterranean cruising her specification for an "icebox of the largest size possible, fitted athwartships in one of the cupboards" must have been welcome. With her twin 30 h.p. Thornycroft engines the distance was no problem, though these have now been replaced by two Perkins diesels.

Even before the war started, W.D. Wills, a distant relative of the tobacco family, who later became a Lieut. Cdr. RNVR, allowed her to be used by the

Royal Navy, for wireless telegraphy training, carrying up to 60 ratings at a time. After the war, Maurice Wooding, a marine surveyor, had her for twenty years and cruised the waterways of Europe down to the south of France. Now her owners, Mr. and Mrs. Lewis who found her derelict in Reading in 1986, have once more painstakingly restored *Tarifa* as closely as possible to her original condition and she will make a fine charter boat.

It is sad, in a way, that these old timers can only survive if they produce an income, but the cost of their upkeep constantly threatens their survival and they have no chance of being put out to grass to rest on their past achievements. But maybe it is better so. Like old soldiers, they would die if they were made to retire, with no further practical function.

Motor Yacht Mermaiden

NAME:	Mermaiden
TYPE:	Motor Yacht
LENGTH:	72ft
BEAM:	15ft
DISPLACEMENT:	73 tons
DRAFT:	7ft
ENGINES:	2 x Cummins 160 h.p.
HULL CONSTR.:	Steel
BUILT BY:	Kiekenend Co., Holland
YEAR BUILT:	1939

First mentioned in the Battle Summary amongst the Little Ships which arrived off Dunkirk on 31st May 1940, *Mermaiden* (now named *Amazone*) was still in the thick of it on 3rd June. This was the last day of the evacuation, when 30,000 troops, mostly French, still remained to be evacuated.

She belonged to a Naval officer, Lieut. Cdr. P.M. Filleul, RN, and was commanded that day by Sub-Lieut. L. Beale, RN, with her crew: Petty Officer J. Norton, Leading Stoker W.A.S. Horner, plus one RAF gunner on leave and one "white-haired old gentleman who normally took care of Lord Horatio Nelson's flagship *Victory* at Portsmouth".

Mermaiden was picked by Rear-Adm. Taylor, who for some time sailed in her, to lead a convoy of small, slower motorboats, which had been towed by tugs, to be released off Dunkirk harbour and make their own way to Quai Felix Faure, which was still reasonably intact, to embark French troops. *Mermaiden* made four trips between the harbour and the transport ships at a time when the Germans were already entering the town. Her deck and wheelhouse were riddled by machinegun bullets and she was so crowded that the helmsman could not see to steer. Directions had to be shouted to him over a cacophany of French voices. For this action, her Petty Officer received the DSM and the Stoker was Mentioned in Despatches.

After the war she went back to Lieut. Cdr. Filleul and had two more British owners before she was sold to return to her native Holland. *Amazone*, as she now is, was built in 1939 by N. Kieken & Co. of Warmond, a substantial 37-ton steel vessel.

Frits and Gerda Rouschop of Maastricht, who now own her, have restored her to a condition which should make her the winner in any concours d'élégance. Although she is in constant use and attends many of the reunions of the Association of Dunkirk Little Ships, where she is always much admired, between outings, she is kept in a climatically controlled shed and is pampered like a film star.

Motor Yacht **Fervant**

The Armenian sugar broker who ordered *White Marlin* from Thornycrofts never even took delivery of her. As she was completed at Hampton on Thames in 1939, right on the eve of World War II, she was handed over instead to the Ministry of War Transport at Dover. The Royal Navy called her *HMS Fervant* and assigned her as the communications boat for the Officer Commanding convoys in the area.

During the evacuation she was the launch of the S.N.O. at Dunkirk, under the command of Lieut. Cdr. W. R. T. Clemments. She numbered among her crew Douglas Kirkaldie, the coxswain of the Ramsgate lifeboat *Prudential* who was mentioned in despatches. And she was one of the last naval vessels to leave Dunkirk harbour.

Back at Folkestone, she was copper-sheathed, had rubbing strakes added and was taken to Archangel where she helped with the convoys to Russia. Badly damaged on the port bow, *Fervant* was sent home, patched up and kept at Dover until she sank at Strood while at the Small Crafts Disposal Unit. There she was found by Col. F. A. Sudbury, of Tate & Lyle. He got Thornycrofts to survey her, take her back to Hampton on a barge and restore her completely. Although his personal boat, she rapidly became the

NAME:	Fervant
TYPE:	Motor yacht
LENGTH:	50ft
BEAM:	11ft 9ins
DISPLACEMENT:	15 tons
DRAFT:	3ft 9ins
ENGINES:	Gen. Motors twin 140 h.p.
HULL CONSTR.:	Double carvel Teak on elm
BUILT BY:	Thornycroft
YEAR BUILT:	1938-1939

company's communications launch, taking visitors from Tower Pier in London down to the Albert Dock refineries. Col. Sudbury had her superstructure rebuilt and he took *White Marlin* to Henley Regatta fifteen years in succession. She now belongs to Richard and Anne Thompson who keep her at Temple in Buckinghamshire.

In many ways, the Little Ships of Dunkirk are like the soldiers they rescued. War was not their profession and it took them from an entirely different environment into a dramatic event, almost like a bad dream. Then, after it was all over, the Little Ships returned to their previous

existence. But they were never quite the same again. It was the making of some of them, which would probably not have survived and would certainly not have been cherished as they are today, had it not been for their moment of glory at Dunkirk. Others perished and have now mostly been forgotten. Yet, not all of them have a heroic or dramatic story to tell. We know that they took part, or they would not be in

this book. But fifty years on, there are no details and the simple story of how they went to Dunkirk, made a number of journeys from the beaches to the transport ships and finally returned to Ramsgate, becomes repetitive. *Bou Saada* was one of these. Built at Burnham-on-Crouch by W. King & Sons in 1935, she belonged to Edmund Dreyfus, a member of the Royal Burnham Yacht Club. She was requisitioned and went to Dunkirk. No details of her achievements are recorded. After the war she was sold into private ownership and spent some time in Yorkshire where her present owners, Donald and Carolyn Hamilton-Khaan bought her. Donald had been a Petty Officer in the Royal Navy and served in Combined Operations. He landed in Normandy on D-Day and is therefore an experienced mariner who appreciates *Bou Saada's* war record.

Little has been altered on *Bou Saada* except for her re-built wheelhouse and the replacement of her original twin 4-cylinder Morris petrol engines with Perkins diesels. She has had a larger mast fitted which enables her to carry a steadying sail. This provides additional safety if her engines fail. She still has the original shining teak panelling below and is a fine cruising boat which has taken her owners to Belgium, the Friesian Islands, the Dutch canals and the pretty River Ling.

NAME:	B o u S a a d a
TYPE:	Motor Yacht
LENGTH:	33ft
BEAM:	9ft 6ins
DISPLACEMENT:	11 tons
DRAFT:	3.25
ENGINES:	Twin Perkins diesel
HULL CONSTR.:	Teak and oak
BUILT BY:	W. King & Sons, Burnham
YEAR BUILT:	1935

Researching into the background of the Little Ships brings to light many interesting stories about their past occupations, their owners and their names. Francisco de Orellana after whom this Little Ship is named, was a 16th century Spanish soldier. He sailed for Peru in 1535 and in April 1541 was sent ahead of the main expedition to seek provisions, taking a brigantine with 50 soldiers. When he reached the junction of the Napo and Maranon rivers, he deserted the Pizarro expedition. He followed the great river system until he reached the Atlantic. He therefore discovered the Amazon River and named it after the Amazons of Greek mythology, who came to his mind when he encountered a tribe of fighting women near the mouth of the great South American river.

The Little Ship *Orellana* started life as the *Evelyn* in 1907, built by J.T. Crompton in Portsmouth. She was a steam pinnace flying the white ensign. Like most ships of her day, she did not rely entirely on engines, but was rigged as an auxiliary gaff ketch and she is still a good sailing boat today when her steam engine has long been replaced, in 1912 by a Blake 4 cylinder petrol engine, in 1933 by a Detroit-built Gray and more recently by a 100 h.p., 6 cylinder Ford. She remained in the service until the late 1920s when she was owned by H.E. Lamplough of Walton-on-Naze in Essex. She then

had fifteen more owners on the east coast and it was not until 1929 that Lt. Colonel S.G. Allden of Beccles in Suffolk re-named her *Orellana*.

She was recruited for Dunkirk by Ron Lenthall of Tough Brothers at Teddington. Ron's notebook shows her crew as H. Ambler of Twickenham, G. Thomas of London and K.J. Ray of Southwick. The Navy kept her until 1947, but the trail of her subsequent owners goes cold after that until 1972 when the Rev. Terry Fuller bought her from Emil Freeman of Ramsgate and kept her in Cornwall. She is still maintained there by her 1989 owner, John Fincham.

NAME:	Orellana
TYPE:	Auxiliary. Gaff Ketch
LENGTH:	46ft 6ins
BEAM:	9ft 1in
DISPLACEMENT:	14 tons
DRAFT:	4ft 5ins
ENGINES:	6 cylinder Ford 100 h.p.
HULL CONSTR.:	Teak sandwich
BUILT BY:	J.T. Crompton, Portsmouth
YEAR BUILT:	1907

Ketch Motor Yacht Pelagia

When *Pelagia* set out for Dunkirk she had on board Claud Whisstock who built her at Woodbridge, Suffolk in 1932, her retired owner Major Warnford and W.H.A. Whitworth, then headmaster of Framlingham College, Suffolk, where the Major had a son. Whitworth, who came to the college in 1929, had lost a leg whilst in the Royal Flying Corps. and had a wooden replacement. He was also a keen yachtsman, the owner of several boats and a member of the Royal Cruising Club. When the Major decided to do his bit, using his own river boat *Pelagia*, the headmaster was an obvious choice to take along.

Mrs Whitworth, however, protests - as did her husband during his lifetime - that he was no great hero. He feared that a crossing to Dunkirk in *Pelagia* would mean certain death, and anyway felt that his first responsibilities were to the school. He stalled, he would go only if the Chair-man of Governors agreed. The Chair-man agreed readily, and said that he would himself sleep at the school in Mr Whitworth's absence; so then the headmaster felt morally obliged to go!

Of course *Pelagia* had not been officially requisitioned and Claud Whisstock later recalled that when they reached Harwich, the Navy was too busy organising boats already under Admiralty orders to deal with *Pelagia*. There was also concern because there was some suspicion that enemy agents in British Naval uniform were about the quay issuing false orders and causing confusion. The Navy did not want *Pelagia* to set off alone, but as time went by, the Major was anxious to get going. Eventually they were told to sail to Ramsgate from where they would be able to cross in convoy.

In fact, they sailed towards the Sandiette light vessel on a breeze which "gave the Kelvin engine a chance to cool down". They began to encounter boats loaded with troops, and before they could reach Dunkirk, a Naval vessel came alongside, said that the evacuation was almost complete, and told *Pelagia* to return to Ramsgate.

She has been a river cruiser for a succession of owners ever since. *Pelagia* last changed hands in 1988, after two years blocked up ashore, and is now owned by John Holman who keeps her at Faversham, in Kent.

NAME:	Pelagia
TYPE:	Ketch motor yacht
LENGTH:	29ft
BEAM:	9ft
DISPLACEMENT:	10 tons
DRAFT:	3ft
ENGINES:	Renault RC25D diesel
HULL CONSTR.:	Carvel
BUILT BY:	Whisstocks, Woodbridge
YEAR BUILT:	1932

Many of the Dunkirk Little Ships came from the Thames which was then alive with well-found cruising boats built only just before the war and ideal for the task. The Thames is still where some of the 'lost' Dunkirk ships are to be found, often by a member of the Association with an eye for a boat from the thirties. John Knight, the Association's indefatigable Archivist then gets to work looking into their records, registration forms and the Dunkirk documents in his collection. Sometimes, the details which emerge are heroic, often amusing and, on occasion, even a little scandalous!

Deenar started life as a Naval steam pinnace in 1917 and served valiantly at Dunkirk. When her post-war owner moved to South Africa, she was bought by a confirmed bachelor, M. Russell-Snook who enjoyed recalling the wild parties on board with girls whose names sometimes hit the headlines in the less salubrious Sunday papers. He felt that the pictures taken on board in those days would not be fitting for a serious book like this!

When Mr. Russell-Snook moved to Cornwall, the glitter went out of *Deenar's* life and she was left at Weybridge Marina gradually deteriorating and filling with water until boatyard owner Terry Tappin hauled her out on to the bank. There, in 1984, David and Andrew Smith took pity on her and have since been trying to put her to rights. They have renewed her decks, her wheelhouse and her cabins in the style of the 1920s when she was recognised as a Dunkirk Little Ship.

NAME:	Deenar
TYPE:	Naval Pinnace
LENGTH:	32ft
BEAM:	8ft
DISPLACEMENT:	
DRAFT:	2ft 6ins
ENGINES:	3.8 BMC
HULL CONSTR.:	Double skinned teak
BUILT BY:	The Admiralty
YEAR BUILT:	1917

Motor Yacht **Wanda**

Reginald Yebsley built *Wanda* at E.F. Elkins' Christchurch boatyard in 1935 for Henry Maxim, the head of a tailoring firm associated in business with Austin Reed. Mr. Reed was the owner of *Reda* (see p. 104) long before she went to Dunkirk. The two men frequently visited the Christchurch yard during the nine months or so it took to build *Wanda*. There were at most a dozen men working there

(see p. 104)

and they were more accustomed to building small sailing boats. The motor yacht *Wanda* was well within their capability as craftsmen, but stretched their facilities.

Reg recalls how pleased they were with the boat, a double-ender with a canoe stern into which they installed two Morris Isis engines. Her original owner used her mostly in the Solent and remained on friendly terms with the builder. Whenever the weather forced him to leave *Wanda* at Cowes or Poole, Reg was despatched to bring her home. All that is known of *Wanda* at Dunkirk is that she ferried troops off the beaches during Saturday 1st June 1940. Afterwards, it is believed that she was fitted with a Bofors gun and used on patrol and pilot boat duties in Portland harbour. The Navy let her go in 1946 to a motor engineer at Clacton in Essex and for many years a succession of owners cruised in her around the Medway area. During the 1950s these included the Finch family who subsequently owned *Ryegate II* and *Matoya*, both of them Dunkirk Little Ships.

It is usually men who have love affairs with boats, but in *Wanda's* case, as Bill Finch recalls, it was his mother who fell in love with her and they bought her on the spot! The boat had not been sailed for years and Bill's first job was "to clear out seven sacks full of empty gin bottles". They heard that the previous owner committed suicide the day after he sold her. Over the next two years, *Wanda* had a series of mishaps which disillusioned the Finch family, but when they sold her, she again gave pleasure to subsequent owners.

Since 1978 *Wanda* has been owned by David Rolt whose involvement with boats began in 1945 when he belonged to a Henley rowing eight. Quite by chance he bought *Wanda* 33 years later

David Rolt, ADLS Commodore, 1988/90 (above)

Wanda *returning from the Dunkirk reunion in 1980*

NAME:	Wanda
TYPE:	Motor Yacht
LENGTH:	35ft
BEAM:	9ft 8ins
DISPLACEMENT:	8.7 tons
DRAFT:	3ft 6ins
ENGINES:	2NE Perkins 4.236 diesel
HULL CONSTR.:	Carvel Pitch pine on oak
BUILT BY:	E.F. Elkins, Christchurch
YEAR BUILT:	1935

Wanda *in the Solent, Summer 1989*

from a friend of the cox in that same crew. David Rolt's introduction to the Association of Dunkirk Little Ships was a strange one. He was lunching one day with his friend, J.B. Cannell, who was at that time the Association's Commodore and the owner of *Doutelle,* Cannell was urgently called to the telephone, and when he returned he mentioned that he had just had to make one of the most difficult decisions of his life. This was to cancel the Return to Dunkirk in 1975. The Return of the Little Ships is an event which was planned to take place every five years and began with the 25th anniversary of Operation Dynamo in 1965.

It was at this lunch that David Rolt first learned about the Association and he became very enthusiastic. *Wanda* was well known at Weymouth where David Rolt has his country cottage. She was frequently used at Regattas either as a rescue boat or as a marker vessel and she had taken part in the Cowes-to-Torquay powerboat races during the 1960s. David Rolt also owned a powerboat, but when *Wanda* became available and was confirmed as a Dunkirk Little Ship, he bought her. He became an active member of the Association and soon began to organise the Little Ships lying in the south of England. Since then the Solent Rally is an important annual event in the Association's calendar. By 1980 David was a leading member of

the committee which organised the Return to Dunkirk and he took *Wanda* across for the 45th anniversary in 1985. Three years later, he succeeded Bob Tough as the Commodore of the Association and now flies his twin-tailed Commodore's flag at *Wanda's* masthead.

The Association has been fortunate in attracting flag officers of sufficient energy and stature to take charge of its affairs and to maintain the interest of members who come from a wide range of backgrounds and from every walk of life. But most important of all, is the maintenance of the spirit of the Association which excludes personal self-interest and concentrates solely on cherishing the Little Ships, the memory of those who served in them and of those they rescued.

The original gleaming oak panelling in Wanda's *saloon*

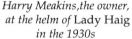

Harry Meakins, the owner, at the helm of Lady Haig *in the 1930s*

S aving lives at sea had long been every-day work for *Lady Haig* when she was towed across the Channel by the Skoot *Hilda* on Friday 31st May 1940. She was commanded and manned by the Royal Navy, but also on board as First Engineer was Reginald Walter, who was mentioned in despatches. *Lady Haig* was badly damaged during her work on the beaches, but luckily survived to be towed back to her home port.

NAME:	Lady Haig
TYPE:	Deal Hoveller
LENGTH:	27ft
BEAM:	7ft 6ins
DISPLACEMENT:	Not known
DRAFT:	2ft
ENGINES:	2.2 BMC diesel
HULL CONSTR.:	Elm and oak
BUILT BY:	Dan Trott, North Deal
YEAR BUILT:	1928

Lady Haig launching into a racing surf in December 1939. with Dick Brown, Charlie and Dave Pritchard, and Bill Brown pushing her out with a long pole.

She was a lifeboat with a difference. Only 27ft long, a clinker-built open boat, she was a 'hoveller' - a name given to unlicenced, privately owned pilot and lifeboats, which went out to wrecks in the olden days, (often to plunder them!) Lady Haig was built for Harry Meakins, the Landlord of the Port Arms in Deal and she was always kept ready for launching off the beach. The notorious Goodwin Sands and the Downs, on the approach to the narrowest part of the English Channel,

have claimed thousands of ships over the years and Harry Meakins then aged 63, and his crew: Dick Brown with his son Jim, his cousins Charles and Dave Pritchard, both in their 70s, Edward Griggs, Thomas and George Baker, both younger men - would turn out at a moment's notice to render assistance. Their lifeboat received no subsidy or grant. They relied for payment on bounties alone. Sometimes they were told in clear terms that their help was not required because, for the ship owners, it incurred a liability.

1939 had been a busy year for *Lady Haig* and other Deal boats. When war was declared, the Downs became a contraband control station and there were often 200 ships at anchor there. Inevitably, some collisions occurred and when air raids started, the Deal

ships were kept busy rendering assistance, taking out stores and medical supplies and landing survivors.

Not long before Dunkirk, Jim Brown, the last of her pre-war crew left in 1989, took part in one of *Lady Haig's* most famous rescues: that of the 6,000 ton steamship *Mahratta* which went ashore on Goodwin Fork during the early evening of 11th October 1939. Fifty years later Jim, now a retired Trinity House Captain with 42 years' service, recalls how they received a telegram from the owners authorising them to go out and take charge of salvage operations. After four days, the efforts of six tugs to re-float the *Mahratta* failed, the weather worsened and as the tide scooped out the sands under her keel, the *Mahratta's* back broke with rivets going off like rifle shots! Wide cracks opened in her hull until her boilers exploded while *Lady Haig* was lying alongside with Jim's father on board. It was then a race against time to get the crew off in a full south westerly gale, with a heavy sea running. The tugs had left her to

Lady Haig had been built for Meakins by Dan Trott and was launched from his North Deal yard in January 1928. When she was not saving lives, she took holidaymakers for pleasure trips round the bay and engaged in light haulage. Jim Brown started in the Trinity House service as a seaman and retired forty-two years later as one of their most respected Masters who also earned fame for the superb and intricate model ships he constructed during his time off.

By a strange coincidence, two of Jim Brown's cousins, who served in the Grenadier Guards, were rescued from the beaches in *Lady Haig*.

After her part in the Evacuation of Dunkirk, *Lady Haig* went back to her peaceful occupation of fishing. She was eventually converted to a cabin cruiser and kept on the River Stour near Sandwich, Kent. On one occasion, she nearly came to grief when she crashed against one of the winches on Deal beach in a severe storm. She was badly holed on the port side and was

Jim Brown, Trinity House Captain in 1982

27th December 1938. Lady Haig rescuing 20 visitors trapped in St. Margaret's Bay, cut off by snow. The crew: Harry Meakins, Charlie and Dave Pritchard, Dick Brown and Jim being towed.

anchor off Deal and *Lady Haig* ferried the crew from the wreck to the steamer *Challenge* in four runs. On their third run, they took the ship's lifeboat in tow with luggage they had saved. As they cleared the bow of the *Mahratta*, they were hit by a big wave and almost capsized. So they slipped the lifeboat, but only after they had rescued ten men from it.

left to rot ashore. This is where her present owner, John Burbridge found her in 1979. They had intended burning her on the beach where she lay. Instead, John Burbridge repaired her, moored her in Margate Harbour and has been using her for fishing and trawling round Sandwich Bay. Now he feels the time has come to pension off the old lady.

Auxiliary Ketch **Skylark**

NAME:	Skylark
TYPE:	Aux. Ketch
LENGTH:	60ft
BEAM:	13.1ft
DISPLACEMENT:	30.51 tons
DRAFT:	5ft
ENGINES:	Gardner 4LK
HULL CONSTR.:	Carvel Teak
BUILT BY:	Thornycroft
YEAR BUILT:	1922

Another of the eleven ships called *Skylark* which took part in Operation Dynamo is now called *Tahilla*. She belongs to Jerry Lewis and his wife Peggy, who is the Hon. Secretary of the A.D.L.S. *Skylark* was built by Thornycrofts at Hampton-on-Thames in 1922 for D. Melville Wills of the tobacco family in Bristol. He used her to travel from there to his estates in Scotland.

At the time of Dunkirk, she belonged to W. Egerton Wilson of Colwyn Bay in Wales, but was kept on the Thames where she was collected with the other Little Ships to go to Dunkirk. After the war, she remained in Admiralty ownership until 1948 and then became a widely-travelled and comfortable cruising ship. Eleanor Samuelson, who owned her throughout the 1960s, came to know the French canals well. They took *Tahilla* down to the South of France, to Spain and the Balearic Islands, Italy, Corsica, Sardinia, Yugoslavia and Corfu. Once, in St. Tropez, they had a near escape when they entered harbour and the wheel came off in the captain's hands leaving him no means of steering! They had a good laugh and escaped damage.

Jerry Lewis, who had business interests in the South of France, found *Tahilla* there in the mid-sixties and used her as a floating office. He had to re-build the coach roof over the engine compartment and the after-deck and, fifteen years later, brought her back home where she is now used as a family cruiser in the Solent.

Motor Yacht Iorana

NAME:	Iorana
TYPE:	Motor Yacht
LENGTH:	40ft
BEAM:	10ft 6ins
DISPLACEMENT:	8 tons
DRAFT:	3ft 6ins
ENGINES:	2 BMC 1.8 diesel
HULL CONSTR.:	Carvel Wood
BUILT BY:	D. Hilliard, Littlehampton
YEAR BUILT:	1935

A gentleman of independent means, E.P. Lewns, designed *Iorana* himself and had her built under his own supervision by David Hilliard at Littlehampton, Sussex, in 1936. *Iorana* is the Tahitian word for welcome; 'hello', 'hail' or 'good-day,' as used by the natives of that Pacific island.

Each summer before the War, Lewns cruised in *Iorana* down to Fowey in Cornwall and on to Falmouth and the Helford River . He used her to fish for tunny off Cornwall and tope - small shark of around 6ft, weighing 45-50 lbs - from Bournemouth, in Hampshire.

In 1940, The Royal Navy collected Mr. Lewns' boat for Dunkirk from Littlehampton. She was not compulsorily acquired until 1942. When Mr Lewns was offered her back by the Ministry of War Transport in 1948, he turned her down, because he then wanted a larger boat. So Fred J. Watts, yacht and boat builder of Parham boat-yard Gosport, bought her, together with a number of other vessels which had been requisitioned by the Admiralty for the duration of the war. She was at his yard in 1949 when engineer Donald Berry found her "very tatty but sound

and unaltered from the original design". The engines had been completely dismantled and packed into boxes and the rudder was missing. But the job just suited him. Having bought *Iorana*, he rebuilt the original engines and had twin semi-balanced rudders cast in admiralty bronze. She had a small wheelhouse and was open at the stern, with light hatch covers across the open cockpit.

In about 1954, the Brooke engines went in favour of a handed pair of Vosper V8s which, at full power, gave 17 knots on the measured mile off Lee-on-Solent. Mr. Berry built a larger enclosed wheelhouse and aft cabin for what was essentially a family boat. He kept her until 1963 at Gosport. From there he enjoyed cruising the Solent and along the south coast of England. When he sold *Iorana*, she became a houseboat, by the mill stream at Windsor, where her owners lived on her for four years. Percy Beaumont, only her fourth owner, has kept her on the Thames at Staines ever since and *Iorana* was the ADLS Commodore's boat 1979-81.

Motor Yacht Papillon

Whilst Cdr. V.A.L. Bradyll-Johnson was in charge of the eastern arm of Dover breakwater during 'Operation Dynamo' many handwritten messages and instructions were sent to him and the naval officers under his command. One of these was the order to 'keep a list of the men in each boat by name, initials and official number. If civilian, next of kin and address are required'. His staff were also told: 'On arrival (of requisitioned boats) make a full list of requirements and defects. Immediate necessities are fuel, water and two days' provisions for the crew'. The various naval officers scribbled brief notes in compliance. Without these notes, which Bradyll-Johnson collected together and kept for many years, the Dunkirk involvement of many vessels such as *Papillon* would have remained unrecorded. These scraps of paper, written in several hands over three or four days, are evocative reminders of the time. They tell us that she arrived for service at Dover on 30th May, 1940 and that her two 4 cylinder Morris petrol engines were 'defective'. Her skipper was E. Somers Holmwood of Kingston by the Sea, Sussex, and his crew S.J. Downes of Shoreham,

NAME:	Papillon
TYPE:	Motor Yacht
LENGTH:	33ft 5ins
BEAM:	8ft 7ins
DISPLACEMENT:	10.5 tons
DRAFT:	3ft 8ins
ENGINES:	2 x 4 cylinder BMC
HULL CONSTR.:	Carvel Wood
BUILT BY:	Leslie W. Harris, Burnham
YEAR BUILT:	1930

B. Hawood of Brighton and Mr. Griffiths of Peacehaven (who was lent to an RNLI lifeboat). She was probably a local boat, since her owner, C.P. Mackenrot, lived at Westcliffe-on-Sea, Essex and she had been built in 1930 by Leslie W. Harris at Burnham-on-Crouch.

No extra fuel was required; another note states that she had 30 gallons of petrol, a full crew, and a minor electrical fault. Another that she had two casks of water, was o.k. for oil and fuel and that the fault in her condenser had been repaired. Then we know she was loaded with six spare tins of petrol and water, and that there was a minor hiccup: her civilian crew were 'uncertain of conditions of service'. She sailed on 2nd June and, when she came back next day, gave up her route order and had her fuel and oil tanks replenished. It is also likely that the men who took her across were volunteers otherwise unconnected with *Papillon*, for instead of being sailed home she was left for collection at Burnham-on-Crouch. *Papillon's* movements as a private yacht after Dunkirk are unknown, and she is now a family boat owned by Richard and Caroline Huggett and kept at Erith, in Kent.

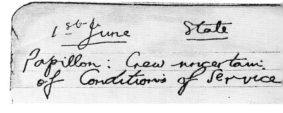

W*hite Heather* was designed by W.G. McBride and built in 1920 by McGruer & Co. Ltd. of Clynder, Scotland as a 21st birthday present for Anna Johnson, daughter of the owner of a Scottish shipping company. It was thought to be such a prestigious project that the foreman at McGruers made a model of the boat. The family also had a racing yacht and *White Heather*, with her powerful Thornycroft petrol/paraffin engine which she had for 34 years, was used to tow the yacht from regatta to regatta.

By the time war broke out, she belonged to W.M.V. Wright of Glasgow. *White Heather* went to Dunkirk on 1st June 1940 and was afterwards abandoned. The Navy requisitioned her as *HMS Manatee* and used her until 1947 in the Solent area. Returned to Mr. Wright, she was sold and became the only Dunkirk Little Ship we know of to have worked her way through a succession of owners all the way from Scotland to the south coast of England. It was one of these owners, Lieut. C.H.H. Brewster, who in the mid-1950s changed her name to *Riis I*, derived from the Dutch, meaning maiden, or first voyage. In 1960, Dr. J.W.E. Fellows found her lying at Conyers Creek on the Medway,

NAME:	White Heather
TYPE:	Motor Yacht
LENGTH:	57ft 6ins
BEAM:	10ft 6ins
DISPLACEMENT:	27 tons
DRAFT:	4ft
ENGINES:	2 x Thornycroft 250 diesels
HULL CONSTR.:	Pitch pine on oak
BUILT BY:	McGruer & Co. Ltd.
YEAR BUILT:	Dumbartonshire, 1920

in appearance like a houseboat. Her original engines had been replaced by Dorman diesels, and in 1972 he replaced these with Thornycroft diesels. He has worked continuously on her over three decades, externally at least keeping her exactly as she was when new. Dr. Fellows was the 8th Commodore of the A.D.L.S. and flew his flag in *Riis I* during this time.

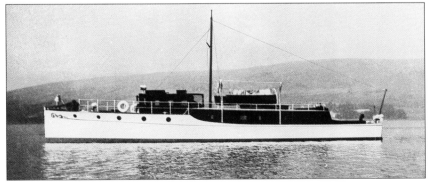

The Little Ships of Dunkirk

So far, in this book, we have described 158 of the Little Ships in detail. Of these, only four had definitely been destroyed, by 1989, although the exact whereabouts of some lifeboats are also unknown. On pages 230-233 twelve more vessels are illustrated and described, less fully. Our total is therefore 170.

What is our definition of a Dunkirk Little Ship? Altogether, some 1,432 vessels took part in the evacuation of Dunkirk. Generally, we have excluded regular ships of the Royal Navy (although we have included *MTB 102*) and merchant ships, the larger transport vessels commandeered by the Admiralty and the tugs. We have not been able to trace any of the Dutch schuits or skoots, as the British called them, which played such an heroic part in 'Operation Dynamo'. Our book has concentrated on the small, privately owned ships, which were

---

The Withdrawal from Dunkirk June 1940
by Charles Cundall,
Imperial War Museum, London

summoned to help, mostly at short notice, in this emergency. Most of these were requisitioned and retained after Dunkirk as patrol boats, barrage balloon boats, for mine spotting and communications work. All surviving ones were offered back to their original owners, where known, or sold into private ownership after the war. Many were never officially requisitioned. Some simply went of their own accord. Some perished, unrecorded and unsung.

The list of Little Ships which follows in this book has been compiled from no less than 21 surviving sources and is the most comprehensive list yet published. The names used are the ones they had in 1940, but the General Index at the end of this book provides a cross-reference between these and their present names. Against each name in our list, letters and symbols indicate our sources, the page numbers of ships comprehensively described in this book. Asterisks mark those which are known to have perished. The fate of the rest is not known.

Symbols used in List of Little Ships

*	lost at Dunkirk
**	known to have been lost since
(xxx)	page numbers of main references in this book

Sources

A	Admiralty List
B	Ministry of War Transport List
C	Divine, A.D., *The Nine Days of Dunkirk*
D	Divine, A.D., *Dunkirk*
E	Dunkirk Veterans List
F	Tough Brothers' records
G	E.F. Elkins' records
H	Admiralty notes of Merchant Vessels lost or damaged, 1939-1945
I	Ships of the Royal Navy lost or damaged 1939-1945
J	Supplement to London Gazette July, 1940
K	Chatterton, E.K., *The Epic of Dunkirk*
L	Masefield, John, *The Nine Days Wonder*
M	Collier, Richard, *The Sands of Dunkirk*
N	Ellis, L.F., *The War In France* and *Flanders 1939-40*
O	Butler, Lt. Col. E & Selby-Bradford, Maj. J., *Keep the Memory Green*
P	Plancher, R., *List of Belgian Ships Used In Operation Dynamo* in *The Belgian Ship Lover No. 69*
Q	Rampart Boatbuilding Company Ltd. records
R	Belgian Seaways List
S	Ministry of War Transport X MT40/36 (PRO Ref)
T	Bradyll-Johnson V.A.L., Manuscript notes
U	Eye-witness confirmation

A

Ship	Code
Abdy Beauclerk	(120)AEST
Aberdonia	(170)U
Ace	BCQS
Ada Mary	ABCDKS
Adeline	BCDKS
Adeline	BC
Advance	B
Adventuress	**ABCD
Ahola	ACDET
Aid	**BCEHKS
Aid II	BCD
Aidie	*ACHKM
Albatross	*ABCDEKS
Aljanor	ABCDEKS
Aloha	BCDEKS
Alouette	**BCDEI
Alusia	(18-19)QT
Amethyst	**AI
Amity	BCDEKS
Andora	BCDE
Andora II	CD
Anee	ACDEKS
Angele Aline	(10-13)CE
Angler	F
Anne	(77)B
Anne	B
Anne	B
Anne	**BFS
Anthony	BCDEFKS
Antoinette	BCDEFKS
Aquabelle	(228)BCDEFKS
Aronia	ACDE
Ashingdon	BCDEKS
Athola	BCDE
Auntie Gus	BCDEKS
Aura	ABCDEFKST

B

Ship	Code
Balquhain	ABCDEKS
Barbara	BCDEFKS
Barbara Jean	*ACHKM
Barbill II	BCDEKS
Basildon	BCDEKS
Bat	ABCDEKS
Beal	**ABCDEH
Beatrice Maude	(47)U
Bee	ABCDEKMS
Belfast	ABCDE
Ben & Lucy	ACDE
Bendor	BC
Berkshire Lass	*O
Bessie	BCDES
Betty	(173)BCDKS
Beverley	*BCDEKS
Bhurana	CDEFKS
Black Arrow	*ABCDEKS
Black Java	BCDE
Blackpool	ABCDE
Bluebird	(188-191)BCK
Bluebird II	(166-167)BCD
Boat	*CDEKS
Bobeli	*ABCDEKS
Bonnibell	*ABCDEKST
Bonny Heather	ABCDEFKS
Bou Saada	(216)BCDEFS
Bounty	(33)ACDE
Boy Billy	*BCDEHKS
Boy Bruce	BCDEKS
Boy Fred	BCDES
B.P. One	BCDE

Ship	Code
Braymar	(143)B
Breadwinner	BCDEHKS
Brenart	BCDEKS
Britannia	*DEHKS
Britannia IV	BCDEKS
Britannic	ABCDFH
Brywyn	BCDEFKST
Byffub	F
Bullfinch	ACDE
Bull Pup	*ABCDKST
Burgoni	BCDKS
Burton	ABCDEKS
Bystander	CDEL

C

Ship	Code
Cabby	(40-41)BCDE
Cachalot	(132)BDEK
Cachalot	BCS
Cairngorm	ACDEFKS
Caleta	ACDE
Camellia	CDEKST
Canvey Queen	ABCDE
Carama	U
Caraid	BCDEKS
Carmen	BCDEKS
Caronia	CDEKS
Caversham	BCDEKS
Cecil & Lilian Philpott	(120)ADKT
Cecile	BCDEKS
Cervantes	BCDEKS
Chalmondesleigh	(156)CEKS
Chamois	ABCDEKS
Chantecler	ABCEKS
Charles Cooper Henderson	(110-111)AET
Charlotte	BCDEKT
Charles Dibdin	(122)AEST
Chico	(74-76)BK
Clara Belle	*ABCDEKST
Claude	ABCDE
Commodore	*ABCDEKST
Commodore	BD
Constant Nymph	BCDEKLNS
Cora-Ann	*BCDEKS
Cordelia	(165)ABCDEKST
Cornelia	BCDE
Corsair	CDEFKS
Count Dracula	(178-179)BCDEKMS
Court Belle II	ABCDEKS
Creole	BCDEFKS
Cruiser	BCDEKS
Curlew	BDKS
Cyb	*ABCDEKS
Cygnet	**(59)BC
Cyril & Lilian Bishop	(113)AE

D

Ship	Code
Dab II	(182)ABCDEFKS
Dandy	BCDEKS
Daphne	(212)BDEK
Dawn	BCDEKS
Deenar	(219)BCDEFKS
Defender	(25-26)ABCDKS
Desel II	(231)BCDEKST
Desiree	**BEI
Devilfish	BCDEKS
Dhoon	ABCDE
Diamond	BCDEKS
Diana Mary	ABCDEKS

Ship	Code
Diante	BCDEFKS
Dianthus	(193)BCDEKS
Dinky	*ABCDKS
D. L. G.	BCDEKS
Dogger Bank	BCD
Dolphin	BS
Doreen	BCDEKS
Dorian	(70-71)BCDEKS
Doris	*AEK
Dover Abbey	U
Dragonfly	(155)BCDEK
Dreadnought II	*ABCDKS
Dreadnought III	*U
Duchess of York	BCDEFKS
Duke	ABCDEKS
Dumpling	*ABCDEKMS
Dwarf	BCDE

E

Ship	Code
Eastbourne Belle	ABCDEKST
Eastbourne Queen	*ABCDKST
Edina	*BCDEKS
Edna	BCDEKS
Edward and Mary	BCDEKS
Edward Nissen	ABCDE
Edward Z Dresden	(121)A
Edwina	*ABCDEKS
Elaine	BCDEKS
Elizabeth Green	(148-149)ABCDEFKS
Ella	BCDEKS
Elsa II	(135)U
Elvin	(207)BCDEKS
E.M.E.D.	(119)ACDEST
Empress	*ABCDEKS
Ena	(42-44)ACDKM
Enchantress	*ABCDKST
Encourage	*BCDHKS
Endeavour	(24)BDK
Enterprise	ABCDMS
Eothen	(126-127)BCDEFKS
Erica	ABCDE
E.R.V.	CDKS
Eskburn	ACDEH
Esperanza	BCDEKS
Ethel Ellen	BCDEKS
Ethel Everard	*AHKM
Ethel Maud	(39)BCDEKS
Evelyn Rose	ACDE

F

Ship	Code
Fair Breeze	*ABCDEI
Fairwind	BCDES
Faith	BCDEKS
Falcon II	(99)CDEKS
Favourite SM 225	BCDEKS
Fawley	B
Fedelma II	(146-147)BCDEKS
Felicity	(153)CDEKS
Ferry King	BCDES
Ferry Nymph	ABCDEKST
Fervant	(215)ABCDE
Firefly	(177)U
Fishbourne	ABCDEK
Fleetwing	BCDKS
Fleury II	(203)G
Floss Hilda	BCDEKS
Folkestone Belle	(202)BCDEKST
Foremost 101	A
Formidable	BCDE
Formosa	BCDEKS
Fortuna	BCDEIKS

The Little Ships of Dunkirk

Benjamin Taylor of Hampton Wick and his daughter Joyce delivered *Aquabelle* to the Royal Navy to go to Dunkirk. Her twin Ailsa Craig diesels with a 100 gal. fuel tank gave her the endurance to tow 5 others back. She was dirty, her hatch covers were broken and the soldiers had left

NAME:	Desel II
TYPE:	Motor Cruiser
LENGTH:	30ft
BEAM:	8ft 6ins
DISPLACEMENT:	5.5 tons
DRAFT:	3ft
ENGINES:	Inboard diesel 80 h.p.
HULL CONSTR.:	Carvel
BUILT BY:	Saunders & Roe, Cowes
YEAR BUILT:	1934

Now named *Delise*, *Desel II* belongs to Rory Maher, at Milford Haven in Wales. But she was once reported to have sailed through the straits of Japan. At the time of Dunkirk she belonged to a Mr. Dudley Stone. As a member of the ADLS she took part in the 45th Anniversary

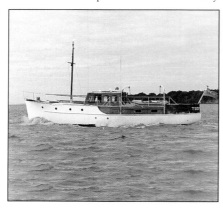

Lieut. R. Nimmo RN, commanded *Forty Two* at Dunkirk and Derek Bromige, her 1989 owner knew the family, but then lost touch. Therefore no more is known aboat the ship's part in 'Operation Dynamo' She is now moored on the river Severn near Worcester. Built for Mr. N. West, her owner at

NAME:	Aquabelle
TYPE:	Motor Yacht
LENGTH:	45ft
BEAM:	12ft
DISPLACEMENT:	12 tons
DRAFT:	4ft 6ins
ENGINES:	2 x Ailsa Craig
HULL CONSTR.:	Mahogany on teak
BUILT BY:	Wm. Osborne
YEAR BUILT:	Littlehampton, 1939

their khaki socks and mugs aboard. Fitted with a gun she went on to defend lighthouses from air attack. After two post war owners she went to France where she now belongs to Patrice Lolostuzzo a canal boat skipper at Aigues Mortes. Our picture comes from the Dimbylow family album.

return to Dunkirk in 1985. Rory Maher, who found her in very poor condition on the river Avon, has now entirely restored her and keeps her across the Severn at Milford Haven in Wales.

NAME:	Forty Two
TYPE:	Motor Cruiser
LENGTH:	46ft
BEAM:	11ft 9ins
DISPLACEMENT:	20.5 tons
DRAFT:	4ft 7ins
ENGINES:	2 x BMC 3.8 diesel
HULL CONSTR.:	Pitch pine on oak
BUILT BY:	Strood Boatbuilders
YEAR BUILT:	1936

the time of Dunkirk, by Strood Boatbuilders in Kent, she is a fine 46-footer whose original 6-cyl Morris petrol engine has since been replaced with twin BMC 2.8 diesels.

Forty Two	(229)ABCDEKS
Fram	BDEKS
Frances	(180-181)BCDEKS
Francis	U
Frightened Lady	ABCDE
F.W. 23	BCDE
G Galleon's Reach	ABCDEM
Gavine	ACDEFKS
Gay Crusader	(233)ABCDEFKS
Gay Fly	BCDEKS
Gay Venture	(34-36)BCDEKS
Gertrude	BCDEKS
Gipsy King	ABCDEKS
Girl Nancy	BCDEKS
Girl Vine	BCDEKS
Glala	(150)CDE
Glenway	(50)ABCDEK
Glitter II	ABCDE
Golden Eagle	ACDEJK
Golden Lily	ABCDEFKS
Golden Spray	BCDEKS
Golden Spray II	*ABCDEKS
Goliath	BCDEP
Gondolier King	ABCDEKST
Gondolier Queen	(145)ABCDEKST
Gondolier III	BCDEKS
Good Hope	ABCDEKS
Good Luck	CDEKS
Gourka	BCDE
Grace	BCDEKS
Grace Darling	BCDEKST
Grace Darling IV	ABCDEKS
Grappler	BCDE
Greater London	(119)ACDET
Green Eagle	*U
Greta	(45-46)BCDEKS
Guide of Dunkirk	(115)A
H Haig	ABCDE
Halfway	ABCDE
Handy Billie	ABCDEKS
Hanora	*ABCDEKS
Harbour Launches:	D1, D4, D7, D9 (all BCDE) DG694, DG715, DG950 (all U)
Haste Away	ABCDEKS
Hawfinch	BCDEKS
Hazard	*BCDEKS
Heather Bell	BCDEKS
Henry Harris	BCDEKS
Hilda	BE
Hilfranor	(58)BCDEFKS
His Majesty	BCDEKS
Holland	ABCDE
Hopper 26	CDE
Hopper Barges:	4, 101, 102 (all BCDE), W24 (D)
Hound	ABCDEKS
Hurlingham	(196)BCDEKS
I Idaho	ABCDES
Imshi	BCDEKS
Industry	BCDEKS
Inspiration II	(92)BCDEKST
Iolanthe	ABCDET
Iorana	(225)B
Iota	BCDEKS
Iote	*ABCDES

230

Irenic	BCDEST
Irma	(208)BCDEKS
Iron Duke	U
Island Queen	**ABCDEHKS

J
Jacinta	*ABCDEKM
James 67	BCDE
Jane Hannah	BCDES
Jane Holland	(122)AET
Janis	*BCDE
Jeff	(199)BCDEKS
Jetsam	BCDEKS
Jockette II	(63)BCEKS
Johanna	ABCDE
Jong	(192)ABCDEFKS
Jordan	BCDE

K
Karen II	F
Karina	BCDEFKS
Kayell	BCDEFKS
Kestrel R.7	ABCDEHS
King Fisher	BCDES
Kingsgate	U
Kingwood	(198)BCDEKS
Kintail	BCDEKST
Kitcat	ABCDEFKS
Kitty	(187)BCDE
Kitty	BCDES
Kongoni	BCDEKS

L
Lady Anita	(96)U
Lady Cable	(142)ABCDEFKST
Lady Delft	(157)U
Lady Gay	(206)U
Lady Haig	(222-223)ABCDEKS
Lady Isabelle	(183)BCDEKS
Lady Lou	(86)Q
Lady Nancy	BCDEKS
Lady Rita	BCDEKST
Lady Rosebery	*ABCDEHKS
Lady Sheila	ABCDET
Lady Southborough	ABCDE
Lamouette	(72)BCDEFKS
Lansdowne	ABCDEKS
Lark	*ABCDEHIKS
Laroc	ABCDE
Latona	(140)BCDEFKS
Llaudania	BCDE
Laurel Leaf	CDES
Lavinia	BCDEKS
Lazy Days	(133)BCDEKS
Leach's Romance	**BCDEHKS
Leading Star	BCDEKS
Leila 4	BCDEFKS
Lent Lily	BCDEHKS
Letitia	(23)ABCDEKM
Letitia	*ABCDEKS
Liebestrawn	BCDEFKS
Lighters:	X95, YC63, (both ABCDE) X134, YC71, YC72 (all BCDE), X209 (D)
Lijns	(64)BCDEKS
Little Admiral	BCDEKS
Little Ann	*ABCDEKS
Little Mayflower	BCDEKS
Little O'Lady	BCDEKS
Llanthony	(60-62)ACEJ
Lord Southborough	(121)AE

NAME:	Gay Crusader
TYPE:	Motor Yacht
LENGTH:	35ft
BEAM:	9ft
DISPLACEMENT:	11.59 tons
DRAFT:	3ft
ENGINES:	Gray petrol 4 cyl.
HULL CONSTR.:	Mahogany and larch
BUILT BY:	Gibbs, Teddington
YEAR BUILT:	1935

Gay Crusader is being restored in a field in Kent, for Ron Matthews who bought her in 1989. Sub. Lieut. T.H. Rodgers was her skipper when she went to Dunkirk and Tough's records show her crew as: B. Kearns, L.R. Missingen and C.H. Newers.. After the war, one

Uffa Fox, famous yachtsman and designer, waxed lyrical when he wrote about Mary Jane in 1938 "A yacht where the owner's wife shares the joys of cruising has a restfulness and peace which is lacking in vessels used entirely by men, so that one constantly expects to see a cat curled up by an inviting fire. . . .Mary Jane is one of the cosiest yachts I've ever slept aboard". He was the guest of Col. Richardson and his wife who had converted her from a naval pinnace. Her hull built to stringent

NAME:	Miss Margate
TYPE:	Motor Cruiser
LENGTH:	24ft
BEAM:	7ft
DISPLACEMENT:	Unknown
DRAFT:	2ft
ENGINES:	Chrysler 20 h.p.
HULL CONSTR.:	Carvel
BUILT BY:	Hoylecraft, Notts.
YEAR BUILT:	1936-37

Built as a hire boat at Margate in 1936, by Hoylecraft of Nottingham, Miss Margate once went to the rescue of a light aircraft whose pilot misjudged a loop and crashed in the sea. Alas, there were no survivors. She was in Ramsgate when harbour master D.R. Price sent everything afloat to Dunkirk

of her owners had a serious accident in her, which badly damaged her starboard bow. Although she was patched up, she was then kept ashore and completely dried out so that her planks opened up. Her next owner had her re-caulked, but when he took her out, she nearly sank. He decided to cut his losses and sold her but the next owner had equally bad luck, this time with her engines, which let him down every time. Despite this long chain of woe, Ron Mathews, her latest owner, is now restoring her to make her once more a proud member of the Association.

NAME:	Mary Jane
TYPE:	Motor Yacht
LENGTH:	42ft
BEAM:	13ft
DISPLACEMENT:	16 tons
DRAFT:	4.5ft
ENGINES:	BMC Commodore
HULL CONSTR.:	Pitch pine on oak
BUILT BY:	Unknown
YEAR BUILT:	1926

Admiralty standards, her accommodation was panelled in Canadian birch and she had centralheating throughout. She owed the comfort of her furnishings to Mrs. Richardson and her daughter who often cruised in her. Now at Deptford, she belongs to David Bowderey of Camberwell.

on 31st May 1940. The smaller ships, were towed by Dutch schuit Hilda. Miss Margate was commanded by George Rickwood of Brightlingsea. After Dunkirk she was put on contraband control. After Edwin Wild had converted her for Broads cruising Michael Cates, her 1989 owner has kept her there.

Built for a London doctor, *Noneta* was part of the Portsmouth Inner Patrol and was sent to the beaches, commanded by Sub Lieut. A.J. Potter-Irwin. This was the first day when small craft arrived there in hundreds. *Noneta's*, second owner was Brig. Sir F.W.C. Featherstone-Godley, Chairman of the British

NAME:	Quest
TYPE:	Motor Cruiser
LENGTH:	30ft
BEAM:	9ft 6ins
DISPLACEMENT:	6.5 tons
DRAFT:	3ft 3ins
ENGINES:	BL Thornycroft diesel
HULL CONSTR.:	Wood
BUILT BY:	Gibbs, Teddington
YEAR BUILT:	1936

Tough's records show her among the boats they took to Ramsgate for the Admiralty. When she was returned, *Quest* was taken to Worcester and her immediate post war owner used her for holidays in Devon. She has since cruised in the Severn and Sharpness canal. *Quest* could have found no better

The motor yacht *Singapore* commanded by Sub Lieut. J. W. Pratt, RNVR, ran aground on the beaches of Dunkirk. Refloated on the rising tide she left with three Frenchmen. On the way they picked up two British soldiers who were 'floating around'. Wine from the French water bottles re-

NAME:	Noneta
TYPE:	Motor Yacht
LENGTH:	63ft
BEAM:	12ft 9ins
DISPLACEMENT:	58 tons
DRAFT:	7ft
ENGINES:	Twin Gardner 6LX
HULL CONSTR.:	Steel
BUILT BY:	J. Samuel White, Cowes
YEAR BUILT:	1934-36

Legion before World War II, who was a keen yachtsman. Rebuilt in 1956 *Noneta* has cruised extensively in the Mediterranean and she now belongs to Joseph Cassar and is based in Malta.

owners to restore her than Maureen and Alex Patch who got Judge's boatyard to restore her hull and they did the rest. They have won three trophies for the best maintained boat in their yacht club.

NAME:	Singapore
TYPE:	Motor Yacht
LENGTH:	32ft 3ins
BEAM:	9ft
DISPLACEMENT:	7.56 tons
DRAFT:	2ft 9ins
ENGINES:	6 cyl. Perkins 100 h.p.
HULL CONSTR.:	Wood
BUILT BY:	Boatbldg & Eng. Ltd.
YEAR BUILT:	Walton on Naze, 1934

vived them. In mid-channel they took three lifeboats in tow but when their engine broke down they themselves got towed home. Now in Greek ownership, the yacht is in Piraeus.

Lorna Doone	BE
Lotus	B
Louise Stephens	(118)AET
Louisiana	ABCDE
Lucy Lavers	(112)ADT
Lurline	(87)BCDEFKS
Lydia Suzanne	BCDEPR
M Madame Pompadour	ABCDEFKS
Madame Sans Gene	*ABCDEKS
Maid of Honour	*ABCDEKS
Ma Joie	*ABCDEKS
Major	BCDEFKS
Malden	BCDE
Maldon Annie	*ABCDEKS
Malvina	BCDES
Marasole	*BCDEL
Marchioness	(197)BCDEKS
Mare Nostrum	BCDEFKS
Margaret Mary	BCDEKS
Margherita	*ABCDEKS
Margo II	(169)G
Marina	BCDKS
Marquis	BCDEK
Marsayru	(84)ACDEFKS
Mary	BC
Mary Irene	BCDEKS
Mary Jane	(232)BCDEKS
Mary Rose	*ABCDEK
Mary Scott	(114)ABET
Mary Spearing	*D
Mary Spearing II	ABCDEKS
Massey Shaw	(88-90)ABCDEKLM
Mata Hari	BCDEFKS
Matilda	ABCDEFKS
Matoya	(131)BCDEFS
Mayflower	BCDEKS
May Queen	BC
Mayspear	ABCDE
MB 278	(176)U
Meander	ABCDEKS
Medora	*ABCDEKS
Medway Queen	(93-95)ACEJKLM
Mermaiden	(214)ABCDEKST
Mersey	BCDEKS
Michael Stevens	(119)ABCDET
Millicent D Leach	CDEKS
Mimosa	BCDEKST
Minikoi	*ABCDEKS
Minnedosa	BCDEKS
Minnehaha	(128-130)U
Minoru II	ABCDEK
Minotaur	ABCDEFKMS
Minx	BCDEKS
Miranda	*ABCDEKS
Miss Margate	(232)U
Miss Ming	BCDEKS
Miss Modesty	BCDEKS
Mizpah	BCDEKS
M.L.8	BCDE
M.L.108	BCDE
Moiena	(82-83)BCDEFKS
Monarch	(54)S
Montague	*BCDEKS
Moss Rose	*ABCDEKS
Motor Boats:	27b & 42 (both BCDE), 43, 101, 243, 270, 275 (all U)

MTB102	(162-164)ACDEJM
MTBM2	CDES
Mouseme	BCDES
Murius	ABCDES
Mutt	BCDEKS
N **Naiad Errant**	(14-16)ABCDEFKLMS
Nancibelle	(52)BCEKS
Nanette II	ABCDEFKST
Narcissa	BCDES
Nautilus A	BCDEFKS
Nayland	(80)AB
Nelson	BCD
Nemo IV	*ABCDEKS
New Britannic	(171)A
New Prince of Wales	
New White Heather	*U
New Windsor Castle	(55-57)BCDEKS
Nin	BCDEKS
Nirvana	BCDEKS
No Name II	BCDEKS
Noneta	(231)ACDE
Norwich Belle	BCDES
Nydia	(97)U
O Ocean Breeze	ABCDE
Offemia	ABCDEFKS
Olivia	BCDE
Omega	(134)BCDEKS
Ona II	(53)BCDEKS
Oratave RX 45	CDEKST
Orellana	(217)BCDEFS
Orient Line Motorboat	U
Oulton Belle	(65-67)CDES
Our Lizzie	(152)BCDEKS
Our Maggie	BCDEHKST
P Palmerston	BCDES
Pandora	BCDEKS
Papillon	(226)BCDEFKST
Papkura	BCDEST
Patricia	(204)AB
Pauleter	ABCDEFKMS
Pearl	B
Peggy IV	*ABCDEKS
Pelagia	(218)U
Petra	BCDEKS
Pioneer	ABCDEKS
Polly	BCDEKS
Pride of Folkestone	BCDES
Prima	ABCDE
Prince	ABCDEKS
Prince of Wales	ABCDEFKS
Princess	BCDEKS
Princess Elizabeth	(174-175)ACDEJL
Princess Freda	(194)ABCDEKS
Princess Lily	ABCDEKS
Princess Maud	*ACDEKS
Providence	(210-211)BE
Provider R19	ABCDEKS
Prudential	(121)AEMS
Pudge	(48-49)ABCDK
Q Q.J. & J.	BCDEKS
Queen	ABCDEST
Queen Alexandra	ABCDEKS
Queen Boadicea	BCDEFKST
Queen Boadicea II	(151)ABCDEKS

NAME:	Singapore II
TYPE:	Motor Cruiser
LENGTH:	32ft
BEAM:	8ft 6ins
DISPLACEMENT:	10 tons
DRAFT:	3ft 2ins
ENGINES:	Ford 4D 58 h.p. diesel
HULL CONSTR.:	Wood
BUILT BY:	Boatbldg. & Eng. Ltd.
YEAR BUILT:	Walton on Naze, 1937

Ever since her 1940 owner had her built for east coast fishing, *Singapore II* was kept in Ipswich. Sub Lieut. F.E. Greenfell took her to Dunkirk and J.B. Patston bought her after the war in '65 for his work as a naturalist. He lived in Lincolnshire and cruised the area of the Fenns and the Wash. A col-

Alive but lost: reported to be in the south of France and last seen at Antibes, *Smolt* is one of the Little Ships we have not been able to trace, though we believe she is still alive. She is another of the boats collected by Tough Brothers at Teddington and taken down to Ramsgate on

NAME:	Snow Bunting
TYPE:	Motor Yacht
LENGTH:	39ft 8ins
BEAM:	11ft
DISPLACEMENT:	7 tons
DRAFT:	4ft
ENGINES:	2 Lister diesel
HULL CONSTR.:	Pitch pine on oak
BUILT BY:	R. J. Prior, Burnham
YEAR BUILT:	1938

Two years after she was built, *Snow Bunting* went to Dunkirk. Then she served as a patrol boat in the Solent until her first post-war owner bought her in a derelict condition. It took hundreds of hours and thousands of pounds to prepare her

lector of steam launches and a boat owner since the 1920s, he established a number of nature reserves. Now *Singapore II* belongs to Richard Moss who keeps her at Woodbridge, Suffolk.

NAME:	Smolt
TYPE:	Motor Yacht
LENGTH:	39ft
BEAM:	12ft
DISPLACEMENT:	11.5 tons
DRAFT:	4.2ft
ENGINES:	Unknown
HULL CONSTR.:	Wood
BUILT BY:	Gibbs, Teddington
YEAR BUILT:	1936

her journey to Dunkirk. After the war she found her way to Brixham in Devon where Mr. and Mrs. J.E. Hambrook found her. She was their home and they lavished on her all the tender loving care she was in need of until she was sold and taken down through the French canals.

to cross the Channel and cruise down through the French canals. Now she belongs to V.S. North who lives aboard with his cat which jumps ship when the engines start.

The Little Ships of Dunkirk

Queen of England	*ABCDEKS
Queen's Channel	ABCDE
Queensland	U
Quest	(229)ABCDEFKS
Quicksilver	B
Quisisana	(141)ABCDEKST

R Rania	(27)Q
Rapide	ABCDEKS
Rayon	BCDEKS
Reda	(104-105)ABCDEFKS
Reliance	ABCDEK
Remembrance	BCDEHKS
Renown	*ABCDEKMS
Resolute	(20-22)ABCDEKS
Ricas	BCDE
Roberta	*ABCDEKST
Robert Cliff	ABCDE
Robina Tennant	BCDEKS
Rocinante	ABCDEKS
Rosabelle	*ABCDEIKS
Rosa Wood &	
Phyllis Lunn	(116-117)ABCDEST
Rose	B
Rose LN19	BCDEKS
Roselyne	BCDEKS
Rose Marie	ABCDK
Rowan	BCDE
Royal Thames	BCDEKS
Royalty	*CDHKM
Rummy II	(161)BCDEKS
Ryegate II	(136)BCDEFKS

S St. Abbs	*ABCDEI
St. Clears	ABCDE
St. Fagan	*ABCDI
St. Olaf	BCDE
St. Patrick	BCEKS
Sally Forth	BCDEKS
Salvage Launch	U
Salvor	(123-124)U
Sandown	CDEJKS
Santosy	ABCDEKS
Sarah and Emily	ABCDEKS
Satyr	BCDEKS
Saviour	ABCDE
Scene Shifter	ABCDEKS
Schedar	BCDEFKS
Sea Falcon	*ABCDEKST
Sea Foam	ABCDEKS
Seagull	BCDEKS
Seagull LN203	BCDEKS
Sea Hawk	BCDEKS
Sea Roamer	ABCDEFKS
Seasalter	ABCDEKS
Seaschool	BCDES
Sea Swallow	BCDEFKS
Seine	ABCDE
Seymour Castle	(144)BCDEKST
Shamrock	*ACDKS
Shannon	ABCDEKS
Sheldrake	BCDEFKS
Sherfield	ABCDE
Shunesta	BCDEKS
Silicia	ABCDEI
Silver Foam	ABCDEKS

Silver Queen	(73-74)B
Silver Spray	B
Silver Spray LI230	BCDEKS
Silvery Breeze	ABCDEKS
Sinbad II	BCDEKS
Singapore	(99)ABDFKS
Singapore I	U
Singapore II	(200)ABCDEKS
Skylark	(224)ABCDEKST
Skylark	U
Skylark I	ABCDEKST
Skylark II	ABCDEK
Skylark II SM281	*BDEKST
Skylark III	*ABCDEKS
Skylark III SM391	*CDEKS
Skylark IV SM5	BCDEKS
Skylark VI	ABCDEFKST
Skylark IX	(201)BCDEKST
Skylark X	(200)BCDST
Small Viking	ABCDE
Smiling Through	BCDEKS
Smolt	(233)BCDEFKS
Smuggler	BCDEKS
Snow Bunting	(230)BCDEKS
Sonia	BCDEKS
Southend Britannia	(78-79)ABCDEKS
Southern Queen	(68-69)ABCDEKST
Southern	
Queen PL17	*ABCDEKS
South Ray	BCDEKS
Speedwell	BCDE
Spinaway	ABCDEFKS
Spindrift	BCDEK
Sprite	BCDE
Starfish	BCDEKS
Stonehaven	ABCDEKS
Suffolk's Rose	BCDEKS
Sultan	ABCD
Summer Maid	ABCDEKST
Sundowner	(102-103)ABCDEFKS
Sunshine R13	*ABCDEKS
Surrey	(184-186)ACDEKS
Sylvia	(137)BCDEK

T **Tamzine**	(125)B
Tankerton	
Towers	ABCDEHKS
Tarifa	(213)F
Tarpon	BCDEKST
Tenias	ABCDE
Thame	**(172)U
Thark	ABCDEKS
The King	(28-29)BCDEKS
Thelmar	(168)BT
Thetis	*ABCDKS
Thomas Kirk	
Wrright	(122):AEST
Three Brothers	BCDEKS
3270	BCE
Thurn	BCDEKS
Thyforsa	ABCDE
Thyme	U
Thyra	ABCDE
Tigris I	**(30-32)ABCDEKS
Tollesbury	(36-38)ACDM
Tom Hill	BCDEKST

Tom Tit	(205)U
Tony LN40	BCDEKS
Tortoise	BCDEFS
Trillene	BCDEFKS
Triton	**BCEKS
Two Rivers	ABCDEKS
Two Sisters	BCDEKS

U Unique	BCDEFHIKS
Usanco	BCDEFKS

V Valerie II	BCDEKST
Vanguard	(209)ABCDEKMS
Vanitee	*ABCDEK
Vedettes	CDEFKS
Venture	B
Vera	B
Vere	(85)B
Victoria	BK
Viewfinder	*ABCDEKS
Viking	(51)ABCDEKS
Viking III	*ABCDEKS
Viscount	(195)BCDEKS
Viscountess	
Wakefield	(120)ACDET
Volante R110	U
Volo	BCDEHKS

W Wairaki	(98)U
Wairaki II	(160)BCDEFKS
Walmer Castle	BCDEH
Wanda	(220-221)CDEGKS
Warrior	(81)ABCDEKS
Warrior	CDEHKS
Watchful	(138-139)D
Wave Queen	ABCDEKS
Welcome	BCDEST
Wessex	BCDGI
Westall	BCDEKS
Westerley	ABCDEKS
Westgrove	BCDE
Westward	B
Weymouth Queen	BCDEKS
White Bear	ACDKS
White Heather	(227)B
White Lady	BCDEKS
White Orchid	**(100-101)BCDEKS
White Wing	ABCDEKS
Whitewater	BCDEKS
Willanne	U
Willdora	(17)U
Willmarie	U
Willnorman	U
Willie and Alice	ABCDEKS
Windsong	(158-159)ABCDEKST
Wings of the	
Morning	ABCDEKST
Winnabet	BCDEKS
Winston	BCDES
Wolfe	ABCD
Wolsey	ACEJ
Wootton	BCDEM

Y Yola	BCDEFKS

Acknowledgements

The histories of the Little Ships, the illustrations and the anecdotes contained in this book have been drawn from sources too numerous to mention. Actual survivors of Dunkirk were scarce in 1989, but we still found many first-hand accounts. Harry Hastings died only weeks after he spoke to us. His son Roland told us about the Thames passenger steamers. Others who could cast back their minds for 50 years or more included Capt. Jim Brown, Tom Bell, Ron Lenthall, Reg Yebsley, Eric Davis, Norman Girling and Bill Chalmers.

Past and present owners of ships generously helped with documents and pictures. Local fishermen, boatbuilders and mariners helped us trace ships and people. Our special thanks are due to Bob Tough who gave us access to his father's records, pictures and the Dunkirk charts reproduced on the endpapers of this book. Bill Finch was a mine of information about the Medway boats and John Tooke about the working barges. Heather Deane of the RNLI and Jeff Morris of the Lifeboat Enthusiasts Society, Kathleen Harrison of Cowes Public Library, Dr. John Bullen and the staff of the Imperial War Museum never failed to respond to our cries for help. Leo Cooper, publisher of military books, gave us much useful advice. Martin Summers allowed us to use *Bluebrd of Chelsea* with Scott Beadle, as skipper, for taking photographs at rallies. Lt. Col. & Mrs M. Harris contributed the late Bernard McDonald's map of the BEF positions at Dunkirk. We have already paid tribute to John Knight, Hon. Archivist of the ADLS, without whose help and encouragement this book could not have been written.

Among the photographers, Beken of Cowes, three generations: founder, son and grandson, must be singled out. Kenneth Beken let us search through his amazing collection, including 100-year-old glass plates and Ken took many of the most recent ones especially for us. But we equally appreciate the pictures from Jack Smith and Derek Weston and the many private ones contributed by present and past owners, their widows and children, many of whom trustingly took them out of family albums so that they could appear in this book. Hopefully, in this way they will survive longer than any of us! Where copyright is uncertain, we have credited those who gave us the pictures. If, in this brief list, I have failed to give tribute to anyone who deserves special mention, I hope that I may be forgiven and that they will be pleased to have contributed to this memorial to the Little Ships and those who made them a proud part of our nation's history.

Christian Brann
Kemble, Gloucestershire,
October 1989

Second generation: Keith Beken

The list which follows is in alphabetic order of photographers, contributors and copyright owners of pictures in this book. The pages on which their pictures appear are given after their names. The letters after the page numbers mean:
  a: above, **r**: right, **c**: centre
  and **b**: below.

ADLS collection: 7b, 25, 35, 79, 85, 116a, 134a, 140, 143, 160b, 161, 174a, 205b, 206a, 222r. **Clive Anderson**: 193. **G.T.Atkinson**: 204a. **J. Bailey**: 135b. **R. & M. Balcomb**: 200. **H. W. Bambridge**: 77. **Ray Barrett**: 152. **Raymond Baxter**: 8c, 181b, 186a & r. **Beken of Cowes:** Cover b, 19, 74, 81a, 86a & b, 89, 90, 105, 107a, 108b, 114a,

Frank Beken, 1880- 1970, founder of a dynasty, with the camera he made himself.

Acknowledgements

Third generation: Kenneth Beken

115b, 117b, 118a, 120a, 122a, 130, 134b, 137, 147, 158, 168, 170b, 173, 174-175, 180a, 182a, 184, 187, 192a, 194b, 202, 210a, 213, 214a, 216a, 221a, 224b, 225a, 227a. **Donald Berry:** 225b. **Brian Blake:** 6a, 17a, 32. **J. Blake:** 66. **G. Borsboom:** 86c. **A.F. Bourne:** 135a. **David Bowdery:** 231c. **E.S.Brandao:** 207. **Christian Brann:** 4a, 16c, 128a, 139b, 181a, 194a, 195b, 196, 197a, 198, 211a, r & br, 220a, 221b. **Kenneth Brewer:** 204b. **Derek Bromige:** 230b. **Capt. J.S. Brown:** 222a & b, 223. **J.B. Cannell:** 44, 101. **Norman Cannell:** 72b, 104b. **Anne Carter:** 53. **Mrs J.P. Carter:** 138b. **Joseph Cassar:** 232a. **Michael Cates:** 231b. **C.J. Cave:** 115a. **W.D. Chalmers:** 178a, 179a. **Mark Child:** 30, 195a, 232c. **R.L.Cornwell:** 124a. **Dr.Robert Cowley:** 183b. **Crescent Shipping Ltd.:** 41b. **F.S.Cooper Collection/ Ray Rush:** 39b. **Eric Davis:** 206b. **Daily Despatch/ Bob Tough Collection:** 128b. **Ian Davidson:** 27. **Aidan de la Mare:** 180b. **Sue Dimbylow:** 230a. **Brian Down:** 153. **Kevin P.Duffy:** 176. **East Kent Maritime Trust:** 102, 103. **Echo, Sunderland:** 17b. **Sandy Evans:** Cover a, 14b, 15. **P.W.Farrant:** 182b. **Howard Fawsitt:** 114b. **Dr.J.W.E.Fellows:** 227b. **Bill Finch:** 131b, 136a. **Mark Fishwick:** 167. **Simon Frost:** 23. **J.K.Fuller:** 165. **Rev. T.J.Fuller:** 217. **M.V.Gardener:** 162, 163. **Frank E.Gibson:** 68, 171. **Mrs. J.Gingell:**

63a. **Cameron Graham:** 60b. **J.C.Graham:** 155. **P.M.Hambrook:** 233c. **Michael Hamby:** 178b, 179c & b. **Tom Hanson:** 139a. **R.V. Harris:** 98. **R. Harvey-George:** 166. **Harry Hastings:** 29a. **Roland Hastings:** 197b, 199b. **Herald Express, Torquay:** 142. **M.K. Hill:** 26. **Dave Hocquard:** 73. **J.M. Holman:** 218. **J.G. Hornshaw:** 81b. **Hulton-Deutsch Collection:** 7a, 156a. **Frank Hutchinson:** 54. **Imperial War Museum:** 2, 6b, 7c, 125, 228. **Interyacht Ltd:** 216b. **Alan Jackson:** 148. **Kent Photonews Ltd:** 226. **W.H. Keyte:** 34b. **Ian F. Kiloh:** 132b. **Paul King:** 170a. **John Knight:** 8r, 146b. **Mrs J.Lamb:** 8a. **Leigh Times:** 21, 22b.

Jack Smith

M.J.P.Lewen: 160a. **Nicholas Lidiard:** 141. **Rodney Lissenden:** 93. **London Fire Brigade:** 88,90. **Stephen Lucas:** 205a. **T.E. Machin:** 65, 67. **Alex McMullen:** 123, 203b, 215a. **David Maude:** 39a. **A.C.Miller:** 20. **John Mills:** 149a, 177, 212. **John Moor:** 111c &b. **H.M.Morris:** 70,71. **J.Morris:** 110a. **Jeff Morris/Life-boat Enthusiasts Society:** 121b. **National Maritime Museum:** 118b. **Norfolk Museums Service, Great Yarmouth:** 138a. **V.S. North:** 233b. **A.B. Nott-Bower:** 132a. **Mrs. E.K. Osborne:** 22a. **R.D. Paton:** 60a, 61, 62. **Steven Peel:** 64. **Picturecard Promotions, Plymouth:** 151. **Planet News/ London Fire Brigade:** 91. **W. Raven:** 133.

John Richards: 183a. **John Ridalls:** 144, 145. **Alan Roades:** 156b. **Isabelle Robinson:** 80. **Nicholas Rorke:** 59. **Richard Rothery:** 117a. **J.F. Rouschop:** 214b. **Royal National Lifeboat Institution:** 109a, 110b, 111a, 112, 116b, 119, 120b, 121a, 122b. **E. Samuelson:** 224a. **Mrs E.Savill:** 24. **John Sharman-Courtney:** 172. **Michael Simcock:** 87. **Keith Slaughter:** 208. **D.R.Smith:** 219. **Jack Smith:** 4b, 8b, 33, 58a, 63b, 72a, 97a, 99, 100, 113, 129b, 146a, 149b, 150, 157, 185, 186b, 203a, 220b, 230c, 233a. **D.B.Stewart:** 96.. **Martin Summers:** 188, 189 c & b, 190, 191. **John Sweeney:** 201. **Anita Tait:** 231a. **Thames Tripping Ltd:** 28, 29b. **George & Meriel Thurstan:** 10, 11, 12, 13. **Bob Tough:** 9b, 31, 129a, 192b. **Turks Launches:** 55, 56-57, 199a. **David Turner:** 52. **Don Waddleton:** 34a. **N.D. Watling:** 58b. **Richard Walker/Studio 70, Swindon:** 14a, 16b. **Nigel Warrington-Smyth:** 210b, 211b. **Dennis Wells:** 92. **Derek Weston:** 37, 40, 41a, 43, 45, 46, 47, 48, 50, 51, 84, 94, 95, 123, 124b, 131a, 136b. **Whisstocks Ltd:** 104a. **Geoffrey White:** 69. **J.White:** 108a. **Doug Whiting:** 209. **J. Wilkie:** 109b. **B.J.Wood:** 126, 127. **M.R.Woods:** 18. **World of Interiors Magazine:** 189a. **Ron Wylie:** 106, 107b. **Richard Young:** 169. **Wassos Zachazakis:** 232b. **E.H.Zandwijk:** 82, 83.

Derek Weston

Abdy Beauclerk **120**
Aberdonia **170**
Adam Mr. 203
ADAT 175
Adesi see *Greater London* 119
Admirals' boats (ADLS) 180-181, 184-186
Admiralty 72, 85, 219, 228
Advance 148
Afrika korps 181
Ailsa Craig engines 77, 85, 230
Ailsa Yard 93
Alabama see *Falcon II* 99
Aldeburgh lifeboat 108, 120
Alderman 49
Aldington, Donald 192
Alexander, Maj. Gen. H. 164
Alexander, Louisa 18
Allard, General 154
Allden, Col.S.G. 217
Alliance see *Lady Anita* 96
Allendale, G. 192
Alusia **18-19**
Amazone see *Mermaiden* 214
Ambler, H. 217
Ambleve 165
Amulree 150
Anderson, Clive 193
Andover II 148
Angele Aline **10-13**
Ankh 150
Anne **77**
Anstey, A.J. 137
Apple Tree, The 152
Aquabelle **230**
Aquila see *White Orchid* 100
Arkian see *Rania* 27
Armed Patrol Service 147
Ashcroft, Gerald 102
Ashton, Victor 144
Association of
Dunkirk Little Ships 8-9, 221
(Flags) 9
Association of St. Mary's
Passenger Craft 69
Astor, Lord 60
Atanua see *Mary Scott* 110
Atley, Capt. 42, 44
Aureol see *Kitty* 187
Auxiliary River Patrol 140
Avanturine 116

Bailey, George 183
Bailey, John 135
Bain, John 82, 98, 160
Baker, G. &. T 222
Balcomb, R. & M. 200
Bambridge, H. W. 77
Barden, A. 158
barge trade 36, 38, 39, 40-41, 42-44, 45-46,47,51
barge yachts 52, 180-181
barges 36-38, 39, 40-41, 42-44, 45-46, 47, 48-49, 50,51
Barnard, Lt. Col. 188
Barnet class 114
Barnett, B. 193
Barrett, Ray 152
Bartlett, Percy 97
Baudoin engines 166
bawley sailing ships 20-22, 23, 24, 25-26
Baxter, Raymond 8, 184-186
Bayle, H.L. 87
Beacon Boat Yard 64
Beadle, Scott 188, 189, 190
Beale, S. Lieut. L. 214
Beatles, The 130
Beatrice Maud **47**
Beaumont, Percy 225
Beckwith, Gary 28
Beech, Mr. 187
Beken of Cowes Ltd. 9, 81
Belgian Seaways List 228
Belgian Ship Lover, The 228
Belgian Ships used 228
Bell, Lieut. S.. 151
Ben & Lucy .. 23, 24, 26
Bennay, Leonce 10, 12
Berry, Donald 225
Betje 194
Betty **173**
Beverley see *Southend Britannia* 79
Blackwell 123
Blake engines 217

Blakes' Cruises 67
Bluebird 74, 188
Bluebird of Chelsea 166, **188-191**
Bluebird II **166-167**
BMC engines 35, 39, 63, 64, 72, 84, 92, 97, 104, 140, 160,161,165, 168, 181, 185, 203, 205, 219, 222, 225, 226, 230, 231
Boats & Cars 140
Bolson, J. & Son 200,201
Bolus, I. & J. 142
Bonadventure 154
Borsboom, G. 86
Boswell, Cdr. 162
Bou Saada **216**
Bounty **33**
Bourne, Fred 135
Bowderey, David 231
Bowley, A.G. 182
Bowman, Len 29
Bradyll-Johnson,
Cdr. V.A.L 66,226, 228
Braemar see *Braymar* 143
Brann, Christian 193
Bray, Mr. 143
Braymar **143**
Breda see *Dab II* 182
Brewer, K. & P. 204
Brewster, Lieut. C.H.H. 227
Briault, Douglas 34
Brightlingsea Belle see
Southend Britannia 78
Brig..ton Belle 93, 174
Brighton Queen 174
Brit see *Watchful* 138, 139
Britannia (Royal Yacht) 204
British Legion 232
Britt II see *Watchful* 138
Broads Cruiser 231
Brockman & Titcombe 125
Bromige, Derek 230
Brooke engines 225
Brooke, J.W. & Co. 182
Brookes, Cdr. Ewart 178-179
Broom, Alf 142
Brown, B. & D. 222
Brown, Ian 173
Brown, Capt. Jim 222-223
Brown Owl Class 98, 160
Brown, S. 213
Brownsea Island 201
Bryher Boat Services 170
Buchanan, Lieut. Cdr. 207
Buckle, A.C. 87
Bukh engines 154
Burbridge, John 223
Burnard, C.W. 173
Burnham Oyster Co. 209
Butler, L. Col. E. 228

Cabby **40-41**, 49
Cable, Lady of Lindridge 142
Cachalot **132**
Cadgwith lifeboat 111
Caleta 150
Cameron Highlanders 26
Campbell, Gina 189
Campbell, Sir Malcolm 74, 166, 167, 188, 190
Camper & Nicholson 33, 61, 74, 81, 150
Cannell, J.B. 100, 101, 221
Cannell, Norman 100, 101, 105
Carama 117
Caresana see *Charles*
Cooper Henderson 106-107
Caronia see *Watchful* 139
Carpathia 102
Cars & Boats Ltd. 185
Carshalton Sea Cadets 206
Carter, Cdr. 73
Carter, K. & A. 53
Caspari, P. E. 187
Cassar, Joseph 232
Castaways, The 175
Cates, George 66
Cates, Michael 231
Cattle, Ted 71
Cave, C. J. 115
Cecil & Lilian Philpott **116**, 118
Challenge 223
Chalmers, Sgt. W. D. 179
Chalmondesleigh **156**
Channel Rover

see *Charles Dibdin* 122
Chapman, R. C. 230
Charlmain 146
Charles & Eliza Laura
see *Salvor* 123
Charles Cooper
Henderson **106-107**
Charles Dibdin **122**
charter boats 10-13, 150
Chase, C. 193
Chase, Irwin 126
Chatham Historic
Dockyard 24
Chatterton, E. K. 228
Chelsea Harbour 193
Cherry, Peter 97
Chichester, Sir Francis 101
Chico **74-76**, 166
Christie, J. 58
Chrysler engines 143, 156, 193, 231
Chrysler Marine Co. 156
Chumley see
Chalmondesleigh 156
Churchill, W. S. 7, 164, 207
citations 71
Clacton-on-Sea
Lifeboat 111, 121, 148
Clapson & Son 207
Clark, Bill 30, 31, 32
Clark, Horace 14
Clarke, Cdr. 206
Clayton, Cdr. P. F. 26
Clements,
Lieut. Cdr.W.R.T. 215
Cliff & Jones 133
Clough, Joe 209
Cobham, Sir Alan & Lady 150
cockle boats see
bawley sailing ships 20-22,23, 24, 25-26
Colberg, E. 167
Cole & Wiggens 24, 177
Collier, Richard 228
Collins, Dr. Charles 160
Colonial Wharf 91
Columbine see *Reda* 105
Co-operative Barge
Yard 51
Commodore see
New Britannic 170
Commodores' Boats
(ADLS) 34-35, 100-101,128-130, 143, 146-147, 180-181, 184-186, 220-221, 225, 227
Conidaw 74, 75
Contraband control 222
Cook, Lieut. A. T. 93, 95
Cook, Dick 147
Cook, Jack 170
Cordelia **165**
Cordon Rouge see *Eothen* 127
Cornwell, Reg 124
Coronation Review,
Spithead 94
Count Dracula 99, **178-179**
Courtney & Newhook 143
Coventry Boat
Builders 183
Cowes-Torquay races 221
Cowley, Dr. Robert 183
Cox, F. G. 160
Cox & King 143
Crabtree, Stanley 81
Crane, Sean 153
Crawford, A 193
Crescent Shipping Ltd. 41, 46, 49
Crested Cock 50
Crested Eagle 148
Crompton, J. T. 217
Crossley, Petty Officer 95
Crump, A. 131
Cummins engines 214
Cundall, Charles 228
Cupid see *Glala* 150
Curtis, Frank 77
Cygnet **59**
Cyril & Lilian Bishop **109**

Dab II **182**
DAF engines 83
Daimler-Benz engines 61
Dalton, G. L. 158
Dalton's Weekly 80
Dann, S. Lieut. F. N. 193
Dansie, Dr. Oliver 116

Daphne **212**
Darby, P. J. 77
Dart Pleasure Cruises 151
Dartmothian see
Seymour Castle 144
Davidson, Ian 27
Davis, engineer 94
Davis, E & G. 206
Davis family 153
Day, G. F. A. 157
Day, Summers 174
de Gaulle, Gen. Charles 145
de Hamel, S. Lieut 50
de Mattos, S. Lieut B. G. P. 68
de Orellana, Francisco 217
Deal, C. J. 97
Deal boats 222
Deards, Robert 46
Deenar **219**
Defense, Min. of 187, 202
Defender 20, 22, 23, **25-26**
Delise see *Desel II* 230
Dench, A. J. 23
Dervilers, Paul 94
Desel II **230**
Devas, Liz 87
Devonia 174
Devonport dockyard 134
Devries Lensch 64
Dianthus **193**
Dickenson, S. Lieut Stephen 110
Dickie's Yard 81
Dimbleby, Richard 26
Dinwiddie Mr & Mrs 131
Dive & Ski Club
of St. Helier 108
Divine, A. D. 84, 142, 146, 160, 166, 228
Dolphin Barge Museum 50, 51
Dorian **70-71**
Doris 49
Dorman engines 227
Doutelle see *White*
Orchid 100, 101, 221
Dow, S. Lieut. J. A. 150
Dowager see *Rosa Woodd*
& Phyllis Lunn 113
Downes, S. J. 226
Downs, The 222
Dragonfly **154**
Drake 123
Draycott, A. C. 96
Dreyer, Cdr. C. W. S. 162-164
Dreyfus, Edmund 216
drug running 82-83
du Cane, Cdr. Peter 162
Duddridge, Col. M. N. V. 159
Duke of Cornwall 114
Duke of Wellington's
Regiment 42
Duffy, T. 176
Dundee Ketch 10
Dungeness lifeboat 106, 120
Dunkirk book 84, 142, 146, 160, 228
Dunkirk (eye witness
accounts) 14-16, 20-22, 23, 30-32, 38, 42-44, 60-62, 75-76, 80, 88-91, 94, 136, 148-149, 158, 162-164, 178-179, 207, 226
Dunkirk Returns to 26, 103, 181
Dunkirk Little Ships,
List of 228-234
Dunkirk Veterans
Association 53, 201

Eagle has Landed, The 164
Eagle steamers 21
East Kent Maritime Trust 103
East Yorks Regiment 42
Eastbourne lifeboat 122
Edward Z. Dresden **121**
Eisenhower, Gen. D. D. 164
Electric Launch Co. 126, 127
Elizabeth Green 8, 146, 147, **148-149**
Elkins, E. F. 203, 220, 221
(records) 228
Ellis, Albert 198
Ellis, L. F. 228
Elphinstone, Sir Lancelot 132
Elsa II **135**
Elvin **207**
E.M.E.D. **119**
Emergency River
Transport Service 56
Emile Deschamps 90

Index

Emms, Sam 140
Empress of India 56, 110
Ena **42-44**
Endeavour 20, **24**, 25
Eothen **126-127**
Epic of Dunkirk, The 228
Ethel Everard 38
Ethel Maud **39**
Evans, Sandy 16
Evelyn see *Orellana* 217
Eves, Joe 80
Excel 123
Exchange and Mart 187
Fairbrother, Capt. John 41
Fairfield, Dennis 59
Fairman, Charles 201
Fairmile Craft 78
Falcon II **99**
Falkingham, T. H. 158
Farrant, P. & L. 182
Farry engines 176
Fawsitt, Howard 114
Featherstone-Godley
    Brig. Sir F. W. C. 232
Fedalma II 8, **146-147**
Felicity **153**
Fellows & Co. 65, 139
Fellows Dr. J. W. E. 227
Felton, H. 36
Ferguson, C. B.& P. 73]
Fermain V see *Silver Queen* 73
ferries see passenger vessels
Ferris & Blank 144
Ferry engines 114, 115
Fervant **215**
Festival of Britain 138
Fiat engines 191
Fierstone Leonard 187
Filleul, Lieut. P. M. 214
filmed Little Ships 26, 152, 164,
    165, 175
Finch, Bill 131, 220
Fincham, John 217
Findley, Mr. 70
fireboats 88-91
Firefly **177**
Fisher, Bud 199
fishing boats 20-22, 23, 24,
    25-26, 125, 142, 152, 209, 223, 225
Flanders, John 154
Fleet Air Arm 180
Fletcher, Arra 109
Fleuret family 203
Flight Refuelling Ltd. 150
Fleury II **203**
Foam Queen 192
Folkestone Belle **202**
Ford engines 24, 25, 55, 68, 73,
    109, 116, 144, 145, 153, 162, 165, 170
    171, 197, 199, 202, 207, 217, 233
Forecast 75
Foreman, A. C. 134
Foreman, Sub Lieut. E. S. 194
Foremost 87 118
Forty Two **230**
Foudroyant 15
Fox, Charles H. 146, 147
Fox, Uffa 231
Framlingham College 218
Frances 8, **180-181**
Fraser, George 17
Fray, Capt. B. G 85
Freddy 28
Free French Forces 145
Freebooter see *Our Lizzie* 152
Freeman, Emile 217
French, Eric 203
French Lieutenant's Woman 152
Fryer, E. G. 49
Fuller, J. K. 165
Fuller, Rev. Terry 217
Fyldea 75

gaff cutters 20-22, 132
gaff ketch 10-13
Galway, J. 98
Gardner engines 33, 70, 134,
    150, 151, 195, 200, 224, 232
Garside, Lieut. E. T. 148, 149
Gates, L. 72
Gay Crusader **231**
Gay Goblin see *Latona* 140
Gay Venture **34-35**
Geba see *Lady Isabelle* 183
General Motors engines 215

Gentle Ladye see *Jong* 192
George, Les 51
George VI 7
George Wheeler Launches 144, 151
German Imperial Navy 178
Gibbs, H. 136, 183, 231, 232, 233
Gibson, Mike 108
Gilbert & Pascoe 210
Gill & Sons 172
Gill Bros. 40
Gingell, Joan 63
Girl Guide see *Guide of
    Dunkirk* 111
Girl Guides Association 111
Glala **150**
Glendenning Cdr. J. 80
Gleniffer engines 65, 75, 87, 88,
    89, 102, 160, 202
Glenway **50**
Gloster Aircraft 140
Goddard P. & C. 76
Golden Era see *Llanthony* 62
Gondolier Queen **145**
Goodman Sub. Lieut. T. E. 84
Goodwin Sands 222, 223
Goole Shipbuilding Co. 166
Gorlestone 166
Gort General Lord 33
G.R.1740 165
Gracie Fields 174
Graf Spee 159
Graham, Cameron 60, 154
Grand Duchess 56
Graves, J. D. 93, 95
Great Britain 193
Great Yarmouth & Gorlestone
    Lifeboat 110, 114, 115
Greater London **119**, 121
Greater London Council 91
Green, B. & B. J. 177
Greenfell, Sub. Lieut. F. E. 233
Greiner, C. & A. 178, 179
Greta **45-46**
Grey Mist 74
Griffiths, Mr. 226
Griggs, Edward 222
Grimwade, skipper 209
Groenier, B. & D. 11
Groves & Gutteridge 107, 108, 113
    18, 122
Guide of Dunkirk **111**

H.A.C. 42
H. & T. Marine 189
Hackforth-Jones, Mr. 207
Hall, F. 24
Hambrook, Mr. & Mrs. J. E. 233
Hamby, Michael 99, 179
Hamilton-Khaan, D. & C. 216
Handy Billy engine 135
Hanora 148
Harbour Defence Patrol 150
Hardy, Lieut. Col. 182
Haresign, Dennis 53
Harewood, Admiral 159
Harland & Woolff 161, 176
Harpur, Bert 137
Harris, Leslie, W. 226
Harris., Cdr. W. V. H. 74
Harris, R. V. 98
Hartlepool Diving Club 17
Harvey, Dr. R. V. 33
Harvey, Ted 26
Harvey-George, B. & S. 167
Hassall, I 98
Hastings, Harry 30-32, 195
Hastings Lifeboat 109
Hastings, Roland 195, 198
Hastings, Warren 30, 32
Hawkins, Jack 165
Hawood, B. 226
Hayes, Marshall 72
Haywards Boatbuilders 20, 21
Haywood Boatbuilders 25, 54
Hebe 33
Henley Royal Regatta 101, 215
Heron, Lieut. 47
Hibbs Sailmaker 45
Hicks, Alec 69
Highlander engines 207
Hilda 222, 231
Hilfranor **58**
Hill, Gaynor 190

Hilliard, David 59, 159, 225
Hills, W. 58
Hilton, Bob 136
Hindenburg 178
Hissons, V 58
H.M.S. Barnham 176
H.M.S. Basilisk 174
H.M.S. Calcutta 80
H.M.S. Erebus 176
H.M.S. Golden Eagle 150
H.M.S. Grafton 80
H.M.S. Hamford 140
H.M.S. Icarus 121
H.M.S. Iron Duke 176
H.M.S. Keith 33, 174
H.M.S. Kellet 119
H.M.S. King Alfred 81
H.M.S. Manatee see *White
    Heather* 227
H.M.S. M.M.S.41 149
H.M.S. Queen Elizabeth 176
H.M.S. Raglan 176
H.M.S. Resolution 176
H.M.S. Seriola 33
H.M.S. Sir John Moore 176
H.M.S. Verity 75
H.M.S. Vernon 162
H.M.S. Wakeful 72
H.M.S. Windsor 75
Hockin, Bert 142
Holdaway, Terry 169
Holman, John 218
Holmwood, E. Somers 226
Holton Heath Depot 201
Horn Bros. 73
Hornby engines 36
Hornshaw, J. & M. 81
hovelling 222
Howard, J. 39, 87, 181
Hoylecraft 231
Hugget, R. & C. 179, 226
Hulbert, Jerry 208
Hurlingham **196**, 197, **198**
Hurrell, John 59
Hurst 136
Hurst Castle & Cruises 153
Husk, J. & Son 131, 145
Hutchinson, Frank 54
Hydrogen 50
Hythe Lifeboat 120

Iceland Naval Base 204
Imperial War Museum 125, 146,
    187, 202
Ingle, Wing Cdr. Alex 82
Inspiration II **81**
International Marine Radio 135
Iorana **225**
Iris see *Southend Britannia* 78, 79
Irma **208**
Island Queen 153
Isotta Fraschini engines 162

J-class yachts 20, 36
Jackson, Alan 149
Jackson, P. J. & R. F. 200
Jacobs, Arthur 55, 56, 199
Jameson, J. J. 131, 213
Jane Holland 122
Janick see *Bluebird II* 167
Janthea see *Reda* 104-105
Janice 151
Jarrett, William 51
Java 80
Jean see *Angele Aline* 10
Jean see *Thame* 172
Jeff **199**
Jefferson, Wing Cdr. Tom 192
Jeffries, Mr. 178
Jenkins, K. & L. 170
Jockette II **63**
Johnson & Johnson 23
Johnson, Anna 227
Jolly, Lieut. 94
Jones, S. & J. 187
Jong **192**
Joscelyne, Vincent 20
Judges Boatyard 232
Julian, R. J. F. 165
Jurd, Lesley 35

Kaye, Arthur 105
Kearns, B. 231
Keeble & Sons 209
Keep the Memory Green 228

Keith 163
Kelvin engines 17, 19, 20, 21,
    41, 49, 70, 209, 218
Kelvin Hughes 135
Kenia 92
ketches 34-35, 59, 98, 134, 143,
    152, 158-159, 160, 217, 218, 224,
Kiekenend Co. 214
Kiloh, I. & J. 132
Kinder Star 158
King, E. G. & Son 206
King, Harold 23
King Edward VII 28
King, Paul, 190
King, W. & Sons 216
Kingston Bridge Boatyard 200
Kingwood 197, **198**
Kirkaldy, Douglas 124, 215
Kitty **187**
Kiwi 143
Knight, Howard 117
Knight, John 8, 9, 146, 147, 149,
    185, 187, 202, 219
Knowles 49
Knowles, Hugh 72

L'Aventure see *Dragonfly* 154
Lady Anita **96**
Lady Aureol see *Kitty* 187
Lady Cable **142**
Lady Delft **157**
Lady Frances see *Frances* 8, 180-181
Lady Gay **206**
Lady Haig **222-223**
Lady Isabelle **183**
Lady Lou **86**
Lady Roseberry 48, 49
Lamb, Cdr. Charles 8, 180, 181,
    185, 186
Lamb, J. & J. 181
Lambe, J. E. 165
Lambert, Wing Cdr. Leonard 99
Lamouette **72**
Lamplough, H. E. 217
Landscaper 79
Larkin, P. & E. 107
Latham, Ricky 63
Latona **140**, **187**
Launch & Boat Co. 137
Lawrence, T. B. 113
Lazarus, M. V. 133
Lazy Days **133**
Leather, John 45
Leach, J. D. 154
Lenthall, Ron 104, 105, 217
L'Esperance see *Lucy Lavers* 108
Letcher, T. C . 194, 202
Letitia **23**, **24**, 25
Lewis, E. & P. 213
Lewis, J. & P. 224
Lewns, E. P. 225
Leyland engines 133, 194, 196, 198
Leyland, Lieut. 160
Lidiard, Nicholas 141
lifeboat (ships') 204
lifeboats 106-107, 108, 109, 110,
    111, 112-113, 114, 115, 116, 117, 118,
    119-122, 123
Lightoller, C. H., & family 102, 103
Lijns **64**
Lindy Lou see
    Cyril & Lilian Bishop 109
Lister engines 171, 233
Little, James 50
Little Ann 146
Little Ships (participation) 7
Llanthony **60-62**, 84
Loch-Lack, J. E. 203
Loggins, C. 84
L'Oiseau Bleu 188
Lolostuzzo, Patrice 230
London & Rochester
    Trading Co. 40, 41, 48, 49, 51
London Fire Brigade 91
London Gazette 228
London River Yacht Club 86
London - Cowes race 143
Long, Bill 110
Longfield, E. W. & S. H. D. 67
L'Orage see *Surrey* 8, 184-186
Lord Southborough **121**
Lord, Walter 84
Louise Stephens 110, **114**, 115
Lowestoft Lifeboat 115
Lucas, Stephen 205

Lucy Lavers **108**
Lund, Cdr. C.A. 81
Lundy, Lieut. C. A. 33
Lurline of Ipswich **87**
Lusitania 126
Lutzow 178
Lydd 148

Ma Joie 209
MacAllister, Petty Officer 95
McBride, W. G. 227
McCracken, Dr. 77
McGruer & Co. Ltd. 127
McKay, Colonel 42
McKenzie, Bob 166
McLearon, W. 42
McMeak, William 129
Machin, Tom 67
Mackenrot, C. P. 226
Mada see *Fleury II* 203
Maher, Rory 230
Mahratta 223
Mallett, Felix 45, 46
Mansell, Charles 86
Mansfield, P. 98
Marchioness **197**
Marcuse, Gerald 96
Margate Lifeboat 121
Margherita 31
Margo II **169**
Marine Transit Ltd. 196
Maritime Trust 91
Maritime Vessels Pres. Soc. 91
Marinner, John S. 82
Marsayru **84**, 192
Mary Jane **231**
Mary May 49
Mary Scott **110**
Masefield, John 15, 16, 101, 228
Mason, Sub. Lieut. J. 75
Massey Shaw **88-91**
Mathews, Ron 231
Mathews, W. 170
Matoya **131**, 220
Maude, D. & J. 39
Maxim, Henry 220
May, S. 91
Maynard, F. 171
M.B.278 **176**
Meakins, Harry 222, 223
Mears, J. T. 76, 195, 197, 198, 199
Medway Queen **93-95**
Medway Queen Pres. Soc. 95
Medway Queen Trust 95
Medway Yacht Club 168
Mehatis see *Lady Gay* 206
Melinda Margot see *Tom Tit* 205
Melsom, L. 213
Mercedez Benz engines 173
merchant vessels, records of 228
Mermaiden **214**
Metropolitan Fire Brigade 88
Michael Stephens, **115**
Mighty horse 151
Milland, H. 48
Miller, Dusty 22
Miller, J. N. & Son Ltd 75
Millington Drake, Sir J. & Lady 159
Mills, D. & J. 212
Millson, C. E. 168
Milson, L. 131
Mine Watching Patrol 76
Minnehaha **128-130**
Minns, Jonathan 210, 211
Minton, G. H. 72
Miracle of Dunkirk 84
Miskimmin, Fred 58
Miss Margate **231**
Missingen, L. R. 231
Mitterrand, President J. 145
M.L.286 see *Eothen* 127
Moelfre lifeboat 123
Moeltke 178
Moiena 81-83
Monarch **54**
Montgomery, Maj. Gen. B 7
Moody, A. 116
Moor, John 111
Morgan Giles Ltd. 142
Morris engines 14, 18, 27, 59, 86, 100, 148, 173, 206, 216, 220, 226, 230
Morris, Maj. M. P. 59
Moss, Richard 233
Motor Boat Magazine 85, 98, 189, 213
Motor Ship & Motor Boat 127

Mott, C. & N. 142
Mount's Wharf 129
M.T.B.50 75-76
M.T.B.102 **162-164,** 228
mulberry harbours 144
museums 50, 51, 118, 125, 132
Mutt 199
My Babe II see *Lady Anita* 96
My Queen see *Gondolier Queen* 145

Nachman, P. 150
Naiad Errant **14-16**
Nancibelle **52**
Nautilus Diving Club 24
National Maritime Museum 118
Naval Fire Service 150
Naval Historical Branch 165, 202
naval pinnaces see pinnaces
Navigator see *Aberdonia* 170
Nazi propaganda 9
Nayland **80**
Neate ,P. & R. 118
Nelson, Admiral Lord 139
New Britannic **171**
New Windsor Castle **55-57**
Newbery engines 81
Newers, C. H. 231
Newhaven Lifeboat 116
Newson, Fred 164
Nichol, D. R. 149
Nightingale, Ralph 14
Nimmo, Lieut. R. 230
Nimrod see *Betty* 173
Nine Days of Dunkirk, The 228
Nine Days Wonder The, 228
19th Field Regiment R.A. 42
Noakes, Harry 23
Nomad 184
Noneta **232**
Norfolk Broads 65-67
Norris, Steve 46
North V. S. 233
Northcott, Gunner, A. J. 19
Norton, Lieut. G. L. 78
Norton, Petty Officer J. 214
Norwich Belle 66
Nottac see *Irma* 208
Nydia **97**
Nyula see *Betty* 173

Odham's Wharf 59
Oemering, Ron 29
Olivier, G. D. 84
Olly, Seaman 95
Omega **134**
Ona II **53**
Onedin Line, The 152
Onslow, Countess of 74
Operation Dynamo 7, 165
Orellana **217**
Oriole 174
Osborne family 23, 26
Osborne, William 14, 92, 96, 230
Oulton Belle **65-67**
Our Lizzie **152**
Ouseburne Water Sports Ass. 17
oyster fishing 209

Packard, P. M. A. 173
paddle steamers 93-95, 174-175
Padgette, Dorothy 156
Page, Alfred 44
Paling, Dave 38
Palmer, A/S Samuel 14-16
Pamment, D. & E. 136

Papillon **226**
Parham Boatyard 225
Parker, Graham 190
Parry, Owen 45
Parsons engines 107, 113
Partington, Judge Adam 63
passenger vessels 24, 28-29, 30-32, 54, 55-57, 65-67, 68-69, 73, 78-79, 93-95, 138-139, 142, 144, 145, 151, 153, 156, 171, 174-175, 194, 195, 196, 197, 198, 199, 200, 201, 202, 231
Patch, A. & M. 232
Pathfinder 180
Patricia **204**
Patston, J. B. 233
Paul, R. & W. Ltd. 36, 42, 44
Pavillon, d'Or 103

Pay, Anthony 143
Payne, Alison 151
Payne, H. 53
Pearce, Maurice 202
Pearson, Ian & Doreen 137
Peel, Stephen 64
Peggotty see *Nayland* 80
Pelagia **218**
Pender, Frank 69
Perfect, N. 85
Perkins engines 12, 14, 45, 53, 58, 80, 86, 87, 98, 123, 136, 143, 147, 152, 157, 164, 176, 178, 182, 187, 189, 190, 206, 210, 211, 216, 220, 232
Perkins, R. J. & Sons 80
Peters, E. L. 213
Petter engines 23, 159
Philcox, Henry 113
Phillips, Cliff 194
Phillips, Mr. 208
pinnaces 34, 70-71, 85, 102-103, 126, 176, 178-179, 217, 219
Pipe, Ron 209
Pipkin, Denise 52
Pittaway, Alf 142
Plancher, R. 228
Pleasure Steamers Ltd. 66
Pombal, Marquis of 207
Poore, Hugh 50
Porbeagle engines 107, 113
Port of London Authority 192, 195
Porter, Harold 23
Porthleven Boatbuilders 152
Portsmouth Inner Patrol 232
Portsmouth Yard Boatbuilders 70
Potter-Irwin, Sub. Lieut. A. J. 232
Prater, D. & G. 169
Pratt, Sub. Lieut. J. W. 232
President Briand 112
Price, D. R. 231
Priddle, Charlie 170
Princess Elizabeth **174-175**
Princess Freda 31, **194**
Prior, R. & J. 209
Prior, R. J. 233
Pritchard, C. & D. 222, 223
Pritchard, Jack 161
Providence **210-211**
Prudential **117**, 215
Public Record Office 202
Pudge **48-49**
pulling and sailing vessels 123

Quai Felix Faure 214
Queen Boadicea II **151**
Queen Elizabeth 49
Queen Mary 49, 174
Queen Victoria 28
Queen's Silver Jubilee 164
Quest **232**
Quick And The Dead,The 140
Quisisana **141**

Rainbow, Paul 192
Rampart Boatbuilding Co. 18, 19, 27, 86, 187, 228
Ramsay, Vice Admiral Bertram 7, 22, 162, 163
Ramsgate Lifeboat 117, 124, 215
Rands, Alec 41
Rania **27,** 148
Raven, D. & W. 133
Ray, Henry 91
Ray, K. J. 217
Red Funnel Line 174
Reda 101, **104-105,** 220
Reed, Austin 104, 105, 220
Regal Lady see *Oulton Belle* 67
Reliance 20, 25
Renault engines 218
Renault J. L. 166
Rennie, Ian 72
Renown 20, 23, 24, 25
Reporter see *Jane Holland* 122
Resolute **20-22,** 23, 24, 25, 26
Returns to Dunkirk 26, 103, 181
Richards, J. & R. 183
Richards, Paul 206
Richardson, Cdr. H. du P 121, 231
Rickwood, George 231
Ridalls G. H. & Sons 145
Ridett, Alan 95
Riddle of the Sands, The 102
Riis I see *White Heather* 227
Rika 188

River Dart Steamboat Co. 144
River Emergency Service 196
Roades, H. & A. 156
Roberts, William 123
Robinson, Capt. 170
Robinson, Isabel 80
ROCC Computers Ltd. 58
Rochester Barge Co., 40, 45
Rodgers, Sub. Lieut. H. H. 231
Roe, Gareth 84
Rogers, A. E. 192
Rolt, David 220-221
Rommel, Maj. Gen. Erwin 7, 181
Roper, Cyril 144
Rosa Woodd & Phyllis Lunn **112-113**
Rothery, Richard 117
Rouschop, Frits 214
Rouse, G. & H. 134
Route 'X' 75, 204
Rowe, Chris 59
Rowehedge Ironworks 111
Rowse, A. A. 59
Roxborough, Vice Adm. Sir J. 179
Royal Boatbuilding Co. 169
Royal Burnham Yacht Club 216
Royal Cruising Club 218
Royal Flying Corps. 218
Royal National Lifeboat Institution 106-107, 108, 109, 110, 111, 112-113, 114, 115, 116, 117, 118, 119-122, 123-124
Royal Navy Ships, records of 228
Royal Worcestershire Regiment 26
Rummy II **161**
Russell & Newberry engines 117
Russell, Thomas 94
Russell-Snook, M. 219
Ryan, Tony 46
Ryegate II 131, **136**, 220

sailing clipper 99
Salter Bros. Ltd. 195, 196, 197, 198
Salvor **123-124**
Sambre 165
Samuelson, Eleanor 224
San Francisco Chronicle 199
Sanders, R. 132
Sands, Stewart 168
Sands of Dunkirk, The 228
Sarah Hyde 26
Sargeant, Ginge 189
Saunders & Roe 230
Saunders, S. E. 117, 121
Scapa Flow 178
Schneider Trophy 134
Schollaert, Gerard 10
schuits 7, 26, 228
Science Museum 132
Scripps engines 70
Scrutton, Claud 147
Sea Leech II see *Dragonfly* 154
Seal, Lieut. J. S. 151
Sears, Caroline 82
Seasalter 209
Selby-Bradford, Maj. J. 228
Senang see *Latona* 140
September Tide see *Moiena* 82
Severn Motor Yacht Club 134
Seymour Castle **144**
Sharman-Courtney, Lieut. Cdr. John 79, 172
Shaw, Sir Eyre Massey 88
Shoreham Lifeboat 112
Short Bros. 68
Silver J. A. 82, 83, 98, 100, 160
Silver Jubilee Procession 100
Silver Queen **73**
Simcock, Michael 87
Simpson, J. & G. 97
Singapore **232**
Singapore II **233**
Sissons engines 196
Sittingbourne Shipbuilding Company 52, 168
615 Water Transport Co. 164
Skentelbert, K. R. 205
Skipjack 174
Skylark **224**
Skylark IX **201**
Skylark X **200**
Slack, David 165
Slaughter, Keith 208
Small Boats Service 200
Small Crafts Disposal Unit 215
Small Vessels Pool 85

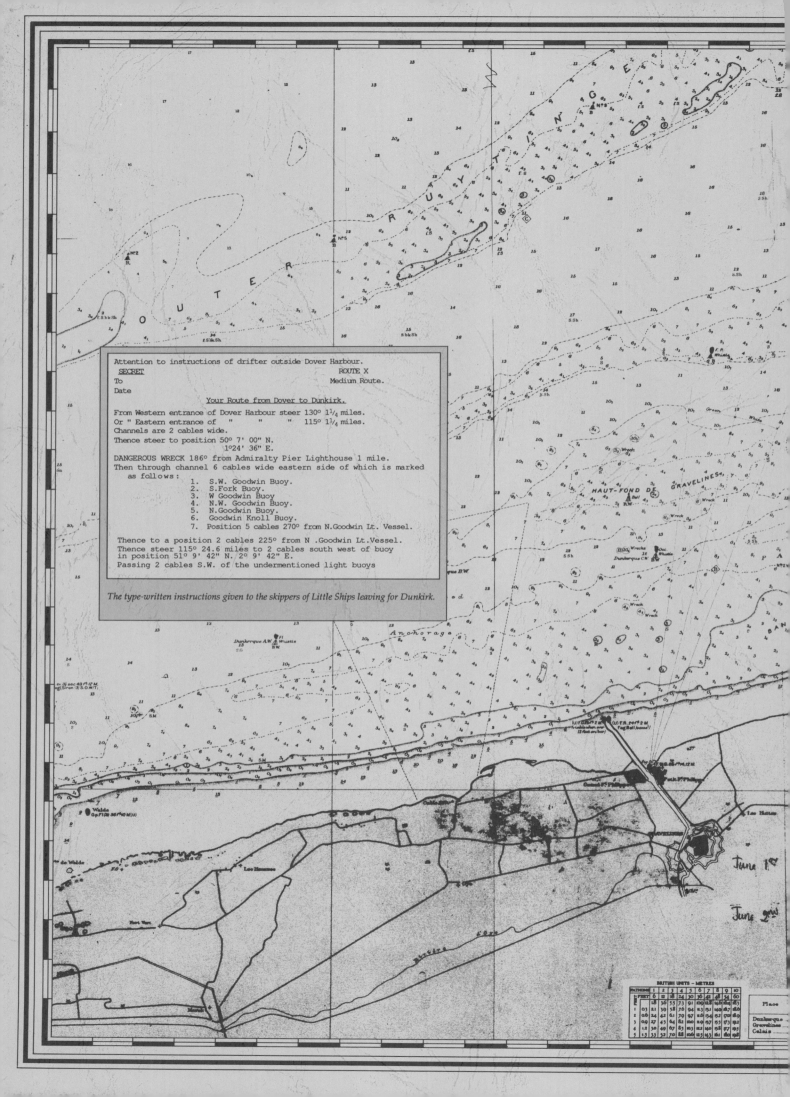

Attention to instructions of drifter outside Dover Harbour.

SECRET   ROUTE X

To   Medium Route.

Date

Your Route from Dover to Dunkirk.

From Western entrance of Dover Harbour steer 130º 1¼ miles.
Or " Eastern entrance of   "   "   115º 1¼ miles.
Channels are 2 cables wide.
Thence steer to position 50º 7' 00" N.
                      1º24' 36" E.

DANGEROUS WRECK 186º from Admiralty Pier Lighthouse 1 mile.
Then through channel 6 cables wide eastern side of which is marked
    as follows :
                  1.   S.W. Goodwin Buoy.
                  2.   S.Fork Buoy.
                  3.   W Goodwin Buoy
                  4.   N.W. Goodwin Buoy.
                  5.   N.Goodwin Buoy.
                  6.   Goodwin Knoll Buoy.
                  7.   Position 5 cables 270º from N.Goodwin Lt. Vessel.

Thence to a position 2 cables 225º from N .Goodwin Lt.Vessel.
Thence steer 115º 24.6 miles to 2 cables south west of buoy
in position 51º 9' 42" N. 2º 9' 42" E.
Passing 2 cables S.W. of the undermentioned light buoys

The type-written instructions given to the skippers of Little Ships leaving for Dunkirk.